COMMERCIAL

LENDING

TO THE

SMALL AND

MIDDLE MARKET

BUSINESS

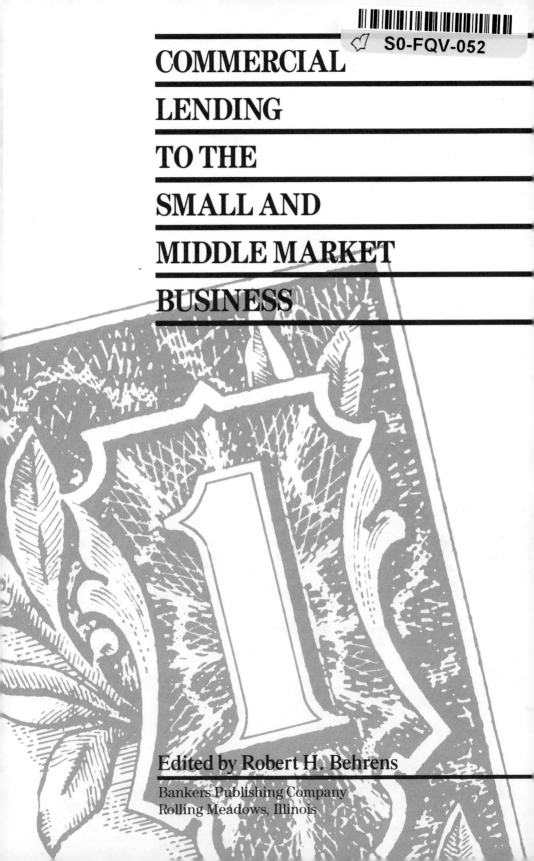

S0-FQV-052

Edited by Robert H. Behrens

Bankers Publishing Company
Rolling Meadows, Illinois

Selected portions of this text have been reprinted with permission from *Bankers Middle Market Lending Letter*, presently published by Faulkner & Gray, Inc., New York, NY.

Copyright © 1990 by Banker's Publishing Company, Rolling Meadows, Illinois.

All rights reserved.

This book or any parts of it may not be reproduced in any form without written permission from the publisher.

Printed in the United States of America.

No. 552   ISBN: 1-55520-131-8

Contents

Introduction

Lending may well be considered the heart of the commercial banking business. Loans constitute the largest single asset category of commercial banks, and in almost every banks interest on loans is the largest single source of revenue. Because the loan portfolio represents such a major portion of a bank's assets and generates the majority of its income, every bank is vitally concerned with the quality of its loan portfolio and the proficiency and professionalism of its lending operations. If the bank has a high-quality, well-managed loan portfolio, it will almost invariably prosper. On the other hand, a low-quality, poorly administered portfolio will lead to significant losses, and may even result in the ultimate failure of the bank.

This book is a collection of articles originally published in *Bankers Middle-Market Lending Letter* which addresses issues of vital interest to lenders. Although the emphasis is on commercial lending. there is also much information of interest to loan administrators, loan review officers—and consumer lenders. The material in this book is divided into nine sections covering general banking topics. general lending topics, loan documentation, dealing with collateral, Article 9 of the Uniform Commercial Code, lending to small businesses, dealing with problem loans, loan review—and lender liability issues.

Most of the articles contained in this work were authored by Kathleen Victory, editor of *Bankers Middle-Market Lending Letter*, and by contributing editors Robert H. Behrens and James W. Evans. Other contributing authors include John B. McCarter, Dennis McCuistion, Don Wright, Frank C. Jen, and Steven L. Cranfill, all experts in their particular area of banking.

This book is intended as a convenient reference on a wide spectrum of lending topics which will provide the reader concise, basic, authoritative information in an easily readable format.

1

General Banking Topics

This section contains four articles covering topics of general interest to bank management. An article on protecting the bank from insider fraud describes the characteristics of vulnerable employees, gives examples of several types of fraud, and makes recommendations for protecting the bank from this kind of problem. Bank fraud, and especially that perpetrated by insiders, is a significant and growing problem. For each dollar lost from burglary or robbery, banks lose almost fifty dollars as a result of fraud and embezzlement. These crimes are usually difficult to detect because they often involve insiders. Total 1988 losses by financial institutions were in excess of $1\frac{1}{2}$ billion. Federal Bureau of Investigation statistics also indicate that fraud losses in the thrift industry quadrupled from 1987 to 1988, reaching a high of $587 million. Due to the sheer magnitude of the losses involved, protecting itself against insider fraud and embezzlement should be a major concern of every financial institution.

A second article discusses dealing with bank examiners, who perform a necessary function that often causes irritation and frustration to the banker due to the differing perspectives of the banker and examiner. Bank examiners are primarily concerned with the safety and soundness of the bank. Bank management, while also concerned with safety and soundness, must of necessity also be customer service and profit oriented. These differing perspectives often create tension between examiners and bank managers, and this problem is often magnified if the examiners are inexperienced. Further, as regulators have become more oriented toward evaluating management capability as a factor in bank safety and soundness, management has been subjected to greater scrutiny from examiners. As a result, management, and especially the chief executive officer, may be severely criticized if the bank is not in compliance with regulatory standards. Despite their frustration and apprehension, bank managers must deal with examiners on a professional and rational basis. To assist the banker in accomplishing this objective, specific suggestions are offered to facilitate the credit examination process.

The third article discusses the Community Reinvestment Act and its implications to the bank. CRA is considered from both the banker's and regulator's perspective. Compliance with the requirements of the Community Reinvestment Act is essential, and regulators have given notice to the banking industry that CRA compliance is being reemphasized. When a bank applies for a new facility, for relocation of an existing facility, or similar action, its CRA compliance record is given significant consideration by regulatory authorities. Many community action and consumer advocacy groups have become adept at using CRA as a lever on banks which, in their perception, are not adequately meeting the needs of low-income neighborhoods and other consumer constituencies. These same groups are actively urging Congress to further expand the coverage of the Community Reinvestment Act. In some instances, banks have considered the demands of these groups to be "blackmail." This article gives an overview of CRA and also makes specific recommendations for preventing protests from community activist groups.

The final article, based on a comprehensive study performed by the Comptroller of the Currency, explores the reasons why banks fail and identifies the required characteristics of a successful banking operation. Bank failures have reached post-Depression highs in the past several years. The majority of these failures have occurred in areas dependent on the agricultural and energy industries, with the Southwest and the Great Plains being especially hard hit. Interestingly, the Office of the Comptroller of the Currency (OCC) study indicates that, contrary to common belief, economic factors are not the major cause of bank failures. Rather, the study seems to indicate that poor management and insider abuse may be the primary causes of failure. The study concludes that a strong, capable chief executive officer is one of the essentials for a safe and sound bank. This article also contains a thirteen-point formula for a successful bank, outlining the essential ingredients such as adequate capital; a strong, active board of directors; and adequate management information systems.

Preliminary statistics for 1989 indicate that both bank failures and the number of banks categorized as problem banks are diminishing. This, however, should not reduce the efforts of the banking industry to continue to improve its performance.

Protecting the Bank from Insider Fraud

Although most bankers will occasionally feel concern about possible bank robberies, the banking industry actually loses many times more money to insiders than it does to armed robbers. According to the Federal Bureau of Investigation (FBI), financial institutions suffered $1.6 billion in losses from bank fraud and embezzlement in 1988, compared with $46.8 million in losses resulting from robberies and burglary.

Due to concern about the magnitude of the problem, an Interagency Bank Fraud Enforcement Working Group was created, comprised of representatives from each of the federal financial institution regulatory agencies, the United States Department of Justice, the FBI, and the Farm Credit Administration. In addition, bank examiners are receiving more training in detecting evidence of fraud. The FBI has also increased the number of agents working in the financial area by approximately 30 percent.

3

Characteristics of vulnerable employees

Bank fraud or embezzlement cases are hard to detect because they usually involve insiders, and as a result are often not reported. The defalcation often involves a trusted, long-term employee of the financial institution. In some instances, the theft may continue for many years before it is discovered. Individuals who embezzle from the bank are not stereotypical "criminal types" who frequent sleazy bars and consort with other felons. Rather, they usually lead respectable lives and are often churchgoers who are active in community affairs. Many bank employees who become thieves, however, share certain common characteristics:

1. An extravagant lifestyle inconsistent with either their financial means or family background.

2. Unusual personality traits such as being a loner, being very secretive about their past, or telling conflicting stories about academic background and past employment.

3. Longstanding resentment of their circumstances, including family background, financial status, and relationship with their current or past employer.

4. Hesitancy to take vacations, paid holidays, or even sick leave.

5. Extreme reluctance to allow someone else to deal with "their" customers.

6. A perceived family situation which creates ongoing demands for money such as a spouse who demands an upscale lifestyle or children who insist on having new cars. These demands may exist more in the employee's mind than be actual demands made by family members.

7. Discrepancies in biographical information on a job application, especially regarding education and reasons for leaving previous employment.

8. Tendency to work considerable overtime and consistently take work home, even when workload should not require it.

9. Insistence on keeping certain files under their exclusive control and reluctance to let other people look at them.

Audits seldom uncover fraud

Many bankers believe their bank will be protected from insider fraud due to periodic external audits and regular examinations by various supervisory agencies. In truth, very few defalcations are uncovered either by external auditors or by examiners, because it is not the primary function of either an audit or a bank examination to uncover fraud. Most cases of insider fraud are discovered either by internal auditors or by customers. In some instances, the perpetrator may have a subconscious desire to be caught, and therefore leaves incriminating evidence where it can be easily discovered.

The average perpetrator begins with a small theft, usually intending to replace the money; i.e., a temporary loan. When he or she realizes that the theft has been easy and has not been discovered, a larger theft usually follows, leading to a series of defalcations extending over a period of months or years. Covering up these actions takes considerable work, which may explain why insiders who are stealing from an institution commonly work overtime and/or take work home with them. As the defalcation grows, it usually becomes extremely stressful to keep the scheme going. In many instances, the culprit is relieved to be caught and usually admits the crime after an initial period of denial.

The case of "Fred"

"Fred" had been a junior loan officer at a local bank for several years and was discharged because of a "personality conflict"

5

with a senior officer of that bank. He readily obtained a new job as a loan officer with another bank in the same community. In that position, he processed routine loan applications and was also responsible for handling payment vouchers for the loan department's operating expenses. He also had ready access to the department's blank money order supply, over which the bank maintained little internal control.

For some time he performed his duties well, but then began stealing funds by inflating the amounts to be paid for various supplies the loan department purchased. If the department received a $1,500 bill from a printer, "Fred" would write an expense check for $1,500 to the supplier. He would then run through a debit ticket for $2,500 and write a $1,000 money order to himself or to one of several local stores at which he had charge accounts. In this manner, the department's internal accounts always balanced. "Fred's" defalcations continued for two and a half years, and ultimately also involved the creation of a number of fictitious loans. Although the total amount embezzled reached nearly $260,000, "Fred's" theft was not discovered during that time period, even though the bank had several credit examinations and external audits. Apparently, no one ever reviewed the loan department's copies of its money orders, nor did anyone notice that the department's cost of supplies had multiplied considerably during that same period of time.

Note that "Fred" did not need the money, as both he and his wife had good-paying jobs. Most of the stolen funds were spent on new furniture and antiques. As is typical in these cases, "Fred's" wife had no knowledge of his theft. Interestingly, the thief's spouse is often unaware of the problem, and is told a plausible, but untrue, story about the source of the funds. Unfortunately, even if the spouse is entirely innocent, he or she may be liable for any unpaid tax and penalties owed on the stolen funds, if he or she has filed a joint income tax return with the perpetrator.

Although "Fred" was outwardly a very quiet and unassuming person, he tended to maintain a lifestyle that was beyond his financial means. As his criminal activities increased, he began to spend an increasingly large amount of his workday covering up the evidence of his fraud. As a result, he had a series of confrontations with the bank's executive vice president, during which he demanded that he be provided with additional support staff. During their final confrontation, the executive vice president lost his temper and fired "Fred."

In a fit of rage, "Fred" cleaned out his desk, dumping part of its contents in a wastebasket and the remainder in a garbage container behind the bank building. Another employee found the material, including copies of bank money orders and various loan documents, in the garbage container, and reported the situation to a superior. As a result, "Fred" was apprehended and ultimately confessed his theft. He was convicted and is currently serving a term in a federal penitentiary.

Customers may detect fraud

In another case, the CEO of a community bank was confronted by an elderly customer who complained that some valuable coins had been stolen from her safe deposit box. Attributing the problem to "forgetfulness" on the part of the customer, the CEO took no action. It was only after the bank received similar complaints from other customers that it instituted an investigation. This investigation ultimately revealed that a young officer who periodically worked in the safe deposit box area had managed to make wax impressions of a number of customers' keys, from which he made duplicate keys to gain access to the customers' safe deposit boxes.

Tougher bank fraud enforcement

In an effort to facilitate better reporting of insider thefts, the Bank Fraud Enforcement Working Group has developed a

7

uniform criminal referral form for use by all financial institutions subject to the regulatory jurisdiction of the Working Group's member agencies. It has also developed an automated system to monitor and track criminal referral information submitted to an agency by its examiners and the finan-

How your bank can protect itself

1. Do more thorough background checks on prospective employees.

2. Consider using professional screening or psychological testing of prospective employees for key positions.

3. Require every employee to take two full, consecutive weeks of vacation each year.

4. Watch for the employee who shows unexplained stress or who develops unusual personality traits.

5. Compartmentalize operations to the greatest extent possible so that one employee does not have total control over a specific function.

6. Use the bank's audit staff to spot-check the bank's various operations on an irregular basis, instructing them to be sensitive to unusual transactions or account entries.

7. Request that the audit staff periodically select a loan account at random, examine the credit file, and develop an audit trail for all transactions on that account. Pay particular attention to any loan account handled exclusively by one officer.

8. Prohibit officers and employees from keeping credit files or other files in their desks on a more or less permanent basis. This may require a checkout procedure for files.

9. Don't take customer complaints lightly. Each one merits investigation, even if the complaint appears to be bizarre.

10. Don't hesitate to use a polygraph test if there is a problem but recognize the test's limitations.

cial institutions it regulates. In cooperation with the Working Group, the Department of Justice has developed and implemented a significant referral tracking system. This system keeps track of all referrals from the various bank regulatory agencies that involve amounts in excess of $200,000 and/or in which (1) a senior officer or director of a financial institution is a suspect, or (2) there is a concern that an activity might undermine the integrity of the supervisory process.

Bank examiner training has also been greatly enhanced through the expansion of the Examination Council's White Collar Crime Course and joint FBI and Banking Agency Training Courses. The Working Group has developed a series of uniform instructions for all agency examiners assigned to assist in criminal investigations to enable them to perform their duties more thoroughly. The Department of Justice has also made white collar crime involving financial institutions a top priority for investigation and prosecution by the FBI and the various offices of the United States attorneys.

Because a bank suffering from an insider theft may incur a serious loss, bank management should ensure that internal audit staffs are well-trained and alert to any unusual transactions or book entries. The bank should also establish procedures to limit any one employee's control over a specific function, and enforce its vacation policy. Supervisors should be sensitive to any change in an employee's personality traits, work habits, or lifestyle which may be indicative of developing problems. Lastly, banks should improve their procedures for screening and investigating prospective employees.

Dealing with Bank Examiners

Even the most confident banker usually feels a certain amount of trepidation upon learning that the examiners have just arrived at the bank. Although bankers recognize the important and necessary role bank examiners play in maintaining the soundness of the commercial banking system and the confidence of the public in it, few relish the periodic visit by a team of bank examiners. A credit examination always causes the bank's staff a certain amount of inconvenience, since staff personnel will be asked to produce certain credit files and other information, and will also spend a significant amount of time answering examiners' questions.

Most banks have little concern about the inconvenience involved. Rather, they worry about the possibility that examiners will classify loans which the bank thought were acceptable, criticize some of the bank's policies and procedures, and critically review the bank's capital structure. If the bank fails to meet required standards, it may be instructed to "clean up" its classified and nonaccrual loans, institute more stringent credit criteria, or improve the quality of its credit analysis and credit files. It may even be instructed to increase its capital. At worst, the bank may be requested to adopt a board resolution or may receive a memorandum of understanding requiring it to meet certain performance criteria within a stated timeframe.

Emphasis on weak and problem banks

National banks are examined by the Office of the Comptroller of the Currency (OCC), while state-chartered banks generally are examined by the Federal Deposit Insurance Corporation or the Federal Reserve System. In most cases, a state-chartered bank is also examined by the commissioner of banking of the state in which it operates. In some instances, FDIC and state examiners will perform a joint or concurrent examination. In the past, banks were routinely examined on an annual basis. Because the number of troubled banks has significantly increased in recent years, however, the bank supervisory agencies have concentrated their efforts on weak banks or banks with problems. To a great extent, they have depended upon analyses of reports furnished by sound banks, with less on-site examinations of these banks. As a result, many strong, healthy banks now have an on-site examination conducted only once every two to three years. The supervisory agencies, however, have not downgraded the importance of such examinations. "Despite the progress made in recent years in improved reporting required of banks, better statistical analysis, and off-site review, there is still no substitute for getting a firm feel for the bank's condition through an on-site examination," says James P. Kielczewski, deputy regional director of the FDIC's Chicago regional office.

Kielczewski notes that there are four primary purposes for bank examinations. The first of these is the maintenance of public confidence in the integrity of the banking system and its individual banks. "Such confidence is clearly essential, because the system's customers serve as the source of funding, without which banks would be unable to meet their most fundamental objective of providing financial services," he says. The second purpose for examinations is to determine the bank's adherence to laws and regulations. Third, examinations play an important role in protecting the financial integrity of the deposit insurance fund. Finally, the bank examination supplies the supervisor with an understanding of the nature, relative seriousness and ultimate causes of a bank's problems, and thus provides a factual foundation for soundly based corrective measures.

Rating system used by examiners

The Uniform Financial Institutions Rating System, commonly referred to as the CAMEL rating system, was adopted by the FDIC in November 1979, and is also used by the OCC, the Board of Governors of the Federal Reserve System, the Federal Home Loan Bank Board, and the National Credit Union Administration. The acronym CAMEL refers to five key bank performance areas: Capital adequacy, asset quality, management, earnings, and liquidity. This rating system has proved very useful to bank directors and officers in helping them gain a perspective on the condition of their institution. Banks are rated in each category on a scale of one to five (one being the best rating) and then an overall composite rating is compiled. Any institution with a composite rating of four or five is considered a problem bank.

Many state banking departments have adopted the CAMEL rating system, which is intended to be a uniform method for reflecting an institution's financial condition and operating soundness. The FDIC has disclosed its composite ratings to state nonmember banks for a number of years, as have most state banking departments. The OCC has also recently begun disclosing this information to national banks.

Differing perspectives: banker vs. examiner

Some of the problems that arise between bankers and examiners result from differences in their perspectives. Richard M. Jorgensen, president of Marine Bank of Champaign-Urbana, Illinois, observes that while bank examiners are concerned solely with the safety and soundness of a bank, bank management is also charged with adequately serving its customers and generating a profit for the bank's stockholders. "Examiners need to understand that the bank must deal with people and run a profitable operation," says Jorgensen. "In many instances, if a bank were run exactly as examiners wanted, the bank would neither serve its customers nor generate a return to its stockholders." Jorgensen believes that some examiners have too narrow a perspective in this regard.

A number of bankers also express concern that because of rapid staff turnover at the examining agencies, many examiners lack experience and training. "Too many bank examiners have little more than six months' experience in examining loans and are lacking in credit knowledge," states Thomas M.

Teschner, senior vice president of Southside Bancshares Corporation in St. Louis, Missouri, and a former Missouri state examiner and national examiner. "Their comments during the loan critique are not helpful to the banker due to their lack of experience and training." He is concerned that too many of the best bank examiners are lost because they can obtain betterpaying positions elsewhere in the banking industry. He also feels that the examiners' approach is inadequate in some instances, because they simply react to existing problems rather than try to detect potential future problems.

David A. Bacon, loan review officer at First National Bank of Shreveport, Louisiana, and a former OCC examiner, believes that examiners should be more willing to accept the banker's approach to the workout of a bad loan. They also need to spend more time listening to the banker's input, since he is the one most knowledgeable about the loan. Bacon thinks examiners should spend more time reviewing collateral files, which are often overlooked entirely during the examination. In general, he feels that most examiners are very professional in their approach, but that their mindset is often determined by directives from the agency which they represent; as a result, they tend to be arbitrary in implementing these directives.

FDIC Deputy Regional Director Kielczewski believes that most problems between examiners and bankers stem from a lack of communication and differences of perspective. "Problems can generally be minimized if they are discussed early on, rather than at the close of the examination. Examiners sometimes have problems with a lack of accessibility to the bank's CEO and other key officers. In some instances, the examination is impeded by the banker's failure to provide requested documentation in a timely fashion."

Kielczewski also observes that while it is not a substitute for examiner analysis, "a good loan watch list may expedite the examination to a significant degree." Kielczewski also stresses the importance of good credit files. "Proper and currently maintained files not only enable the orderly transfer of responsibility for the credit within the bank, but also make the examiner review and officer (and/or director) review more expedient and decreases follow-up time in loan discussions. Examiners find that complete and current credit files are a good indicator of management performance."

Making an exam run smoothly

Bank management can do a number of things to ensure that an examination goes smoothly. First, see that examiners have adequate facilities in which to work. Examiners are almost always cooperative in moving from one area of the bank to another if necessary, as long as that area is adequate and comfortable. Bank management should also ensure that bank personnel are cooperative and furnish requested information promptly. Complete and up-to-date credit files will help avoid unnecessary questions. A realistic, complete watch list of weak and problem loans will also be of assistance, since examiners want assurances that the bank is making an adequate effort to recognize the problems in its portfolio.

The bank's CEO and senior officers should make themselves readily available to answer examiners' questions. Management has a right to disagree with an examiner, but always in a courteous and professional manner. Most disagreements arise from differences of opinion regarding the quality of specific loans. Attempting to convince an examiner that a bad loan is really "acceptable" is almost always an exercise in futility. If a loan is bad, it's better for management to admit that fact and then outline its plans for correcting the problem. If a true difference of opinion exists, the bank should listen fully to the examiner's criticisms and then state its case in clear, concise, and factual terms. If its comments fail to change the examiner's mind, the bank has no choice but to accept his decision.

If management is not satisfied, however, it may make written comments in response to the examiner's transmittal letter.

In summary, bankers recognize the important contribution that bank examiners make to the maintenance of the soundness of the banking industry. Bankers also recognize that credit examiners can be of considerable assistance to management in identifying problems and recommending improvements in bank performance. On the other hand, bankers are concerned about bank examiners who are inexperienced, unwilling to consider the banker's perspective, or who apply their directives in an arbitrary manner.

CRA: Blackmail or Community Development Tool?

Of increasing concern to many lenders is the use of the Community Reinvestment Act (CRA) by consumer and business activists to elicit credit commitments for various projects. Is it a form of coercion, as some bankers have alleged, or a legitimate community development tool? CRA, enacted by Congress in 1977, was supposed to encourage banks to participate actively in economic development activities at the community level and discourage them from rejecting loan applications from low-income neighborhoods. The act enables groups or individuals to protest mergers, aquisitions, branch expansions, and geographic relocations of financial institutions to ensure that CRA guidelines are met. By charging that banks haven't served a community's needs, activists can delay a proposed transaction. To avoid delays, banks often pledge financing for projects if the groups drop their objections.

Money for projects like low-income housing is being pried out of banks and other lenders by neighborhood activists using the CRA, according to a recent article in *Business Week*, "The 'Blackmail' Making Banks Better Neighbors" (8/15/88). In 1987 community groups filed fifty-three separate CRA protests to bank regulators, but private agreements reached under the threat of such filings outnumbered formal complaints by as much as four to one. Although more than one banker has dubbed the practice a form of blackmail, consumer groups complain that regulators have rejected only nine of 40,000 bank merger requests on CRA grounds since the law was enacted. Banks have pledged more than $5 billion, mainly in loans for low-income housing, over the past three years. For example, Wells Fargo Bank of California is providing low-cost financing for a shelter for battered women in San Francisco. First National Bank of Chicago is helping to finance work on the headquarters of the National Training and Information Center, a community action group.

The regulators' view

Regulators say the activists play an important role in seeing that community service requirements are met. The Federal Reserve says the activists are helpful in assessing how well banks are meeting their obligations. "CRA was enacted in the belief that financial institutions have a responsibility to meet the credit needs of their entire local communities, including the low- and moderate-income neighborhoods, consistent with the safe and sound operation of the institution," said Martha R. Seger, member of the Board of Governors of the Federal Reserve System, in a speech before the House Banking Committee in March 1988. She noted that the federal supervisory agencies also have responsibilities under the act: To encourage financial institutions to meet the communities' needs, to assess the community lending records of the institutions they supervise as part of their examinations, and to take into account the institution's record when considering certain applications.

Seger expressed concern that CRA has become, over the years, "synonymous with home lending in the minds of many. The regulation, however, does not reflect such a leaning.

16

It reflects the very strong belief that a long list of other forms of lending are just as important to the communities of this nation. This is particularly critical to the Federal Reserve, since many banks have chosen not to specialize in home lending, preferring not to engage heavily in the long-term mortgage market. We believe, however, these banks still play a valuable part in meeting other needs of their communities."

Describing the Fed's compliance examination program, Seger noted that state member banks were examined at least once a year when the program was begun in 1977. "Over the years we have increased the interval between examinations so that at present, banks with a better than satisfactory rating are generally examined every eighteen months. Some of the best performing banks may have as much as twenty-four months between examinations. Banks with less satisfactory records are examined at one-year intervals or more frequently."

According to Federal Reserve statistics, there were thirty-five applications protested under CRA in 1987, while in 1984 there were just three. Of the 112 cases the board reviewed between 1978 and 1987 involving CRA protests, twenty-eight have resulted in the applicant committing to the board to take specific actions to correct problems with its record. "It has been the board's belief that, as a general matter, working in a positive vein with these institutions, rather than simply turning down the application, was consistent with the law's mandate that we encourage these institutions to meet the credit needs of their communities," said Seger. "Moreover, it was not always clear in these cases that the applicant's CRA record was poor enough to deny the application."

"Of course, we have not always waited for a protest to prompt a close review of an applicant's record," Seger added. "When we have found problems in an applicant's CRA examination record, either through our own examiners or those of another agency, we have conducted the same kind of review we conduct in a protested case."

17

Preventing protests

Bankers should be aware that community activists and small businesses alike are being urged to use CRA to get what they want. Take, for example, an article in the June 1988 issue of *In Business*, "Power to the Borrowers." The article encourages small businesses to band together in their communities to get banks to make commitments. It cites the example of Maryland Citizens Action Coalition and other Washington, D.C.-area groups that got three banks to agree to lending commitments of $100 million over five year's. Smart banks will do what they can to fight the perception that they're unresponsive to small business and community needs.

What can banks do to forestall CRA protests? The ideal solution, of course, is to have a community service record that both the bank and the community can be proud of. But how to document that, and how to best communicate it to community members most likely to make an active protest? Janice Smith, director of the FDIC's Office of Consumer Affairs, provided several suggestions at an ABA conference last year. She advised bankers to use a special form used by some examiners to preview an institution's CRA efforts. The form delineates a bank's efforts to determine and meet a community's credit needs. The questionnaire is not a substitute for a CRA exam, but a bank can use the form to highlight its accomplishments. Also, remember that while groups often stress just the quantity and dollar amount of loans made, statistics can't tell the whole story of how a bank is responding to its community. It's up to the bank to provide other examples of how it's providing credit and other important services to the community.

Why Banks Fail

During 1988 a total of 221 commercial banks failed or required regulatory assistance, breaking 1987's record of 203 failures. A high proportion of these failures occurred in states such as Texas and Oklahoma, which continue to suffer adverse economic conditions related to the agricultural, energy, and commercial real estate industries. Such facts have led many bankers to conclude that adverse economic conditions are the primary cause of bank failures. However, this does not explain why, of two banks located in a community that is experiencing economic difficulty, one will fail while the other will continue to operate successfully and even prosper.

A recent comprehensive study of bank failures by the Office of the Comptroller of the Currency (OCC) published in the *Comptroller's Quarterly Journal* (Vol.7, No.3) indicates that factors other than economic conditions may have a material effect on the success or failure of a bank. In fact, the OCC study, which analyzed 171 failed banks, 51 rehabilitated banks, and 38 healthy banks, indicates that economic decline was a significant factor in only 35 percent of the bank failures studied. Further, a depressed economic environment was the sole significant cause of failure in only 7 percent of the banks studied. This statistic is interesting in view of the fact that a fairly high proportion of the banks studied were in the OCC's Midwestern and Southwestern districts, areas that have suffered from adverse economic conditions to a greater extent than other areas of the country.

Characteristics of failing banks

The problem and failing banks studied by the OCC had many characteristics in common. All had poor-quality assets, especially in their loan portfolio, with consequent deterioration of capital position as a result of loan charge-offs and oper-ating losses. Sixty-three percent of these banks had CEOs who clearly lacked the professional expertise, experience, or integrity required to make their banks succeed. Almost 60 percent of these failing banks also had boards of directors that lacked necessary banking knowledge, were uninformed, or

19

were inattentive to the bank's affairs. In addition, these banks generally lacked functioning systems (such as a loan review operation) for the identification of developing problem loans. Fifty-eight percent of the healthy banks surveyed had a problem loan identification system, but the same was true for only 9% of the failed banks. Similarly, 50% of the healthy banks and 65% of the rehabilitated banks had well-defined loan policies, while only 4% of the failed banks had such policies. Another characteristic of the failed banks was overly aggressive growth relative to the environment in which the bank operated. Eight of every ten failed banks analyzed were judged to have had a board or top management that was to some extent overly aggressive. Symptoms of an overly aggressive stance included rapid growth in loan portfolio, inappropriate lending policies, overly liberal credit standards, and lax collection practices. A significant number of loans outside of the bank's primary business area, undue reliance on large volatile deposits, and inadequate liquid assets were also characteristic of these overly aggressive banks. However, an aggressive, growth-oriented philosophy is not itself a danger signal. An aggressive philosophy combined with strong management, prudent policies, and adequate controls may be a very successful strategy. It is only when growth becomes excessive in relation to management capacity, staff capabilities, and funding resources that it becomes dangerous to the bank's future health.

Insider abuse was also a factor contributing to the failure of 35% of the failed banks studied by the OCC. Material fraud also played a part in 11% of these failures. Insider abuse usually involved poor oversight and control, inadequate supervision of key officers, excessive loans to officers and directors or their close associates, failure to adhere to loan policies, unwarranted concentrations of credit in one industry, and inadequate supervision of the purchase of loan participations from other institutions. Other indicators of insider abuse are undue dependence on the bank for income or services by a board member or shareholder, inappropriate transactions with affiliates, and unauthorized transactions by executive officers, especially in the lending area.

Other characteristics displayed by the lending operations of problem banks included excessive financial statement exceptions, such as lack of a current financial statement or a business cash flow projection. In general, such exceptions are a cause for examiner concern if found in more than 7% to 10% of total loan files. Interestingly, significant credit exceptions were also found in a high percentage of healthy banks, and therefore appear to create little damage if the bank's other lending practices are prudent.

Another problem area involves collateral documentation and perfection. A high incidence of collateral exceptions, such as failure to file or record liens, incorrect collateral descriptions, failure to perform a lien search, lack of any meaningful attempt to establish collateral values, and failure to obtain insurance loss payable clauses were also characteristic of problem banks. Such problems obviously contribute directly to a bank's loan losses since they may prevent the bank from realizing the proceeds of the collateral in which it assumed it had a perfected lien.

Importance of good management

Management weakness played a significant part in the decline of 90% of the problem banks evaluated by the OCC. In fact, the study concludes that a strong CEO is probably the most important factor in the success of a bank. In 90% of the problem banks that were rehabilitated, the replacement of the bank's CEO was one of the significant factors involved in rehabilitation. However, the study also makes clear that, in addition to a capable CEO, the bank needs a management team with adequate diversity and breadth of experience to deal with the many complex aspects of a commercial banking

21

operation. A management team that has developed within the bank over a long period of time may appear to be competent, but may be trained in the same outdated methods. In fact, they may be unable to keep up with change, and may have "one year's experience twenty times," rather than the diverse experience required for modern-day bank management.

Although strong management is essential, a bank managed by one dominant decisionmaker who may control both the bank's board and officer staff with an iron hand is often a candidate for problems. A CEO who is too dominant may fail to obtain adequate staff and board input before making decisions, fail to develop adequate successor management, and be unable to retain the strong, diverse officer staff essential to a successful banking operation.

Formula for a successful bank

A number of conclusions can be drawn from the comptroller's study regarding the required ingredients for a successful bank:

- The bank must have adequate capital. Capital serves as a buffer between operating losses and insolvency. The stronger a bank's capital position, the more adversity it can withstand. A bank's capitalization also determines the amount of time it has to correct weaknesses or to outlast an economic downturn.

- The bank must have a strong, active board to oversee management and to ensure that appropriate plans and policies are developed and enforced.

- Competent management is crucial. This includes both a strong, professionally qualified CEO and a management team with a wide range of expertise in all areas of banking.

- The bank must have a well-developed philosophy that is understood not only by top management and the board of directors, but also by all bank personnel.

- The bank must have a long-range growth plan that clearly outlines its long-range goals and objectives.

- The bank must have well-defined, written policies covering all aspects of its operation.

- The bank must have adequate management information systems to keep management well informed and to ensure compliance with all policies and regulations.

- There must be adequate control over all key functions and departments. A strong audit function is an absolute necessity.

- The bank must have a workable system for identifying loan problems at an early stage and then be able to deal with these problems in an aggressive manner.

- The bank must have adequate training programs for all personnel to insure competency at all levels, from the CEO to the tellers.

- The bank must define its market area and then do its utmost to serve the needs of its customers within that area.

- The bank must generate profits adequate to provide both capital needed to support growth and a reasonable return to its stockholders.

- The bank must always remember that it is a service institution and that to survive, it must provide prompt, efficient, courteous service to each and every customer.

2

General Lending Topics

Professional lenders must have diverse knowledge of a wide range of topics if they are to perform in a competent manner. This section contains articles devoted to a wide spectrum of general lending topics, ranging from a discussion of how a good loan decision is made to dealing with a leveraged buy-out. The first article addresses the importance of making a good initial loan decision. The initial decision is the banker's best opportunity to avoid future problems. This requires both adequate technical expertise on the part of the lender and the development of enough information regarding the status of the loan applicant for the lender to fully understand the situation. If the lender never really understands the borrower's financial position, repayment capacity, and general willingness to meet obligations, then it is unlikely that the lender will be able to make a good initial decision. Bankers also create potential loan problems by overestimating the debtor's management ability and by failing to critically assess projections of future performance submitted by the borrower. In addition to complete financial information and projections, the lender needs information concerning the quality of inventory and receivables, the type and condition of the borrower's equipment, and the credentials of its management. The importance of an actual visit to the premises of the borrower and adequate appraisals of equipment and real estate is also stressed. It is essential that there be a realistic evaluation of the liquidation value of the proposed collateral. In the case of a new business, the development and proper analysis of this essential information becomes especially critical. There is no doubt that the ability to develop the required information, analyze it properly, and consequently make a good initial loan decision will minimize the bank's loan problems.

Cash flow is the topic of the second article. Every professional lender recognizes that since only cash repays loans, adequate cash flow is the essential ingredient for a sound and workable loan. Historical income and expense information is usually the basis for cash flow projections submitted by a loan applicant. However, the lender must realize that acceptable past performance does not guarantee adequate future cash flow, and it is future cash flow, not past performance, that will repay the loan the lender is making today. Lacking adequate cash flow, the lender must fall back on collateral, and, as all experienced lenders are aware, obtaining loan repayment by liquidating the collateral is an undesirable alternative for achieving repayment of the loan. Cash flow projections should therefore always be evaluated with a critical eye by the prospective lender. The article also examines the effect of cash flow problems on the debtor's business, such as diminishing account balances and overdrafts, and failure to pay suppliers or to pay taxes in a timely manner. These problems usually result in the debtor approaching the bank with an unanticipated "working capital" loan request. Finally, the article deals with alternatives that may be employed to solve a cash flow problem. Since cash flow is such a vital ingredient in every workable loan, it is essential that the lender be knowledgeable in this area.

Many bankers fail to understand the importance of periodic visits to the premises of the borrower, or worse, perceive these visits to be "social calls" that are a waste of time. In reality, periodic calls on the borrower are an important technique for monitoring and supervising both the loan and the collateral which secures it. The third article addresses the importance of such visits and emphasizes the information that the lender may gain from them. A periodic visit will ascertain the amount and condition of the borrower's inventory; verify the location of collateral; provide information regarding the condition of the debtor's premises; indicate the attitude of employees; and provide information regarding the type of customer with which the debtor deals. Some banks' policies require annual visits to the premises of each commercial borrower, and if the loan is considered to be a potential problem, then visits may be required as often as every sixty or ninety days. Obviously, subsequent to the visit, all pertinent information that has been gained should be recorded in the credit file. Most borrowers are pleased that the bank has enough interest in their business to make a visit, and in most instances, the calling officer is given a positive reception. In those cases where the calling officer receives a negative reception, the bank should immediately begin to consider the existence of potential problems. An experienced calling officer can become quite adept at gaining information in an unobtrusive manner, and such information will be of considerable assistance to the bank in monitoring and supervising the loan.

The fourth article discusses the use of the bank's board of directors in developing a high-quality loan portfolio. In addition to formulating policy and overseeing the management of the bank, a bank's board can perform many other useful functions. In most communities, the bank's directors will be acquainted with many prospective borrowers and can provide valuable input regarding these loan applicants. Further, the board can assist management in identifying the credit needs of the community and in formulating the means for meeting those needs, an important step for complying with the provisions of the Community Reinvestment Act. The bank's board can also effectively monitor the bank's lending program and provide guidance to management concerning the quality of the bank's portfolio and the thrust of its lending programs. The board should also ensure that the bank has an adequate loan support system and that procedures for loan documentation are adequate. In summary, an active, knowledgeable board of directors can be a tremendous asset to a bank and can be a critical factor in the performance of the bank's loan portfolio and the bank's profitability.

Credit inquiries are addressed in the fifth article. Most bankers dislike handling credit inquiries. On the other hand, bankers also recognize that the free exchange of credit information among institutional lenders is an important factor in the loan decision-making process. Therefore, most banks want to cooperate in the exchange of information, but are apprehensive about the many pitfalls involved in doing so. There is no legal requirement that a lender furnish credit information to any other lender, but if it chooses to do so, it must make full and accurate disclosure of the pertinent facts. If, either by intent or through negligence, the bank misleads an inquirer, it may be liable for the resulting damages. Hence, it is critical that banks set up comprehensive procedures for responding to credit inquiries, and ensure that staff follows those procedures. The article outlines a number of pitfalls that banks may encounter, and further suggests policies and procedures which will be helpful to the bank that is either reviewing or establishing procedures in this area.

The sixth article discusses the problems that banks may encounter in making unsecured loans to upscale customers. Because its upscale customers, usually young professionals, are generally excellent account customers, and because competition for their business is intense, the bank may feel impelled to extend significant amounts of unsecured credit. This decision will be based on the customer's strong cash flow and significant account balances against which the bank may exercise the right of setoff. This article discusses the various pitfalls that the bank may encounter in extending unsecured credit, such as problems with contingent liability, unpaid taxes, credit card debt, and the segregation of funds in protected accounts such as IRA or Keogh accounts. The importance of the borrower's integrity is stressed, especially if an unsecured loan is being made. Finally, the article establishes guidelines for the extension of unsecured credit, stressing integrity, strong financial position, adequate cash flow, competent management of finances, etc.

A banker's acceptance is a bill of lading or invoice which is accepted or guaranteed by a commercial bank on behalf of the buyer. The seventh article discusses the use of banker's acceptances to finance domestic transactions. This financing technique has appeal to the customer both because it is a new idea and because it is usually priced competitively. This article describes the eligibility requirements and the documentation required for a banker's acceptance financing. It will be helpful to the commercial lender who is not familiar with banker's acceptances, and who may want to consider offering this financing alternative to some of the bank's better customers.

"Get the CEO out of Lending" is the title of a challenging article that explores the relationship between the bank's CEO and its lending operation. Since many chief executive officers were originally lenders, it may be difficult for CEOs to extricate themselves from the lending function. This article points out that it is the responsibility of the CEO to provide overall management and guidance to the total banking operation, and that overinvolvement in the lending operation may be detrimental to the performance of his other duties. Even in a small bank, the CEO probably does not have much time available to devote to lending. The article also points out, somewhat tongue-in-cheek, that the CEO usually makes the poorest loans, and then identifies specific reasons this may be true, including the fact that the CEO probably has less time to adequately process a loan request than do the loan officers. Further, the article makes it clear that managing a bank is a difficult and complex job that requires the full time and attention of the CEO. Lastly, the article makes recommendations for getting the CEO out of lending, which in a small institution may require a significant public relations effort. The article presents several alternatives for accomplishing the ultimate objective of freeing the CEO from any lending duties. It contains a number of ideas and perspectives that should be of considerable interest to all chief executive officers who are still involved in the lending operation of their banks.

The Comprehensive Environmental Response Compensation and Liability Act (also called CERCLA or the Superfund) has created significant concern among commercial lenders. This federal legislation provides that the subsequent transferee of real estate, such as a mortgagee that obtains title through foreclosure, may become liable for the cleanup of hazardous waste located on that property. In some instances, this liability may far exceed the original loan balance owed on the real estate. Therefore, it is essential for bank mortgage lenders to be aware of this potential liability when considering a loan that is to be secured by real estate which may have a potential hazardous waste problem. In a number of instances, banks have declined to foreclose on real estate pledged to them because of their concern about the potential cleanup cost for which they might become liable as a subsequent transferee. The ninth article discusses both the provisions of CERCLA and the developing body of case law in this legal area. It also makes recommendations for protecting the bank, such as requiring an inspection by an environmental expert prior to the making of any commercial mortgage loan. This article should be of vital interest to any lender involved in commercial mortgage lending.

The final articles deal with leveraged buy-outs. Although many banks are now viewing LBOs with less favor than previously, many institutions have been involved in a significant number of leveraged buy-outs. These articles discuss the basic

30

principles with which the financer of an LBO must be familiar, describe the incentives for doing an LBO, identify the ingredients of a successful LBO, and provide a checklist for evaluating a cash flow basis buy-out. They stress that adequate cash flow and good management are the two essential ingredients for any buy-out. These articles should be of interest to any commercial lender who is considering structuring a leveraged buy-out.

Avoid Trouble: Make a Good Decision Going In

The old adage, "A banker never makes a bad loan, it only turns bad after it's been on the books for a while," is untrue. Many knowledgeable bankers and collection attorneys believe that banks frequently make loans which are seriously flawed at their inception and subsequently become problem loans or charge-offs.

Banks make poor initial loan decisions for a num-ber of reasons. The primary problem is that the bank simply fails to obtain adequate information, therefore never really gaining an understanding of the borrower's financial position, repayment capacity, and general ability and willingness to meet its obligations. In too many instances, banks rely on unverified information furnished by the loan applicant and make little or no effort to verify it or supplement it with information from other sources.

In some cases, the banker succumbs to pressure from an applicant and makes a hasty decision based on inadequate information, without making any meaningful analysis. Problems are also caused by the bank overestimating the ability of management, by accepting overly optimistic projections of future performance, failing to evaluate collateral properly, and neglecting to structure the loan properly. This article will discuss the various steps a bank may take to improve the quality of its decisions on new loan applications.

Information, please

Since inadequate information is a major cause of poor loan decisions, the loan officer should never make a decision or a recommendation to a loan committee until he or she has obtained adequate information about the borrower and its financial affairs. How much information is enough? That depends on the size and complexity of the loan. However, in almost every instance, the loan officer should obtain the following information from the applicant:

FINANCIAL INFORMATION. Financial statements should take top priority. The loan officer should obtain both a current balance sheet and balance sheets for at least two prior years. He or she should also examine income statements for the current period and for at least two prior years. Beware of the applicant who is hesitant or unwilling to furnish income and expense information, since this may indicate a business that is unprofitable or performing in an otherwise unsatisfactory manner. The lender should also be concerned about the quality of statement information, since incomplete or incorrect information may misrepresent the financial status of the business—and therefore mislead the lender. In some instances, especially where the requested loan is large, the loan officer may have to demand better quality information before a decision can be made. Lenders are often far too hesitant to criticize the quality of information submitted by applicants and to request more adequate information, for fear they will lose the loan to a less demanding competitor.

PROJECTIONS. Since the funds for repayment of a loan made now will be generated by the business's future performance rather than by its past history, the lender *must* obtain projections of income, expenses, and capital needs for at least two years or the term of the loan. Sound projections are excellent indicators of a business's ability to produce the cash that will be needed to pay off the loan. While operating projections will

32

indicate the amount of cash the business will probably be able to generate to repay the loan, projections of capital needs indicate the amount of funding that the business will require in future years to acquire needed assets such as equipment and manufacturing facilities.

AGED LISTINGS OF RECEIVABLES AND PAYABLES. If a business has a substantial amount of accounts receivable, an aged listing of those receivables may be an excellent indicator of their quality. An aged listing of payables will give the prospective lender an indication of who the business's major suppliers are and how promptly they are paid.

EQUIPMENT LISTING. If a business owns a substantial amount of equipment, obtain a listing of that equipment. This is especially important if the equipment is to be used as collateral for the loan.

ORDER BACKLOG. In the case of a manufacturing business, obtain information about its order backlog, since this is an excellent indicator of future sales activity and the extent to which the business has penetrated its market.

MANAGEMENT'S CREDENTIALS. A lender must obtain sufficient information about the ability and past experience of management, since management's capability is a key indicator of the company's success potential.

Information from outside sources

The loan officer should also utilize various outside sources to verify and supplement the information that has been provided by the loan applicant.

PUBLIC RECORDS SEARCHES. Perform a Uniform Commercial Code search in both the appropriate state and local filing offices. If the borrower operates in more than one state, make a search in each of those states. The lender should also perform a judgment and tax lien search.

33

CONTACT WITH INDUSTRY SOURCES. A business's suppliers are usually the first to recognize that a business is having financial problems. Therefore, the prospective lender should contact several of the applicant's major suppliers to obtain credit information. Some industry associations also compile operating statistics similar to Robert Morris Associates' (RMA's) *Annual Statement Studies*, which may be helpful in comparing the applicant's performance with industry averages.

A VISIT TO THE APPLICANT'S PREMISES. Before making a substantial loan to a new borrower, visit the borrower's premises. The loan officer may gain a new perspective on how the business actually operates and learn much about the capability and adequacy of the business's employees. The officer will also have an opportunity to learn about the business's customers and facilities. A visit to a business's premises is a crucial and often overlooked step in the loan decision-making process.

APPRAISAL. If the collateral is real estate or equipment, the lender should require a professional appraisal to establish a realistic collateral value. Lenders are often far too hesitant to ask loan applicants to furnish appraisals, even though this information is often essential in determining the lender's collateral margin.

The next step

Once the lender has accumulated sufficient information, the information must be organized so it can be analyzed and conclusions can be drawn about the acceptability of the loan application. The lender must compile the information in such a manner that comparisons can be made between current and past information, and trends can be identified. This generally involves the preparation of a "spread sheet," which enables the analyst to identify the changes in each statement item from one balance sheet and income statement to the next. Such an analysis makes it relatively easy to trace the progress (or lack thereof) of a business over a period of several years. The end result of this analysis should be the identification of the relative strengths and weaknesses of the applicant's business.

The applicant's projections of future performance should also be examined with a critical eye. Applicants often tend to overestimate sales volume and underestimate expenses. As a result, actual net cash flow may be considerably less than shown in the applicant's projections. Projections should always be tested against the past performance of the applicant, and the borrower should be required to explain how it will achieve any significant improvement in projected performance over past actual performance. Bankers generally have been far too willing to accept unsubstantiated, overly optimistic projections from borrowers instead of reasoned estimates of future performance.

It is also crucial to assess properly the capability of the borrower's management. Since adequate management is probably the most important factor in the success of a business, the workability of the lender's loan is directly related to the ability and integrity of management. If it appears that management's credentials are suspect, proceed with caution.

Be especially cautious in the case of a new business with inexperienced management. People with a high degree of technical knowledge may not necessarily have the knowledge and attributes required to be successful business managers. Many bankers have learned from experience that an excellent construction foreman or a highly skilled laboratory technician does not always succeed as a business manager. Therefore, it is as important to obtain adequate information about the skills and experience of the business's manager as it is to obtain adequate information about the business's financial status.

The banker should also proceed cautiously when dealing with a business in an industry with which he or she is not

35

familiar, since it may be very difficult to identify potential pitfalls that are characteristic of a particular industry. For example, several years ago the author's bank agreed to finance a newly formed manufacturing company which produced substrates (aluminum blanks from which rigid computer disks are made), even though the bank had little knowledge of the computer hardware industry. Although the company was well managed, the loan became a problem due to excess capacity and softening demand in the industry. Had the bank been more familiar with this particular industry, it might have foreseen the problem.

Another important factor in making a good initial loan decision is the proper evaluation of the collateral that will secure the loan. Although a banker often does an excellent job of analyzing the financial information, he or she may make little effort to verify collateral valuations. Loan applicants have a tendency to overestimate the value of their assets, so asset valuations shown on the balance sheet may bear little relationship to the actual liquidation value of those assets. At the very least, the bank should inspect the proposed collateral be-fore making the loan. As noted earlier, in some instances a professional appraisal may be required. Many banks could significantly reduce their loan charge-offs simply by devoting more time and effort to developing realistic collateral valuations.

Finally, the loan must be properly structured if it is to be workable. The maturity of the loan should be determined by its purpose and by the date at which cash flow pledged as repayment will be available. For instance, if a short-term loan is made to finance Christmas inventory for a retailer, it seems logical for the banker to propose a single pay note maturing in early January. If the loan is to finance the purchase of a drill press with a useful life of fifteen years, a five-year term loan would be reasonable. However, a five-year term loan for the purchase of Christmas inventory would be inappropriate and would create problems for both the bank and the borrower.

In summary, a lender may avoid many future problems by making a good initial loan decision. This requires the development and proper analysis of adequate information about the borrower, a realistic assessment of the business's future performance, valid judgments about management's capability, a realistic analysis of the bank's collateral position, and proper structuring of the loan.

Cash Flow: The Vital Ingredient

As oil lubricates a fine machine, so cash flow lubricates the whole lending process to make it work smoothly. Cash flow provides the funds for repayment of a loan; if a loan is repaid in full in a timely manner, then whatever its weaknesses may have been, the lender generally considers it to be a good loan. On the other hand, no matter how honest the customer may be, or how well-collateralized the loan, the loan will not work as anticipated without adequate cash flow for repayment.

A lender's judgment of the borrower's capacity to repay is therefore extremely important, and this involves a realistic assessment of the cash flow generated by the ongoing operation of the borrower's business. Note that funds produced by the sale of capital assets necessary for the operation of the business are *not* normal cash flow, since this will disrupt or curtail the business's operation. Rather, cash flow is derived from the sale of products or services, and collection of the resulting accounts receivable. Cash flow may also derive from other sources, such as interest received or tax refunds.

Cash flow is the key

How does a lender judge a business's capacity to generate cash flow, i.e., capacity to repay? When dealing with an established business, the lender may do so in two ways. First, the lender can study records of the business's past performance, utilizing information in annual income statements and records of bank deposits. Second, the lender should study projections of future performance in the form of cash flow projections. Information from income statements is valuable because it gives the lender a picture of the business's past capability to generate repayment, and provides a relatively sound basis for projecting future income, expenses, and repayment. Records of deposits to the borrower's bank accounts provide an accurate picture of the cash the business actually generated during a given time period.

The lender should remember, however, that it is future performance, not past performance that will determine the amount of repayment available for the loan he is about to make. Cash flow projections that intelligently estimate the future availability of cash for repayment may be more important to the lender than historical performance data. Such a projection normally covers a twelve-month period, and is broken down on a monthly basis, showing beginning cash, estimated cash receipts and cash disbursements, and ending cash for each month. In some cases, a projection for one or more additional years will also be prepared, but on a less detailed basis.

In the case of a new business, or one in which a substantial expansion or other change in the nature of the business has taken place, historical income and expense data may be of little relevance, even if available. Since the lender cannot readily use historical data to test projections of future performance in such a case, assessing repayment capacity becomes much more difficult. For this reason, lenders generally are less inclined to lend to a new business or one that has significantly changed or expanded its operations, often demanding a Small Business Administration guaranty, additional collateral, or other changes in loan terms to compensate for the lack of proven ability to produce cash flow.

Deciding how much is enough

What constitutes adequate cash flow in a given situation? Every business must generate sufficient cash income to replace inventory and to pay all normal operating expenses and income taxes. It must produce enough additional revenue to provide an adequate return to its owners and to repay debt in an orderly manner. The amount of debt repayment required will depend upon the type of debt owed, its terms, and the demands of the holders of that debt. Ideally, a business operation should also produce sufficient cash flow to enable it to establish cash reserves to provide funds for the replacement of fixed assets, protect against future adversity, and fund future growth.

When analyzing repayment capacity, a lender must always remember that only cash repays loans! Unsold inventory, uncollected accounts, and work in process are only potential repayment and do not become actual repayment until converted to cash. The lender must project available cash income and the amount of cash needed to meet obligations. This is the basis of *all* cash flow projections.

The founders of new businesses, usually entrepreneurs who are optimistic by nature, have a tendency to overestimate the rate at which sales will develop, while they underestimate the cash costs of operating the business. This presents a potential trap for the unwary lender who fails to view the businesss's cash flow projections with a critical eye. As cash flow from sales develops more slowly than projected, and as expenses absorb more cash than expected, the bank may be forced to choose between loaning the business substantially greater amounts than it originally intended (resulting in substantially greater exposure) or letting the business fail. This is often one of the most difficult of all credit decisions.

To avoid this problem, the lender not only must critically review the cash flow projections submitted by the applicant, but may also be required to counsel him or her in their preparation. This could include furnishing the borrower with information and forms, or involve advising him or her to retain an accountant to help prepare the projections. The lender should avoid becoming too directly involved in this process, lest the projections become the thinking of the lender rather than that of the applicant.

Effect of cash flow problems

What happens when a business begins to experience cash flow problems? First, its cash balances will be significantly diminished. The result will be overdrafts—usually the bank's first "red flag" that a cash flow problem is developing. Second, the business will delay its payments to suppliers, resulting in an increase in the amount of accounts payable on the company's balance sheet. Also, it may result in the bank receiving an increasing number of credit inquiries from concerned suppliers. Third, the business may cease making its state and federal tax payments, which will ultimately result in tax liens, tax levies against the debtor's accounts and other assets, and severe penalties. Despite the dire consequences, a hard-pressed businessman may use this alternative as an "easy" way to meet this week's payroll, to purchase needed inventory, or pay his own salary. Fourth, the debtor will probably approach its bank (or another institution) and request an additional "working capital" loan. If the debtor fails to receive such a loan, it is likely that he will soon be delinquent on his existing loans. This progression indicates that several third parties, such as suppliers and the Internal Revenue Service, may be aware of the debtor's problems before the bank is, unless the bank is actively monitoring average balances and overdrafts in the debtor's accounts.

Most working capital loan requests are entirely justifiable, resulting from a seasonal need to increase inventory, fund an unusually large job, or carry additional receivables. Such requests are ordinarily handled in a routine manner by commercial banks. It is the unanticipated request, with only a vague explanation as to why the funds are needed, that should alert the lender to possible cash flow problems.

Solving a cash flow problem

What can a business do to increase its cash flow? A number of steps may be taken in most cases, including accelerating collection of receivables, increasing inventory turnover, reducing cash operating expenses, delaying payments to suppliers, and lengthening debt maturity. Collecting receivables more promptly makes cash available sooner to meet cash obligations. By increasing inventory turnover, the business can increase its sales volume and also increase its receivables and cash flow without any additional investment in inventory. A reduction in cash operating expenses, such as eliminating the monthly lease cost of an unnecessary vehicle or office machine, obviously reduces cash needs. Delaying payments to suppliers will temporarily increase cash flow but may have an adverse effect on the business's relationship with its suppliers; for that reason it is usually a poor solution to a cash flow problem. Extending debt maturity will increase cash flow by reducing the amount of required debt service payments, but lenders generally will not consent to such a renewal or extension unless the debt is well secured and they believe the business will ultimately succeed.

All the steps mentioned above are, at best, temporary solutions. The ultimate formula for adequate cash flow is simple: The business must generate adequate sales volume, maintain adequate gross profit margins, control its overhead and operating expenses, turn its inventory frequently, and promptly collect its receivables.

There is a significant difference between profits and cash

flow. A failing business may have substantial cash flow if it is liquidating its inventory, receivables, and equipment. A profitable but rapidly growing busi- ness may be very hard-pressed for cash, since rapidly increasing inventory and accounts receivable will act as a "sponge" to absorb a substantial amount of cash flow. Profits are essential for the long-term survival and growth of a business, but in the short term, a debtor's ability to repay is determined by cash flow rather than profits. Cash flow is the vital ingredient for a workable loan which cannot be replaced by collateral, or by reliance on the borrower's character or past performance.

Visiting the Borrower: More Than a Social Call

A visit to a borrower's place of business is a valuable source of information for a lender. Middle Market Lending Letter asked two experienced lenders what they look for when they visit borrowers.

"A good lender can learn a lot from an inspection," says Bob Behrens, president, The First National Bank of Ogden, Illinois. "It's important to look at the inventory. Is it current, or is it obsolete? When I was a naive young loan officer, my employer sent me to inspect the inventory of a heavy equipment dealer. The earth movers and tractors were all in a line outside in the yard. I decided to start at one end of the line and work my way down. I happened to look up and see another man in a suit with a clipboard doing the same thing. It turned out that he was the representative of another creditor which also had an interest in the collateral. The moral of that story is to beware of someone else who appears on the scene and seems to have an interest in the same collateral as you do."

"Inventory is an area of danger for lenders," says Clyde Draughon, Jr., group vice president, Trust Company Bank, Atlanta. "There's the classic horror story about the auditor who jumped into a grain elevator, expecting to go down three feet, but sailed down forty. The lender should look for inventory that could be borrowed. How often does the company take physical inventory? What has been their experience at year-end, plus or minus? Where is the inventory located? What's the policy on returns and allowances, and how do they follow turnover?

"We like to meet with the CEO and the financial officer and chat about what the company does and its needs," says Draughon. "It's good to have a general discussion and talk about the numbers, tour the plant, then sit down and do a recap. During each part of a meeting, I try to get a feel for the management and its style. As far as collateral, it's helpful when we can glance at an aging of accounts receivable. I also glance at a couple of their large accounts and any large past due accounts. This helps me get a feel for what's a major problem, what's not.

"As we sit there or walk around, information is flowing," Draughon continues. "Is the inventory in order, in boxes or broken cases? Is there evidence of a lot of returned goods? Is the plant well maintained? The housekeeping is a big issue. What do they say about slow-moving items?"

Trust your instincts

"We also look at the employees in a business," says Behrens. "What is their attitude? What kind of customers does the business have? If it's a retail type of business, what kind of people walk in off the street? Is it a presentable plant? Is it clean, well kept, recently painted, or messy and neglected? I also like to try to visit with the bookkeeper or in-house accountant, independent of the manager or owner. I like to see what the ledgers look like, what accounting system is used day to day. Does the end of the month statement come out on time, or are they behind? I always notice if people get nervous or uneasy when I talk to the bookkeeper. Does the

43

tour of the borrower's facilities direct you away from certain areas? Good loan officers are adept at sensing those attitudes.

"Our bank's policy is to go out and visit the customers," Behrens notes. "For a business that's doing well, we try to visit annually. We may visit a business we're concerned about every sixty to ninety days. If you're observant, you begin to feel whether things are upbeat or not. You can develop a gut feeling about a business. I remember walking into one business and the manager said, 'Let's go sit in your car, there's no privacy in here.' I saw that as an attempt to hide something. It turned out that the business was in deep trouble, with inventory missing. My gut feeling was right.

"Most good businesspeople are pleased that you have enough concern and interest to make a visit to their business," says Behrens. "Ordinarily, we get a very positive reception. That may change if there's something wrong at the business. If they're gracious but 'too busy' to take the time to meet with you, it makes you wonder if you're getting close to something they don't want you to see. There are three responses to that situation. You can leave after seeing what you can in a few minutes. You can ignore their protestations and insist on taking a tour anyway. Or you can say, 'I'll be back next week.' The disadvantage of this approach is that it gives them a chance to hide what they don't want you to see. Sometimes I've pretended to be unaware of the borrower's reluctance and said, 'Let's take a tour anyway.' You have to play it by ear and use your experience."

The case of the ugly cow

While most of a bank's business customers are honest, there are notable exceptions. "The perspective of a twenty-seven-year veteran is tinged with some cynicism," says Behrens. "Don't ever to-tally believe what you see, because there are all kinds of ways to pull the wool over your eyes. Even though there's equipment in the yard, they might have borrowed or leased it from someone else for a few days. I know of a case where a company did just that to have an earth mover for the loan officer to see.

"In another case, all of a business's inventory was stored in two-foot-square cartons which were stacked six or eight high in a huge rectangle. The manager said that this was all the inventory—but the stack was hollow on the inside. If you discover that something's going on, it's best to confront the borrower with the problem and ask to sit down with him and try to work out the problem. Usually, when the debtor knows the game is up, he's willing to work out a solution.

"In another episode in my youth," Behrens recalls, "my employer sent me to count a herd of cattle which were running loose in a large area of woodland. The borrowers rounded up the cattle and drove them by me so I could count them. After awhile I woke up to the fact that they were running the same cattle by me, time after time. The only reason I caught on was that one of them was the ugliest animal I ever saw—it looked like a Texas longhorn. After I saw a third one that was identical, I realized there couldn't be three of them."

"Every loan officer develops a unique style of asking questions," says Draughon. "If you can develop a pattern, you're asking the same general questions as you move from industry to industry. In a visit, you're trying to flesh out the numbers. You never know a business until you go out and see it. Before we do business with a company, I'll go out with the loan officer and visit the company. You like to hear their goals, and with most entrepreneurs you can count on two or three hours. We follow up monthly reports with a call because it gives us a chance to ask questions and point out any discrepancies and potential problem areas. Sometimes a visit will show you that you don't want to do any business with a company. The tip-off is a messy, disorganized physical plant and a mishmash of inventory.

45

"What you're looking for is a balance between the numbers, the physical condition of the place, and the management team," Draughon concludes. "There should be no tremendous negative that can't be overcome somewhere else. Once you know a business, you re looking for changes in trends. To get the most out of a visit, lenders must apply experience from other situations, use their common sense, and listen to their gut feelings."

Using Your Board of Directors to Develop a High-Quality Loan Portfolio*

A few years ago, I attended a director's loan committee meeting in a good-size bank. The bank's new management declared that it had decided to terminate the consumer and installment lending it had been doing and would be a "middle-market commercial lender." Along that line, management asked the directors to accept or reject four loan applications.

I thought that someone would certainly object to this. If directors do not have anything to say about the thrust of the bank's lending program, what do they have a say about? On the other hand, if they spend all their time in the director's loan committee meetings analyzing three or four loan applications, who is supervising the bank's overall lending program from the standpoint of the board? In this case, it turned out that no one was.

In a small community, directors know many of the prospective borrowers and can provide good input. Even there, why should directors take on the responsibilities for which they are paying the bankers? There should be a clear understanding between the director's loan committee and the board as to what the committee is to do. For a director's loan committee

*This article is written by Don Wright, president of Don Wright Associates, a bank consulting firm in Dallas, Texas.

to report that it has met and examined 127 loans is ridiculous. It is impossible to examine 127 loans in an hour and a half. Instead, the director's loan committee should be instrumental in helping the bank to make quality loans through the steps outlined below.

DIRECTORS SHOULD PARTICIPATE WITH MANGEMENT IN THE DEVELOPMENT OF A LOAN POLICY AND RECOMMEND IT TO THE BOARD FOR ADOPTION. Loan policy should define the thrust of the bank's lending program. If, for example, the bank is involved in interim construction lending, what kind of builders are acceptable? Must a builder have a track record? What kind of liquidity is expected? Are raw land loans a normal part of the lending program, and to what extent?

Nothing here should suggest that the policy will put the lender in a straitjacket. Instead, the policy as it applies to interim construction lending will force the board to look at whether there should be a large expansion in interim construction lending, if the market is in luxury homes or middle-priced homes, and how well-qualified the bank is to do this business. Its policy should similarly apply to other areas of lending.

THE DIRECTOR'S LOAN COMMITTEE SHOULD BE ENGAGED IN MONITORING THE EFFECTIVENESS OF THE BANK'S LENDING PROGRAM. True, all of this is after the fact, because the loan has been made. However, if the loan committee says, "We would not like to make any more loans like this," it will certainly have an effect.

DIRECTORS AND MANAGEMENT SHOULD ESTABLISH OBJECTIVES AS TO ASSET QUALITY—which primarily means loan quality. How can directors judge asset quality? One great regulator said directors should be aware of delinquency and what is being done about it. A reasonable delinquency figure in your bank today depends upon the kind of loan. Single-family residential loans, for example, would not be likely to

47

have a high delinquency rate. Whatever the target is, the board should know the current delinquency figure. If it is over the target, the directors should be told what is being done about it.

What level of loan charge-offs is your bank willing to have? None, of course, but that's hardly practical. As a bank CEO in a large city, I was always aiming at one-fourth to one-half of one percent of average loans outstanding. Many times we didn't hit it—but it certainly helped to have a target. If losses rise above the target, directors should ask what is being done and receive regular reports.

What is a reasonable volume of criticized loans compared with the bank's capital? When the examiner sits in the board meeting and says in a doleful voice, "Fifty percent of your capital is impaired by classified loans," is that good or bad? The answer depends greatly on the nature of the classifications. A group of substandard loans is more desirable than a lesser amount of doubtful and loss loans. Some bankers have suggested that when their total of classified loans reaches 50 percent of capital, an alarm should ring. This includes all classifications, including those on which your bank does not expect to have any loss.

During a bank examination, one or more critiques will be held, most of which will concern loans. DIRECTORS SHOULD FEEL FREE TO ATTEND EXAMINATION CRITIQUES AS OBSERV- ERS, NOT PARTICIPANTS. It is important for directors to attend after there has been a change of management or when there's difficulty in the loan portfolio. This will allow the director to see what the officers know about their loans and their general reaction. Directors should compare the loan classifications with those of the previous examinations. What happened to last year's substandard loans? Did they graduate to the nonclassified category or fall to doubtful or loss? Is the bank's loan portfolio getting better or worse, and again, what is being done?

Keeping current on loan quality

I've conducted about two dozen "retreats" with management and directors and have spoken before many director's seminars for state banker associations. One of the most common questions is, "How can we keep more current on our loan quality?" Directors are increasingly aware that if bad loans are being put on the books, heavy losses can be built in before the next examination.

The board has a legitimate interest in whether the bank has an adequate loan support system and should be aware of any criticisms as to documentation, insurance, and filing. Many banks are developing an internal loan review division which reports to both management and the board. Some have done this by hiring a retired examiner or banker. Some have had a great credit officer who could say "no" and be overruled only by the CEO or the board.

Other banks have passed the loans around; that is, I examine your loans and vice versa. In one case, the chairman and part-owner of five banks insisted that every bank develop its own problem loan list. This program has teeth in it because if an officer charges off a loan that wasn't on the list, he'd better think that's quite a serious matter. Such a monitored list and the progress on it should at least be available at every board meeting. In troubled banks, directors should receive a written report each month. The good old experienced CEO once did all this in a small bank. But many CEOs are not as experienced now, and lending is more difficult today.

Looking for "red flags"

In addition to the previously mentioned steps, directors should have their "antennae" out. Here are some possible red flags the director should spot.

1. Is the bank paying above the market rate for deposits? If so, why will that bank's borrowers pay more interest

than they would need to pay to others? Perhaps they don't plan to pay the principal.

2. Does the bank have a concentration of credit, either to a person or an industry? Alert managements and boards are increasingly aware of this and are taking steps to have this reported, either in the monthly director's report or by the internal or external auditors.

3. Is the bank generally performing at a level below its peers? I recommend that directors select a group of comparable banks, order the Uniform Bank Performance Report on them, and every three to six months devote a part of the board meeting to making the comparison.

4. Is the bank taking fewer losses than other banks in similar situations? This may be a tip-off that loan losses are being concealed.

5. Is the bank growing too rapidly? I am for growth. However, where will a bank put all its high-cost money and make a profit? The answer, in nearly every case, will be loans. So a bank's profitable growth will be limited by its ability to make sound, profitable loans with reasonable liquidity and without a concentration of credit. It should be obvious to managements and boards that there is a limit to any bank's ability to get and digest new loans.

Of course, directors should not be making loans or urging loans upon the banker. When the director brings in a prospective borrower (which he should do), he should tell the banker what he knows and then leave the decision up to the bankers themselves. It is, however, important for the banker to tell the director what happened and why. An informed board of directors can help improve a bank's loan quality.

Seven steps for directors

1. Participate in the development of the bank's loan policy.

2. Monitor the effectiveness of the bank's lending program.

3. Help establish asset quality objectives.

4. Attend bank examination critiques as observers.

5. Be aware of results of the internal loan review process.

6. Be alert for "red flags."

7. Leave the loan decisions to the loan officers.

Handling Credit Inquiries: Proceed with Caution

The handling of credit inquiries is fraught with legal pitfalls; as a result, most bankers feel uncertainty and even trepidation when dealing with this area. Bankers generally agree that the availability of good credit information is vital to both the commercial and consumer lending process, and wish to cooperate in the exchange of information among financial institutions. In order to accommodate the needs and wishes of its commercial customers, the bank may also want to respond to requests for credit information from other interested third parties, such as suppliers.

A commercial bank has no legal obligation to respond to a credit inquiry, and may refuse to respond to any request for credit information. However, if the bank chooses to respond to an inquiry, it must make full and accurate disclosure of the facts in a manner that does not mislead the inquirer. If, either by intent or through negligence, the bank fails to make full and accurate disclosure, it may be liable to the mislead third-

51

party inquirer for any resulting damages. Obviously, unsatisfactory accounts and deteriorating credits will cause the most problems when the bank is replying to requests for credit information. Since the utmost care and discretion are required when dealing with problem accounts, the bank's response to a credit inquiry in such a case should not be left to a clerk. Instead, an officer having the proper training should handle the request.

Consider, for instance, the case of *GMAC v. Central National Bank of Mattoon,* 773 F2d, 771 (CA-7th 1985). Bob Smith Oldsmobile-Cadillac-GMC, Inc., an automobile dealership, had been a customer of Central National Bank of Mattoon for several years. The bank provided the used car "floor plan" for the dealership with GMAC providing financing for the new car inventory. The dealership also had its deposit accounts with Central National which, on numerous occasions, had allowed substantial overdrafts. The policy of GMAC was to send periodic credit questionnaires to banks and trade creditors doing business with its various dealerships. Central National completed and returned several of these questionnaires over a two-year period, usually indicating no overdraft experience. After the dealership failed, GMAC sued the bank for fraud, alleging that its losses were proximately caused by the bank's misrepresentation of the dealership's financial status. The court found that the bank had misrepresented the credit information provided GMAC in order to protect its own loan position and assessed substantial damages against the bank.

What to disclose?

If the bank chooses to respond to a request for information, what facts should be disclosed? In the case of a deposit account, the bank will normally disclose the date opened, average balances (normally expressed by range, such as "hi-five figure," rather than by specific numbers), and its experience regarding overdrafts. When describing its lending relationship, the bank will ordinarily disclose the date its credit accommodations were opened, high credit, balance currently outstanding (again expressed by range), whether secured or unsecured, and the number of times the account has had payments delinquent. The bank should provide only factual information regarding its own experience, and should not generally disclose financial statement information.

The bank should always refrain from making comments regarding opinions, hearsay, and information received from third parties. Be especially careful to avoid disclosing even verified information received from third parties, since doing so may result in the bank being classified as a credit reporting agency as defined by the Fair Credit Reporting Act. Subjective comments concerning the customer's character or management ability should also be avoided. For example, even positive comments such as "their character is excellent" or "they are first-rate businesspeople" are generally inappropriate.

Telephone inquiries

Many banks refuse to respond to telephone inquiries. Others will respond to telephone requests from other financial institutions, but require written requests from all other parties. The greatest problem with telephone inquiries is that the bank will have difficulty verifying the identity of the caller. Banks often employ a call-back procedure under which the caller is required to identify himself and leave a telephone number, after which the bank calls back with the requested credit information. However, this procedure is far from foolproof. If the bank chooses to respond to telephone requests, it must make every effort to identify the caller and determine the reason for which credit information is requested. It must also have a procedure for recording in the credit file the

53

pertinent information concerning the inquiry and the facts disclosed in the bank's reply. A printed form (see sample below) for recording such information can be quite useful, and the use of such a form is recommended. Bank officers often have an impulse to respond to a telephone request by relying on their memory instead of doing the appropriate research. This is a dangerous practice that will ultimately create serious problems.

Prior to returning a telephone call to the inquirer, some banks will contact their customer to obtain permission to divulge information. This is probably the best means of

---

Telephone Credit Inquiry　　　　　　　**Date:** July 20, 1987

---

1 **Bank Customer:** C & B Construction Co.

2 **Inquirer & Location:** Karper Steel Fabricators, Moline, IL

3 **Individual Calling:** Karen Stuart

4 **Title:** Asst. Credit Manager

5 **Phone Number:** (309) 412-3666

　Information Granted

6 **Loan History:** Since 7/82　　Hi credit-low six figures

　Current balance-hi five figures　　　Secured　As agreed

7 **Account History:** Since 4/82　　Mid five figure coll.balance

　One OD past 12 months

8 **Amount Involved—Inquirer:** $16,000

9 **Purpose:** Order for fabricated steel

(use back of card if any additional information is needed)

---

limiting the bank's liability in responding to a credit inquiry. Such action will also help the bank avoid the problem of violating various state statutes which require the bank to deal with the customer's affairs in a confidential manner.

Policies and procedures

Every bank should have written policies and procedures for handling credit inquiries and should ensure that its staff is familiar with these guidelines. Since most bank personnel do not relish handling credit inquiries, the task is often relegated to the most junior member of the staff. So, although senior personnel may be familiar with the bank's policy and procedures, the junior loan officer or accounting department clerk who actually handles these inquiries may be much less well

---

Handling credit inquiries: Seven key questions

1. Does your bank have well-defined policies and procedures for handling credit inquiries?

2. Do the staff people who handle inquiries understand and comply with your policies and procedures?

3. Does the bank retain a written record of all responses to credit inquiries?

4. If your bank responds to telephone requests, does it have a call-back procedure?

5. Are credit inquiries on troublesome accounts referred to an officer trained to handle such requests?

6. Does the bank have adequate educational material and conduct periodic training sessions in this area?

7. Does the bank have adequate procedures for dealing with requests for information from governmental agencies?

---

informed. The bank's procedures should ensure that in every case, the identity of the inquirer is established, the reason for the request is ascertained, only permissible information is disclosed, and a permanent record of the inquiry and the bank's reply is placed in the credit file.

It is imperative that bank personnel handle inquiries properly if the bank is to avoid significant liability. To ensure that this is done, every bank should periodically conduct in-house workshops for personnel involved in handling credit inquiries. Educational materials in this area of banking are readily available. For instance, Robert Morris Associates has a training program entitled *Just the Facts*, which includes a videotape, program guide, and other useful materials. RMA's *Information on Deteriorating Accounts: Handle with Care* is a useful text covering the exchange of credit information on borderline accounts.

The time and effort required for the bank to become adept in handling credit inquiries will pay significant dividends to the bank in controversy and litigation avoided.

The Upscale Loan: How Safe If Unsecured?

Many banks have identified an exciting new market for banking services: high-salaried upscale young professional people—the "yuppie" market. This market includes people like the twenty-eight-year-old attorney in a big-city law firm who has an annual salary of $75,000, the thirty-four-year-old physician who has a six-figure income, and the young professional married couple, each of whom earns $60,000 or more per year. People in this category are prime candidates for deposit account services, investment services, and loans.

Despite their high incomes, these individuals may require substantial borrowings to finance housing, furnishings, automobiles, vacations, and investments. The bank may not only be called upon to extend a real estate mortgage loan of

$200,000 or more, but may also be requested to make loans aggregating $50,000 or more for consumer and investment purposes. In many instances, the bank will make these loans on an unsecured basis because the borrower will insist on it, citing his or her high income and cash flow as justification.

Because these young professionals are usually excellent account customers, and competition among financial institutions for their business is intense, the bank may feel compelled to extend significant amounts of unsecured credit. This is usually done by relying upon a continuing strong cash flow stream and the bank's right of setoff against the borrower's accounts, which may contain substantial balances when the loan is made. However, the bank's reliance upon these factors as a basis for a substantial unsecured loan may be tenuous. For one thing, the borrower may lose his or her job. This may not be a serious problem, since a highly trained professional can usually obtain new employment relatively easily. Also, in the case of a couple who are both highly salaried, the temporary loss of employment by one of the spouses may not greatly jeopardize either their lifestyle or the bank's loan. There are, however, other potential problems which may seriously jeopardize the bank's ability to collect its loan. These may be broadly characterized as lack of integrity, unidentified fiscal pitfalls, and erosion of financial stability.

Importance of integrity

Obviously, the borrower's sense of integrity and his or her dedication to paying the loan as agreed are essential in any lending transaction. This is the "character factor" often referred to by bankers. This sense of integrity, however, is absolutely essential in the case of an unsecured loan, where the bank cannot fall back upon collateral as a secondary source of repayment. Before making an unsecured loan, the bank should carefully examine all the information it has obtained regarding the prospective borrower, including financial statements, consumer credit reports, and information from references. Any indication of unsatisfactory past performance—including collection accounts, tax liens or judgments, and previous loans rated "slow pay"—should alert the bank to a possible problem in this area. Failure to disclose all outstanding indebtedness in a financial statement is another "red flag," as is the borrower's hesitancy to answer pertinent questions regarding his or her financial position.

Fiscal pitfalls

In some instances, the borrower will be subject to potential fiscal pitfalls which may not be evident in his or her personal financial statement. Contingent liabilities, which may not be disclosed in the financial statement at all, or at best may be disclosed in a very cursory manner, are one of these pitfalls. Contingent liability may result from the borrower's investment in a partnership, since a general partner is liable for the debts of a partnership. Even if the prospective borrower is a limited partner, he or she may be subject to assessments under the terms of the limited partnership agreement. Therefore, the disclosure of an investment in either a general or limited partnership in the borrower's balance sheet should result in an inquiry by the lender as to the amount of contingent liability involved. The borrower may also be a guarantor of obligations of relatives or others.

Liability for unpaid state and federal taxes may represent another fiscal pitfall. It is not uncommon for a highly paid professional person to be subjected to a federal tax audit, which in some instances may result in significant additional tax liability. This may also result in an Internal Revenue Service levy against the deposit accounts of the borrower, which will prohibit the bank from exercising its right of setoff against those accounts.

Another fiscal pitfall lies in the area of Individual Retirement Account, as well as Keogh, pension and profit-sharing plans. A high percentage of a typical professional's net worth is often represented by funds invested in accounts of this kind. In analyzing the prospective borrower's net worth, the bank should recognize that such accounts are usually insulated from the claims of creditors, and therefore may be inaccessible to the bank when it attempts to collect its loan. A lender should also be concerned about a prospective borrower who obtains credit from numerous sources. A large amount of credit card debt is especially significant, since this may be indicative of the borrower's inability to manage his or her finances in a prudent manner.

Erosion of financial stability

A borrower may have a strong financial position and adequate cash flow when the loan is made, but there is no guarantee that his or her financial stability will endure throughout the life of the loan. In fact, many events which are often beyond the borrower's control may result in the erosion of the borrower's financial stability. A borrower may be forced to pay debts incurred by his business partners, may lose substantial assets in a property settlement with a former spouse, be subjected to a judgment for unpaid alimony and child support, or be faced with the legal costs involved in defending himself or a family member against criminal charges resulting from the use of narcotics. Imprudent investments in risky ventures may also significantly decrease the borrower's financial strength. In some instances, a hard-pressed debtor may also attempt to hide assets, or engage in fraudulent conveyance of assets, in an attempt to protect them from his creditors.

Dealing with the one-person corporation

Many professionals, such as attorneys, physicians, and accountants, may have a professional corporation in which they

Guidelines for extension of unsecured credit

1. The borrower's integrity is crucial. If there is any evidence of past failure to honor obligations in a timely manner, the bank should not extend unsecured credit.

2. The borrower should have a history of satisfactory performance. Exercise caution in extending unsecured credit to first-time borrowers.

3. The borrower should have a strong financial position and a strong debt-to-worth ratio. This indicates that if adversity arises the borrower will have equities to fall back on. It is also usually indicative of prudent financial management.

4. The borrower should have strong repayment capacity and adequate cash flow to pay for living expenses, to service all debt, and to establish a cash reserve to cover emergencies.

5. The loan should ordinarily be for a relatively short term. Obviously, the longer the term of the loan, the greater the chances of a problem developing.

6. The borrower should deal with relatively few creditors and should have only a modest amount of credit card debt. Numerous creditors and substantial credit card debt are often indicators of poor financial management.

7. The borrower's lifestyle should be commensurate with income.

8. The borrower should manage his or her finances in a conservative manner. High flyers who invest in get-rich-quick schemes are seldom good candidates for unsecured credit.

9. Borrowers who exhibit symptoms of emotional and financial instability should be avoided. These symptoms may include drugs, alcoholism, and gambling.

are the sole stockholder. It is essential for the bank to recognize that the individual and his corporation are two entirely separate entities. To understand the borrower's overall financial situation, the lender must obtain financial statements from both the individual and the corporation. A lender should also be aware that an individual is not liable for the debts of his corporation, even though he is the sole stockholder and officer. Therefore, if a loan is being made to such a corporation, the bank should require the individual involved to cosign or guarantee the loan.

In summary, although the upscale market is a fertile field for new business, bankers should recognize the potential problems involved in the extension of significant amounts of unsecured credit in such a situation.

Using Bankers' Acceptances to Finance Domestic Transactions

Bankers' acceptances have long been used to finance international transactions. Federal Reserve regulations were relaxed in 1982, and banks may now use BAs to finance domestic transactions under certain conditions. Middle market lenders like the idea because they can use BAs as a way to differentiate themselves in their new business prospecting. BA domestic financing appeals to the customer both because it is a new idea and because it is priced competitively.

"A price of a BA rate plus a 150 basis point surcharge would be approximately equivalent to the prime rate today," says Clyde O. Draughon, group vice president, Trust Company Bank, Atlanta. "Because the prime rate is an administrative rate and a BA rate floats freely with the money market, there is often a wide differential between BAs and prime. In some cases, the BA rate plus a surcharge could be below prime. Use of BAs can result in a better loan price for the customer, if he meets the Federal Reserve's requirements for BA trans-

61

actions. However, this can be a way of cutting your price if you're not careful. By adding a proper surcharge, lenders can make money on the spread."

"The advantage to the lender is that he can accept the paper and discount it into the money market to provide the funding for the transaction. Thus, the lender's money use will be zero and active use of BAs could help the lender improve return on assets and return on equity.

Determining eligibility

"BAs are available to anyone who buys or sells in excess of twenty-five miles of their business location and who uses a common carrier (not one of their own) to ship. If they purchase goods using a common carrier and ship with their own carriers, only the purchase side of the transaction would qualify for BA financing.

"To be eligible for BAs, the volume must be related to the underlying transactions," Draughon continues. "Transactions can be on either the selling or purchasing side. For simplicity's sake, we normally issue BAs with a maturity of 30 days, although maturities can range from five days to several months. We limit the volume to the monthly total of qualified sales or purchases. The time period can be extended beyond a month and the volume increased, but the record-keeping can become involved, so we keep to a month.

"Theoretically, the bank does not need to keep records on qualified transactions, but can rely on the borrower to make sure that the transactions are eligible. However, if the volume of BA financing exceeds the eligible transactions, the arrangement could be subject to attack by the Federal Reserve," warns Draughon. "Because of our desire not to become embroiled in a dispute between the borrower and the Federal Reserve, we ask the customer to keep records on the activity—such as sales or purchase reports—and to furnish us with a copy.

The customer does not have to keep detailed records such as copies of invoices but can use a summary report. Ineligible transactions can be financed, but the bank must keep a 5-percent reserve against these transactions. Therefore, most banks limit their financing to eligible transactions.

"To set up BA financing, the bank needs a formal agreement with the borrower that spells everything out. Each transaction must be covered by an eligibility certificate. Because of the handling involved, it is generally not profitable to finance BAs for less than $1 million." Banks must sell off BAs in large enough increments to get a good price reselling them on the short-term money market.

"We lend to distributors and manufacturers, who request part of their line of credit on a BA basis," says Draughon. "We use BA financing in conjunction with a line of credit, not as a major part of lending. If you have a $14 million line of credit, you could put half of it on a BA basis. One of our customers has been using BAs domestically for the past year, and we're talking to three others."

What is a Bankers' Acceptance?

A BA is a bill of lading (or invoice) between the seller and the buyer, which is accepted (or guaranteed) by commercial banks on behalf of the buyer. Once the buyer's bank has accepted the invoice for payment, it is negotiable and can be discounted as a bearer instrument (i.e., bought at a discount by a bank or other investor) prior to maturity, including rediscounting this paper at the Federal Reserve's discount window.

(From *Modern Banking*, by Austin, Hakala, and Scampini. Bankers Publishing Co., 1985)

Get the CEO Out of Lending*

"By the time a bank reaches $50 million in assets, the CEO should not be lending money. If possible, the transition should be made much earlier." I've made those statements to directors, CEOs, and lending officers in several states, and, almost without exception, there is universal agreement—in principle. In practice, it's another story. Actually, many directors and a few CEOs say they never even thought about getting the CEO out of lending. But most CEOs would jump at the chance to spend more time on what should be their major function—running the bank.

There are at least two reasons community bank CEOs are primarily involved in lending: economic constraints and tradition. In most smaller banks, the constraints of salary expense seem to dictate that everyone must be "doing something," as opposed to being able to afford someone who "just manages." The CEO is the highest paid employee and generally takes care of the most profitable, and riskiest, portion of the assets—the loan portfolio.

A more subtle, yet equally compelling, reason for the CEO to be a lender is because most CEOs were lenders first. The problem can be especially acute when the CEO was a lender at the same bank prior to becoming the CEO. Much of the lending officer's loan portfolio naturally follows him or her to the top post. The problem is further compounded by the desire on the part of certain, primarily large, customers who feel they can only do business with "the boss." This group of "important" customers usually includes the board members, so the incentives to create an "objective" CEO are reduced, and the perpetuation of CEO as lender continues.

---

*This article was written by Dennis McCuistion, a banking consultant in Irving, Texas, and reprinted with permission from *Texas Banking,* March 1988. © Texas Banking Association.

Why get out?

There are at least two major reasons CEOs must get out of lending: The CEO usually makes the worst loans, and someone has to manage the bank. Let's explore both reasons. In many cases, a person is made CEO because he or she is the best or most prolific lender. Why then would I assert that the CEO is often the worst lender? With apologies to those of you who do excellent jobs as both lender and CEO, my experience is that CEOs become the worst lenders for several reasons.

- There is added "pressure" applied to CEOs. By this I mean social pressure; customers, intentionally and unintentionally, convince the CEO of his or her invincibility and importance. Then, when a loan request follows (perhaps "negotiated" at the club or Rotary meeting), the CEO is, in effect, compromised and may find it extremely difficult to say no.

- The CEO has, because of other time constraints, a tendency to "shoot from the hip." By this I mean that the required credit investigation process is short-circuited. There's no need to get a new credit report, run a trade check, analyze the financials, etc., because the customer has either "banked here forever" or the loan needs almost immediate funding.

- Most banks have one or more loan committees composed of officers, directors, or some combination of the two. When a CEO has gotten out of lending, he or she can truly be the most effective member of the committee by asking pertinent questions, defending or questioning loan officer decisions, and generally running the meeting in a manner which assures that good decisions are made.

- On the other hand, when the CEO has loans to present and past dues to discuss, his or her effectiveness may be lessened for two reasons: 1) It is difficult to point out weaknesses in other loan officers' credits if those same weaknesses exist in the CEO's loans; and 2) other loan officers may be reluctant to criticize loans presented by the CEO. After all, the loan officer would like to keep his job as well as perform it.

For the last eleven years, I have consulted, not only with banks, but with many other businesses as well. Bankers and lenders are exposed to hundreds of businesses, each of which has its own set of opportunities, many of which come cleverly disguised as problems. But in all the businesses I've seen, a bank is the most difficult to run. Why? Because of an assortment of obvious—and not so obvious—reasons.

- TIME: Financial institutions balance every day—they prepare a statement of condition daily which requires that all transactions which arrive during banking hours be processed that business day. Most other businesses prepare monthly, quarterly, or in some cases, annual financial statements, so the pressure to "get things done today" is much less.

- INTIMACY: Money is an intimate commodity. Customers, whether buying it from us or selling it to us, demand instant, confidential, accurate service—and rightfully so. With no offense intended, customers of concrete contractors seldom become emotionally attached to their foundations or driveways.

- COMPLEXITY: The financial services industry is highly regulated, slightly deregulated, almost reregulated, and overwhelmed by new services and changing market conditions. With stop-and-go conditions such as the moratorium, statewide and interstate banking, and the uncertainty of pending legislation, certainly banking "ain't what it used to be." More and more, I hear bankers tell me that banking "just isn't any fun anymore."

- **GROWTH:** Even in bad times, most banks grow—unless, of course, the trade area itself is stagnant or declining. Growth is wonderful—it is the best of times and the worst of times. Just as growth causes problems with cash flow and management in other businesses, so too does growth create extra challenges for bankers. Many bankers are qualified to be CEOs of a $10 million bank, fewer can effectively run a $50 million bank, fewer still a $250 million bank. Sometimes I wonder if anyone can actually run a multibillion dollar bank well. Why? Because the ability to manage people becomes the most important quality that a CEO must possess—it is no longer enough to be a good loan officer.

The management skills necessary to run a bank are generally not possessed by bank CEOs. By the time bankers become CEOs, they generally will not go back to school to learn, relearn, or refresh themselves on management skills. Many times the CEO also adopts the "Caesar Complex," which simply means that the CEO can do no wrong, else he or she would not be the CEO. In 1987, I witnessed a close friend and a good acquaintance both lose their CEO positions—and for the same reasons. They refused to get out of lending and learn how to manage their banks. Their organizations were well over $100 million in assets—far beyond the time, in my opinion, when lending must give way to management.

On the other hand, CEO Hubert Aaron of Park Central Bank in Dallas told me that he is already weaning himself from the lending function. His bank is about fifteen months old and $30 million in assets. He recognizes that the demands for dealing with marketing and civic activities; director and regulator relations; staff time, including serving as a mentor to other loan officers; and most especially, doing strategic planning for the bank are all a necessary part of what a CEO must do. Growth in his bank has been impressive, and it is that growth, coupled with previously mentioned factors, which make getting out of lending a necessity, not a luxury, for the successful CEO.

Reasons to continue

Few CEOs have disagreed with the previous comments I've made. But, as an old Chinese philosopher put it, "To know, and not to do, is not to know at all." Many CEOs cling to lending for other than mere economic or traditional reasons.

- COMFORT ZONE: Many CEOs are most comfortable as lenders. They came up this way, they were good at it, and it is easier to do something that is familiar than to deal with the unique challenge of managing people.

- LACK OF TRUST: Some CEOs simply don't trust their loan officers to make good decisions; as a result, they don't delegate. Most CEOs will not hire anyone better qualified than they are, so if their skills are still rooted in collateral and "good old boy" lending, then their staff probably won't be any better. One of a manager's prime responsibilities is building subordinates and being a mentor to them when needed.

- POWER: How many times does the temptation to be a "deal man" appear? Some CEOs just can't resist the challenge of putting together a complex loan package and being "in on the deal."

Let's assume for now that I've convinced you that the CEO should be out of direct lending, but, of course, remain a very active participant in the function of credit approval. So how do we accomplish the transition?

68

The conservative approach

The usual way of getting the CEO out of lending is to have the CEO stop interviewing any new loan customers. This can work because it doesn't create ill will among the bank's present customers. Handling them is a different, and more difficult, problem.

The typical way of shuffling existing customers to other loan officers is to gradually bring in another officer so that the customer has "dual account officers." As loans mature or new requests are received from existing customers, the CEO informs the customer that another loan officer will become, over time, the primary contact with the bank. The CEO reassures the customer that nothing will change but that the CEO's time is less available for lending. Another positive approach is to tell the customer that he'll get more prompt service from the new officer. That had better be the reality though, or the CEO will get calls from the customer— and this time they'll be irate ones.

The overall goals of the conservative approach are to keep the customer happy, to minimize the stigma of the CEO being "too busy" for him, and to assure the customer that the CEO will still be involved in the lending function and will be available if there is a problem. Can the conservative approach work? Of course. Does it work every time? Of course not, for all the same reasons the problem exists in the first place. The CEO and the board must be committed to the transition. Further, the CEO must learn to support the loan officer's decisions. I've been involved in too many instances where the borrower simply goes over the loan officer's head and the CEO caves in to the borrower's wishes. Not only are the questionable loans funded, but the loan officer may lose respect for the CEO and become totally ineffective in dealing with the customer in the future.

The conservative approach requires the CEO to have a

qualifed staff to which the customer can be referred. In a community bank, this often necessitates the hiring of additional staff to make the transition a smooth one. Either way, the CEO must manage the transition, coach the loan officer, and educate him or her on the customer's background and expectations. In the transition phase, this may even take more time than if the CEO merely handled the transaction personally.

Playing musical chairs

The "musical chairs" approach works wonders—the bank merely hires a CEO from another institution, thus eliminating the problem of weaning away an existing loan portfolio. The new CEO simply refuses to take on lending customers at all. It certainly sounds simple, but it may not be, especially if the previous CEO handled a significant part of the loan portfolio. The customer may now be very nervous. Not only is he being asked to deal with a new face—a junior loan officer perhaps—but the old face is gone. There is no one there to look out for his interest, even indirectly.

As a result, the new CEO finds himself in a double bind—how to stay out of lending and yet still keep the customer. This situation, by the way, is one reason why most of today's customers have more than one banking relationship. The other problem with "musical chairs" is that the new CEO must have changed banks. Promoting from within and a management succession program are usually efforts to eliminate the need to acquire outside talent.

The "Big Bang" approach

The "Big Bang" approach is simply a theory of mine—I've never seen it tried but I believe it would work. The suggestion is to hold a meeting or a party (the Big Bang) to which the

CEO's lending customers and all lending officers and support staff are invited. Make the affair a marketing event capped off by the CEO making a brief talk explaining why he or she is relinquishing any direct lending involvement. Follow that with an introduction, with appropriate background information, of the lending officers available to handle the CEO's accounts. Finally, ask the customers to indicate within, say thirty days, whether they have a preference of loan officers. If not, an officer will be assigned depending upon the probable needs of each customer. The meeting's tone should be positive and upbeat.

As I see it, there are several advantages to the "Big Bang" approach.

- It allows a quick transition—the next day!

- By inviting all customers, it shows them that there is no favoritism and that the CEO is not just getting rid of the "unimportant" ones.

- It can be an excellent marketing tool and an opportunity for the other loan officers to get acquainted with the CEO's customers.

In summary, the CEO should not be carrying part of the loan portfolio once a bank reaches $50 million, and preferably less, in assets. The reasons which argue for this position are the need for time to manage the bank, the problem with the CEO making bad loans, and the reluctance on the part of the CEO to leave the lending comfort zone and re-educate for the management challenge. There are several methods for accomplishing this transition, but the biggest step is convincing the CEO and the board to make the move. If done properly, there is nothing to lose and everything to gain.

Prevent Hazardous Waste from Eroding Your Bank's Capital*

Passage of the Comprehensive Environmental Response, Compensation, and Liability Act (also known as CERCLA or the Superfund) by the U.S. Congress has opened a new window for potential loan losses for bank lenders. This legislation and subsequent court decisions may not only limit realization of collateral values, but may also subject lenders to liability for cleanup of hazardous waste in amounts larger than the original loan balance. There is also the very real possibility that liability for the cleanup of hazardous waste may so deplete the financial resources of a borrower that loan repayment may be jeopardized. Thus, it becomes extremely important for bank lenders to be aware of the impact of environmental control laws and regulations on lending practices.

Potentially responsible parties

Under CERCLA, the costs of cleaning up hazardous waste can be assessed against any one of four potentially responsible parties: the current owner and operator of a site; the prior owner or operator to the extent that contamination was present during the period in which they had responsibility for the site; generators of, or any party who arranged for disposal or treatment of, a hazardous substance; and any party who accepted a hazardous substance for transport to the site.

These rules prompted several banks not to foreclose on real estate pledged as collateral to avoid becoming the owner of a site containing potentially hazardous waste. In one case, a bank inspected a property on which a $55,000 mortgage was

---

*This article was written by John McCarter, a senior vice president with AmeriTrust Company, N. A., in Cleveland, Ohio.

72

deliquent. Although the property was vacant, more than 300 drums containing lead paint and residues were scattered about, and some of the drums were leaking. The cost to remove the drums and clean up the leaking residues exceeded the appraised value of the property. The bank opted to write off the loan and did not take foreclosure action. In other instances, banks have abandoned real estate to bankruptcy trustees and taken general creditor positions to avoid direct responsibility for cleanup costs.

When banks become liable

As a general rule, having a security interest in property as collateral for a debt does not make the lender liable for hazardous waste cleanup. *Ownership* and *operation* of a property, however, can lead to such liability. Potential purchasers of such property may want indemnification against such costs as a condition of purchase. Prior to commencing foreclosure action on any commercial or industrial real estate, a bank would be wise to conduct an environmental inspection to determine the existence of any problem. Such an inspection may be valuable in avoiding liability from future problems.

Liability may also arise from having participated in the management of operations which led to contamination. Banks may be deemed to be "participants" in management if they exercise undue control over operations as a result of liens on receivables, inventory, or equipment. Such control might exist if a bank denied permission to aquire waste control or disposal equipment or processes under loan agreement covenants. The degree of control will be determined by the court based on the facts of each case. A key element in the judicial determination of control is participation or influence over management decisions.

Developing body of case law

There is a developing body of case law in this area. In varying circumstances, banks have been both liable and not liable.

For instance, in *United States v. Mirabile* (1985), American Bank and Trust Company was a real estate lender to Turco, a paint manufacturer. AB&T held Turco's foreclosed property only four months and took steps to secure the property against vandalism. AB&T inquired as to the costs of disposing of drums on the site and visited the site. Girard Bank (now Mellon Bank) was the company's working capital lender, secured by inventory and other assets. Girard established an advisory board to oversee operations and had a bank employee on the company premises daily to monitor operations. When the cleanup of the site took place, the United States Environmental Protection Agency filed a cost recovery action against the new owners—the Mirabiles—and the banks. The court ruled that AB&T was not liable for the costs, but that Mellon had taken an active part in managing the operations and was, therefore, liable.

In another recent case, *United States v. Maryland Bank and Trust Company*, the bank made a loan to the owner of a property on which hazardous waste had been disposed, foreclosed for nonpayment of the loan, and took title to the property. They held the title for four years, and were later deemed liable for cleanup costs because the length of the holding period made them an owner and operator of the property, not simply a protector of a security interest.

The more passive the bank is relative to the situation, the less likely it is to be liable. Since being passive is not always the best way to manage a weak loan situation, however, it is important for the lender to be aware of hazardous waste potential and to take steps to insure that borrowers are in compliance with all applicable environmental laws and regulations.

Extent of the problem

Many business enterprises routinely deal with materials that might cause contamination if not properly handled. Obviously, businesses which utilize radioactive materials, chemicals, or petroleum products in their operations are most likely to have hazardous waste disposal problems. Ashes and other residues from combustion, as well as liquids from washing or plating operations, may also contain hazardous materials. Underground storage tanks are common sources of ground and water contamination.

The national focus on environmental pollution has spawned a host of new businesses dealing with environmental inspection, testing, and cleanup. Although many of these firms are potential bank customers, it is important to recognize the liabilities they may incur from their activities. Insurance will cover some, but not necessarily all, of the lender's risks.

Protecting the bank

Prior to taking a mortgage on real estate, the bank should obtain a title history to determine the likelihood of previous contamination. A current inspection by an environmental expert should be made to determine the present status of the property. The borrower should agree to comply with all applicable laws and regulations with respect to hazardous waste. The most expensive cleanup costs generally result from hazardous material entering the water table and contaminating the water supply.

A number of states have enacted "super lien" statutes which provide for a priority lien on assets of a firm which has been determined to be liable for hazardous waste cleanup costs. Such a lien will take priority over other liens on assets. Such a situation may put a lender in a secondary position to a large, unexpected claim against collateral. Thus, even though a lender may have avoided taking a lien on property with contamination potential, other collateral may be diminished.

Summary

The existence of hazardous waste or contamination may turn collateral from an asset into a liability. The informed lender must take steps to protect the value of collateral and ensure that losses do not exceed the principal balance of the loan.

Awareness of the potential liability and consultation with local attorneys as to the appropriate protective policies and procedures will enable lenders to avoid such losses.

Leveraged Buyouts: The Basics and the Trends

Leveraged buyouts (LBOs) are more popular than ever, so middle-market lenders need to understand the basics and keep up with the latest trends in LBO financing. LBOs are either asset based, cash flow based, or some combination of the two. Many lenders are emphasizing cash flow and basing loans on historical and projected cash flows. A company's record and future prospects are the most important factors. And while strong asset values are important, lenders are not requiring that an LBO loan be backed dollar-for-dollar with assets.

The typical LBO target usually is a privately owned business, a divested division of a public company, or a public company going private. The sale of a privately held company, for example, does not necessarily reflect a distressed situation. The seller may simply be nearing retirement and the LBO is a flexible way for him or her to sell out. In a typical asset-based LBO, the buyer borrows the bulk of the purchase price by pledging the assets of the company he wants to acquire. With asset-based financing, investors can buy a company with more debt and less equity than would be possible from usecured or institutional lenders.

76

Incentives for doing LBOs

Private Companies

- Owners face the problem of converting capital into liquid assets.

- Low equity values have often made public stock offerings impractical as a means of achieving liquidity for small and medium-size businesses.

- LBOs allow owners to sell businesses at competitive prices and establish the value of holdings for estate and tax purposes.

- LBOs can allow employees to gain a significant equity stake in their company.

Divisions or Subsidiaries of Larger Corporations

- LBOs provide a means of divesting assets that no longer fit financial or product strategies.

- The divesting corporation can realize a fair price in a management LBO without having to consider selling the business to a competitor.

- Management gains new incentives through equity ownership.

Public Companies

- Conversion to a private company through an LBO usually results in an attractive price premium for public shareholders.

- A going-private transaction eliminates registration and the other reporting costs of public ownership.

- Private ownership provides an incentive structure for equity-owning management, encouraging management continuity and commitment to efficient operations.

- Private ownership provides the opportunity to increase a firm's private market value through a change in performance objectives.

Adapted with permission from "Leveraged Acquisitions and Buyouts," Capital Markets Group, First National Bank of Chicago.

The buyout is usually structured with a combination of a secured revolving line and term loans along with equity contributions from the buyer. The revolving portion of the buyout, secured by current assets, is not amortized and provides working capital needed for growth while offering operating flexibility. The term loans, secured by fixed assets, can extract much of the purchase price from assets that may be greatly undervalued on the books and provide another source of needed capital.

In theory, the buyer uses as little of his own money as possible by using the lender's resources to finance the purchase. In many cases, the lender must examine two credits since the assets of both the buyer and the seller are being utilized as collateral. The lender must be aware that the company that emerges after the LBO will have changed significantly—both the financial structure and the management organization will be different. The financial risk, at least initially, will be high due to the influx of debt, so the lender must monitor the loan carefully to detect any ominous trends.

Due to their risks, LBO loans should be based on the viability of the company as well as the comfort provided by the collateral. Although liquidation of financed assets is the repayment source of last resort, lenders must give profitability and cash flow sufficiency equal weight. The loan that begins with an abundance of collateral on paper can end up with serious shortfalls and write-offs after liquidation proceedings.

In any LBO, the lender should scrutinize the buyer and seller with equal intensity. The buyer, as borrower, represents where the company is going. The new owners will install new management and bring a new approach to running the operation. The company will rely heavily on their ability for its success. On the other hand, the seller's company is the foundation from which these changes will occur. The lender must determine that the foundation is solid and that the new owners are not starting with any serious handicaps or pitfalls in front of them.

Ingredients for a successful LBO

What makes one LBO more likely to succeed than another? First, the target company should have a proven track record of consistent and profitable operating results. However, the buyer should also be a solid performer. Secondly, the target's line of business should be mature and well established in the market. This reduces the risk of new competitive pressures, product obsolescence, and pressure for heavy capital expenditures to keep pace with rapidly expanding sales. The buyer's managers should have experience in the business being acquired. Ideally, key managers of the target company will remain with the new company.

There should be a small amount of current and long-term debt on the balance sheets of both the buyer and the seller. The heavy debt created by an LBO dictates a balance sheet that can absorb the increase. Income must be sufficient to service the higher debt payments while still meeting trade obligations and normal operating costs. Income statements should show histories of strong cash flow from one year to the next. On a pro forma basis, cash flow coverage for interest charges and debt service should not be much less than 2.5 to 1.

Buyers often look for severely undervalued assets on the seller's balance sheet which have a market value greatly in excess of the depreciated value. These "hidden assets" can be valuable in creating available collateral if needed. Large amounts of depreciable property which can shelter income indicate a potential for "hidden cash flow" for the buyer. Finally, subsidiaries with operations in unrelated industries can be readily liquidated for cash without hurting the acquired company's ongoing operations.

Trends in LBOs

The number of LBOs being done is still increasing, according to Leonard S. Caronia, head of First National Bank of Chicago's Leveraged Buyouts Division. "More investors and lenders are becoming comfortable with them. For example, we helped a local bank with about $200 million in assets finance a small LBO. Lenders are eager to do LBOs and comfortable with financing supported by assets. Lenders are certainly interested: There's almost a feeding frenzy whenever we offer a deal.

"Many transactions are the result of corporations divesting small units," says Caronia. "We're also seeing more private companies selling off to someone they'd like to sell it to, but who might not have the money. In the past, it couldn't have been done, but with an LBO, money is not an object. We're also seeing more LBOs involving general industrial companies. The deals that are working best involve asset-rich companies with plenty of inventory, receivables, and fixed plants. The best candidate for an LBO is a company with assets the buyer can borrow against. A service business doesn't usually have the assets.

"It's also common to see LBOs involving divisions of larger corporations that aren't doing well and that have a market value below what's listed on the company's books. By doing an LBO, a seller can report a higher sale than it would otherwise get. Corporations love it, because they don't take the accounting hit. There's also a change in the big deals: The stock market is so high that we're seeing more recapitalizations than buyouts."

Caronia predicts that the new tax law will not dim the prospects for LBOs. "I see no problem with interest. Lower tax rates will help, but less favorable capital gains treatment could possibly diminish the amount of venture capital coming into LBOs. But I doubt that very much—the venture capitalists are

Checklist for lenders:
Evaluating a cash-flow-based LBO

Lenders should examine the following items (as applicable) when evaluating cash-flow-based leveraged buyouts.

❏ Consistent earnings and stable profit margins

❏ Ability of company to maintain market positions and plant conditions with internally generated funds after allowing for all debt service

❏ Able and committed management

❏ Ability to pass inflationary cost increases to customers

❏ Strength of company's industry position, market shares of key products, and competitive structure of the industry, including insulation from predatory pricing practices

❏ Production costs and volume levels relative to competitors

❏ Diversification of product lines and end uses for products

❏ Requirements for future capital expenditures and R & D outlays

❏ Condition and market value of assets relative to book value

❏ Susceptibility of product lines to cutbacks in discretionary purchases by customers

❏ Size and technology of company

❏ Internal financial controls and information systems

❏ Supplier and customer loyalty

❏ Off-balance- sheet obligations

Adapted with permission from "Leveraged Aquisitions and Buyouts," Capital Markets Group, First National Bank of Chicago.

making too much money in the game for them to pull out. On net, I see no dramatic impact, because the best LBOs aren't capital intensive."

In summary, the key is to look at the cash flow of the company that's being acquired. Can the company meet the debt service—and how quickly can it do so? Paying the debt as quickly as possible is the name of the game in LBOs. It's also crucial to evaluate the management team's history. The lending officer must also know the value, quality, and marketability of the company's receivables. Finally, have some idea of how changes (both favorable and unfavorable) in the business could affect the target company's ability to repay the loan or stay in business.

Leveraged Buyouts: Absolute Concentration on the Basics

Depend upon it sir, when a man knows he is to be hanged in a fortnight, it concentrates his mind wonderfully.

—DR. SAMUEL JOHNSON

Few lending situations concentrate the mind of a borrower or a lender as much as a leveraged buyout. The borrower must turn a marginal company or division into an earnings dynamo to pay off his debt and turn a profit, while the lender must check every facet of the business to ensure that the loan will be repaid.

An LBO uses little equity capital and substantial borrowing to purchase another company or a division of another company. After reorganizing the company, selling some of its assets, or turning the company around, the borrower hopes to pay off the loan as quickly as possible and turn a profit. Needless to say, if the borrower incorrectly estimates the acquired company's cash flow, management needs, tax situation, or business conditions, then both the bank and the borrower are in for a fall.

While financing an LBO entails considerable risks, these can be reduced by scrutinizing every aspect of the deal. "We make sure we know all the details before we present the loan to the loan committee," says David Weener, president of the Boston-based Nucon Capital Corporation. "We make sure we've done all the 'what ifs' before we make the loan.

Cash flow: The heart of the matter

"The key thing to look at is the cash flow of the company that's being acquired, whether the company can meet debt service, and how quickly it can do so," Weener notes. "That means that you have to decipher the true operating income of the company. For example, if the company is a division of another company, will the new company need to buy the accounting, legal, or tax support it had been getting from the parent company? If so, that could affect the debt service and repayment. You have to study all the numbers thoroughly to get a true picture of the deal."

Roger Vandenburg, president of Narragansett Capital, takes a bare-bones approach to analyzing the target's cash flow. "The key is the pretax, preinterest, predepreciation operating profit—on a FIFO (First In, First Out) basis—minus the amount of capital needed to reinvest and maintain the company's present asset base. It all depends on whether the borrower will need money to fund growth or pay debt—and paying the debt as quickly as possible is the name of the game in leveraged buyouts."

Management: The brains behind the company

Evaluating management is another crucial factor in financing LBOs. "We do very thorough background checks on the management team," Weener says, noting that the company checks the management team's previous history with LBOs and other ventures. "We want to know management's relationships with other businesses, and we want to see how well they can keep the show on the road."

People management is not the only consideration. In many cases, repayment of an LBO loan depends on considerable tax advantages—such as accelerated depreciation of the company's assets, debt service, and tax credits—to make the most of the borrower's money. Because the LBO borrower depends on Uncle Sam to help him repay the loan, solid tax advice is also crucial for an LBO's success. "We're strong supporters of CPA firms," Weener says. "LBOs are structured for tax advantages, and good tax advice is a key to the success of an LBO."

Knowledge of the business: The more the better

Since most LBO loans are collateralized by the assets of the target company, the lending officers must know the value, quality, and marketability of the company's receivables. In addition, the lending officers should have a good grasp of how adverse (or fortuitous) changes in the business could affect the target company's ability to repay the loan or continue in business. A lending officer having experience in the restaurant business, for example, has no business in a high-tech LBO.

Leveraged buyouts can help the borrower to create a new and profitable business, the seller to acquire needed capital, and the bank to make aggressive loans while taking on a new company with high borrowing requirements. Without great concentration on the target company's cash flow, the new management team, and the target company's business environment, however, an LBO can spell trouble for all parties concerned even if the loan is heavily collateralized. "We don't want the collateral," Weener points out. "We want timely repayment of the debt."

3
Loan Documentation

The quality of a bank's loan documentation has a significant effect on the quality of its loan portfolio. The promissory note, security agreement, and loan agreement establish the bank's legal relationship with the borrower. Similarly, the bank's legal relationship with third parties involved in the loan is established by the provisions of the guaranty agreement, hypothecation agreement, and/or subordination agreement.

These legal relationships, and the quality of the documentation which establishes them, will not be tested until a loan problem occurs. Then, the adequacy of the bank's documentation becomes crucially important, since it will be challenged, not only by the debtor's attorney, but also by other creditors and the bankruptcy trustee. If its documentation fails to withstand these challenges, the bank may not only lose its collateral, but may be unable collect the loan from either the primary debtor or from co-obligors such as a guarantor.

The first article identifies ten common loan documentation problems. These include the failure of the lender to identify properly what legal entity is or should have been the borrower, failure to ascertain the borrower's correct legal name, and failure to properly set up the signature block and obtain the authorized signatures. Although names and signature blocks appear to be relatively simple matters, these often cause considerable difficulty for lenders, and the exercise of proper care in this regard is essential. To establish what signatures, and how many signatures, are required, the lender needs evidence of authority and capacity in the form of a partnership authorization, corporate resolution, or other documents containing this information. Failure to comply with the provisions of these documents may result in an invalid loan, thus making it difficult to collect from the primary borrower and providing an excellent defense for any guarantor or other third-party obligor. If the loan is secured, collateral documentation is also crucially important. Complete and accurate collateral descriptions are essential, as is the proper filing of the financing statement or recording of the real estate mortgage involved. A real estate title search and/or a Uniform Commercial Code (UCC) search is also essential to ascertain the lender's priority position as to the collateral. Bankers are often lax in obtaining credible documentation regarding the value of collateral, but this is essential if the lender is to evaluate its secured position accurately. Therefore, formal appraisals of real estate and equipment or other information regarding the liquidation value of collateral are a must for a properly documented loan file.

Banks often encounter documentation problems affecting the enforceability of loan guaranty agreements. These may include consideration problems, impairment problems, or problems involving fraud and misrepresentation. A properly drafted guaranty agreement containing adequate waiver provisions and proper credit file documentation of the circumstances surrounding the execution of the guaranty agreement are essential. The bank must also have procedures for ensuring that it maintains its secured position. This includes procedures for the timely filing of continuation statements and for additional filings as required by the UCC if there are changes in the debtor's name or location, or the location of the collateral. Finally, this article stresses the importance of adequate evidence of casualty insurance coverage with the lender named as loss payee. In summary, the article points out that one of the most vital factors affecting the quality of a bank's loan portfolio is the adequacy of its loan documentation.

The second article discusses the use of loan agreements.

86

A loan agreement is a useful tool for the lender who wants to have some degree of control over the borrower's actions during the life of the loan. Loan agreements are commonly used in connection with revolving loans, lines of credit, large working capital loans, and capital term loans. A loan agreement generally will establish conditions that must be met before funds can be disbursed. It will also contain certain warranties, embody both positive and negative covenants, define default, and establish the remedies that are available to the lender upon default. The loan agreement may also contain special provisions which deal with specific concerns of the lender regarding this particular loan. Although a well-drafted loan agreement is a very useful tool in the hands of a lender, provisions which are too restrictive or which give the lender control of the operation of the business should be avoided. In such a case, management, stockholders, or other creditors may bring legal action against the bank, alleging that the bank was responsible for the business's poor performance or failure.

A loan guaranty agreement is another useful tool for the commercial lender. The third article discusses the use of loan guaranty agreements and the many problems that may arise in a lender's relationship with a guarantor. In the past, lenders have often felt that it was unnecessary to communicate with a guarantor of a loan on a continuing basis. This article points out that ignoring the guarantor is unwise, and that the unique three-way relationship that exists between the borrower, guarantor, and lender is very sensitive. When demand is made by the lender, most guarantors are not inclined to pay, and will therefore attempt to raise a multitude of objections to the enforceability of the guaranty. The article discusses the most common defenses often raised by guarantors, which include lack of consideration, fraud or misrepresentation, and impairment of the guarantor's position. Impairment occurs when the lender takes some action that increases the exposure of the guarantor. Such actions might include the release of collateral without the consent of the guarantor, the release of other guarantors, failure to perfect a security interest, or failure to ensure that the collateral is covered by casualty insurance. Another defense often raised by guarantors is failure of the lender to notify the guarantor of the proposed sale of collateral. Under the provisions of Article 9 of the Uniform Commercial Code, a guarantor is absolutely entitled to such notification, and if the lender fails to comply, the guarantor can usually avoid paying the deficiency. Another guarantor defense involves the issue of an invalid underlying obligation. If the lender has failed to comply with the provisions of the partnership authorization or corporate resolution, the loan itself may be invalid or unenforceable against the primary borrower, and consequently may be equally difficult to enforce against the guarantor. Loan guaranty agreements are often documents of convenience for all parties involved, avoiding the necessity of the guarantor having to be directly involved in each successive loan transaction. However, a lender should recognize the pitfalls involved in relying upon a guarantee to collect the loan.

A May 1989 decision by the U. S. Court of Appeals for the Seventh Circuit may make lenders less willing to rely on guarantees from "insiders" in a business. This decision in the *Deprizio* case (874 F2d 1186 [7th Circ.-1989]) affirms an earlier ruling that a trustee in bankruptcy may recover as a preference any loan payments made by a debtor company during a one-year period prior to its bankruptcy, since those loan payments directly benefitted the "insider" guarantor of the loan by reducing the guarantor's contingent liability. In this case the bank was required to disgorge all such payments, which it was unable to recover from the guarantor since he was deceased. It appears that the *Deprizio* decision will have significant repercussions in the commercial lending industry, and that consequently lenders may demand more collateral in lieu of insider guaranties.

The fourth article deals with loan participations. A loan participation represents a proportionate interest in a loan which may be either sold to or purchased from another institution. Although bankers routinely handle participation transactions, misconceptions abound, and as a result problems arise in dealing with participations. There may be a number of reasons a bank wishes to sell a participation. A sale may be made to gain liquidity, to avoid exceeding legal lending limits, or to diversify risk. A bank may purchase participations to increase the size of its loan portfolio and its loan deposit ratio, generally resulting in additional income, or it may buy a participation simply as an accommodation to another bank with which it has a good working relationship.

There are many pitfalls involved in the participation process. First, the lender must realize that purchasing a participation is an extension of credit, and that a credit decision must be made on an independent basis. Problems may arise if there is a significant difference in the credit criteria of the selling and purchasing banks. As a rule, the selling bank will continue to service the loan, and it may not perform that function to the satisfaction of the buying bank. Also, if the loan becomes a problem, controversy may arise between the two banks regarding the manner in which the problem is to be resolved. The article lists eight precautions which should be exercised by a purchasing bank to avoid problems. If handled properly, the bank's portfolio of participations can be of equal quality and just as profitable as the bank's portfolio of direct loans.

The final article deals with domestic letters of credit, which are, with the exception of those covered by a cash deposit, another type of credit extension by a bank. Domestic letters of credit are used to facilitate commercial transactions, enabling the seller of goods who is the beneficiary of the letter to rely upon the bank's creditworthiness rather than that of the buyer, since the bank makes an irrevocable commitment to pay against the letter if its requirements are met. Most letters of credit, including all international letters, are governed by International Chamber of Commerce Publication No. 400 and every lender who issues letters of credit should be familiar with this publication. In those rare instances where Publication No. 400 is not designated as the governing body, the letter will be governed by the provisions of Article 5 of the Uniform Commercial Code.

Another type of letter of credit is the standby letter of credit, which guarantees the performance of an obligation. Unlike a commercial letter of credit, under which it is almost always contemplated that funds will be drawn, a standby letter of credit is usually not drawn against unless the account party has defaulted in the performance of an obligation. Therefore, a draw against a standby letter of credit, by its very nature, involves controversy. Consequently, standby letters often create problems for the issuing bank, which may become embroiled in a controversy between the account party and the beneficiary. Due to the potential problems, every bank should have a written policy re-garding letters of credit and well-defined procedures for their issuance.

Documentation Deficiencies: The Banker's Bane

If all loans worked exactly as anticipated, the quality of a bank's loan documentation would probably be irrelevant. However, as bankers are well aware, some loans in the bank's portfolio will become problem loans. When this happens, the quality of a bank's loan documentation is of crucial importance.

When a bank attempts to collect the problem loan, the debtor's attorney is likely to examine the bank's documentation, attempting to discover some error made by the bank which will enable the debtor to repudiate the debt altogether, or at least prevent the bank from repossessing and liquidating the collateral. Further, the debtor's attorney may attempt to use the bank's documentation as the basis for a suit alleging that the bank failed to act in good faith, coerced the debtor, or otherwise treated the debtor unfairly. To improve their own secured position, other creditors may retain legal counsel to examine the bank's documentation in an attempt to prove that the bank's collateral position is invalid or unperfected. Finally, if the debtor is bankrupt, the trustee may also challenge the loan documentation in an effort to deprive the bank of its collateral, thereby increasing the bankruptcy estate for the benefit of the unsecured creditors.

If a bank is to minimize its loan losses, its loan documentation must be adequate to withstand these challenges. This article will explore the ten most common problem areas in loan documentation.

1. **DEALING WITH THE PROPER ENTITY**
   In some instances, the lender will fail to ascertain which entity is actually the borrower. In a case where there are a number of interrelated entities, the answer may be less than clear-cut. As a general rule, the entity which will actually utilize the funds should be the primary borrower. In some instances, guaranties may be required from one or more of the other entities involved. The lender must also ascertain which entity in fact owns the collateral, and if different, require that entity (as well as the borrowing entity) to execute all security documentation.

2. **NAMES AND SIGNATURES**
   Every legal entity has a proper legal name and may also operate under an assumed or trade name. It is absolutely necessary that the lender use the proper legal name of the borrower in all loan documentation.

Verify a corporation's name by obtaining a copy of its charter or a certificate of good standing. In the case of a partnership, the partnership agreement will disclose its legal name, which is generally different from the names of the individual partners. In some instances, the lender may require a legal opinion from the borrower's legal counsel certifying the borrowing entity's name, legal status, and other pertinent information. Use of an assumed or trade name alone in security documentation is always inadequate, and will result in the lender's failure to establish a secured position.

Banks are sometimes careless in setting up signature blocks on loan documents. The signature block should always clearly indicate the legal name of the borrowing entity, the number of signatures required, and the capacity in which the individuals are signing the documentation. If an individual is to sign in two capacities, such as that of a corporate vice president and also individually, set up two signature blocks. The individual should sign twice, clearly indicating in each case the capacity in which he is signing.

3. EVIDENCE OF AUTHORITY AND CAPACITY

If a bank is making a loan to an individual or a sole proprietorship, no evidence of authority and capacity is required. In every other case, evidence of the authority and capacity of the person or persons signing the loan documentation is required. If the borrower is a corporation, this evidence will be in the form of a certified copy of the resolution to borrow; in the case of a partnership, in the form of a partnership authorization. If the person executing the documentation is acting in a fiduciary capacity, then a copy of a trust agreement, power of attorney, or a court order may be required.

When the bank accepts a corporate resolution or

partnership authorization, it is bound by the provisions of that document. If, for example, the bank fails to obtain the signatures of the proper persons, the proper number of signatures, or lends in excess of an amount authorized, the loan may be invalid as to the corporation or partnership. This situation will also provide an excellent defense for the guarantors of the loan.

4. COLLATERAL DESCRIPTIONS

Although complete and accurate collateral descriptions are crucial, many banks seem to be careless about them. Always be sure to construct carefully collateral descriptions for both the security agreement and financing statement. The use of "canned" descriptions is generally unsatisfactory. A description that is either too explicit or too general may create a problem. The Uniform Commercial Code does not require that collateral be described on an item-by-item basis; it may be described by category in fairly general terms. The lender should be sure that all appropriate categories of collateral, as established by the Code, are covered in the collateral description. The lender should also ensure that, where required, an after-acquired clause is included in the description in both the security agreement and financing statement, since this may significantly enhance the secured lender's collateral position.

5. FILING OR RECORDING

In some instances the provisions of the Code may require that a financing statement be filed in more than one jurisdiction, or both locally and centrally. Therefore, the lender can never assume that because a filing has been made, it has fully perfected its position. In the case of a real estate mortgage, the lender should double-check the description of the real estate involved, and that the mortgage or trust deed has been properly recorded in the county in which the real estate is located.

6. TITLE AND RECORD SEARCHES

When a bank makes a loan secured by chattel or real property, it usually intends to achieve a first priority position. Identifying the existence of prior perfected liens requires a record or title search prior to closing. Even though a prior search has been conducted, always perform a UCC search subsequent to filing to ensure that the financing statement has been filed in the proper office or offices, and that the filing officer has not made an error. If a bank is careless in obtaining the subsequent search, it will have no evidence of its true priority position. If the loan is secured by real estate, the bank should obtain either an attorney's title opinion or a mortgagee title insurance policy to verify its secured position.

7. GUARANTY AGREEMENTS

Banks often encounter documentation problems affecting the enforceability of loan guaranty agreements, which may prevent the bank from collecting from the guarantor if the loan defaults. These include consideration problems, which occur when a guaranty is obtained subsequent to the closing of the loan without the establishment of new consideration for the guaranty. Problems of fraudulent inducement occur when the bank misleads or misinforms the guarantor concerning the true status of the loan to induce the guarantor to execute the guaranty agreement.

Impairment problems arise when the lender takes some action—such as the release of collateral or the release of another guarantor—which increases the exposure of an existing guarantor without his consent. Even though most standard guaranty forms contain waiver provisions regarding such actions, the bank may nevertheless have difficulty enforcing the guaranty if it impairs the guarantor's position. A stale guaranty (one signed quite some time ago) may also present enforcement problems for the bank. As a result, most institutions endeavor to update guaranties on a regular basis.

8. COLLATERAL VALUATIONS

Even though the bank may have properly perfected its interest in the collateral, credit files often contain little or no information concerning the actual value of the collateral. In some instances, information concerning the exact nature and location of the collateral may be so sketchy that it would be difficult for the lender to identify the collateral on a visit to the debtor's premises. Without adequate information regarding the nature and value of collateral, the bank has no way of knowing whether it is actually secured or what its exposure may be if the loan defaults. Therefore, the bank must establish procedures which require the adequate documentation of both market and liquidation values of collateral on an ongoing basis. This may require formal appraisals as well as periodic inspections of the collateral by bank personnel.

9. MAINTAINING SECURED POSITION

Even though the bank initially perfected its position, it must constantly monitor its credit files to ensure that it maintains its secured position and that continuation statements are filed in a timely manner. The bank must also make additional filings (as required by the Code) when collateral is moved to another jurisdiction or the debtor changes its name. This requires both a "tickler" file and ongoing communication with the borrower to learn promptly of any changes in the borrower's status.

10. CASUALTY INSURANCE COVERAGE

The bank's collateral position must be protected by adequate casualty insurance coverage of the collateral, and the bank should be named a loss payee on the insurance policy. Some banks are quite lax in following up to make sure that the borrower furnishes evidence of casualty insurance, and that such coverage is not allowed to lapse. If the lender is a loss payee, it will generally be notified of any policy cancellation.

In summary, one of the vital factors affecting the quality of a bank's loan portfolio is the adequacy of its loan documentation. To avoid loan documentation errors, a bank needs complete and well-defined procedures, an adequately trained staff, and a dedication by top management and staff to the maintenance of high-quality standards.

The Loan Agreement: A Lender's Tool

Every loan invariably involves a promissory note, the document that establishes the fundamental legal relationship between the borrower and the lender. A secured loan will also include a security agreement which further establishes that legal relationship. In some cases, a third document—the loan agreement—will further define the legal relationship between the borrower, the lender, and occasionally with third parties such as guarantors and hypothecators. Loan agreements were originally used primarily in connection with term loans involving an ongoing, long-term relationship between the two parties. The lender was primarily concerned about the prudent operation of the debtor's business over a relatively long period of time. In such an instance, the term loan agreement ensures that the lender has a certain amount of control or veto power over the actions of the borrower during the term of the loan. This, in fact, is the primary purpose of all loan agreements.

Bankers have recognized that a well-drafted loan agreement is beneficial in other lending situations; as a result, loan agreements are now commonly used in connection with revolving loans, lines of credit, and large working capital loans. If a loan is relatively weak, a strong loan agreement may give the lender a comfort factor and a degree of control over the actions of the borrower, making the loan workable and acceptable despite its weaknesses.

Loan agreements are generally divided into a number of sections that are designed to accomplish the following:

1. Recite the terms of the loan or credit facility.

2. Establish conditions that must be met for funds to be disbursed.

3. Contain warranties that information and representations furnished by the borrower are true and correct.

4. Require the borrower to perform certain actions which are helpful in maintaining the lender's position.

5. Require the borrower to furnish certain information periodically to the lender.

6. Require the borrower to refrain from certain actions which may be detrimental to the lender's position.

7. Contain provisions defining default.

8. Establish the remedies that are available to the lender upon default.

The following are specific examples of provisions that are often included in each of these sections of the loan agreement.

Loan terms

This section includes the name of the borrower, the name of the lender, and usually will include the names of third parties

97

involved, such as co-signers or guarantors. In many cases, these third parties will actually be parties to the loan agreement. This section also recites the amount to be loaned, the term of the loan, interest rate, collateral to be pledged, guaranties required, repayment agreement, use of loan proceeds, and any other terms pertinent to the loan.

Conditions precedent

These are conditions which must be met prior to the disbursement of funds, and generally include the following requirements:

1. The execution of a promissory note, security agreement, guaranty agreements, financing statements, and any other documentation required by the bank.

2. If the borrower is a corporation, the submission of a certificate of good standing.

3. Submission of a properly executed borrowing resolution if the borrower is a corporation, or of a properly executed authorization to borrow if the applicant is a partnership.

4. An opinion from the borrower's legal counsel certifying that the borrower is in good standing; is legally organized; has complied with all state, federal and local laws; and that it is not involved in litigation, etc.

Representations and warranties

This section will generally contain such provisions as:

1. A warranty that all financial statements submitted to the lender are genuine and fairly represent the financial position of the borrower, and that other representations made to the lender are true and correct.

2. A warranty that the borrower has good title to all assets.

3. A warranty that the borrower has complied with all federal, state, and municipal laws and is not involved in litigation.

4. A warranty that the borrower has filed all necessary tax returns and has paid all taxes due.

5. A warranty that the borrower is not in default on other obligations. and that there are no outstanding judgments, injunctions, statutory liens, or federal or state tax liens.

6. A warranty that the borrower possesses all licenses, permits, franchises, patents, copyrights, trademarks, etc., to conduct the business as it is presently conducted.

Positive covenants

This section generally contains provisions that require the borrower to:

1. Periodically furnish certain financial information to the lender.

2. Promptly advise the lender of any change which affects the management structure of the borrower.

3. Promptly notify the lender of any probable or pending lawsuit or legal action.

4. Keep its insurable assets insured by financially sound and reputable insurance companies.

5. Keep all assets and properties in good repair and condition.

6. Cooperate with the lender in any field review or audit of the borrower's records that the lender may wish to conduct.

7. Promptly advise the lender of any change or event which will materially affect the financial condition or performance of the borrower.

8. Use all loan proceeds for the specific purposes for which the funds were requested.

9. Grant the lender a security interest in the collateral.

10. Agree, upon request of the lender, to deliver such additional notes, guaranties, security agreements, or other documents necessary to complete the loan.

11. Appoint the lender as its attorney-in-fact for the purpose of executing any financial statements, continuation statements, or other documents which may be required for the lender to perfect and maintain its security interest.

Negative covenants

These are actions that the borrower is prohibited from undertaking during the life of the loan agreement unless it obtains the lender's consent. This section of the loan agreement may contain provisions such as:

1. The borrower will not sell or lease any of its property or assets, other than in the normal course of business.

2. The borrower will not declare or pay a dividend, make a capital distribution, or purchase or redeem any of its capital stock without the lender's consent.

3. The borrower will not repay loans from owners or shareholders.

4. The borrower will not pay any profit-sharing or bonuses, or increase the compensation of any officer or director, in excess of an amount agreed to in the loan agreement.

5. The borrower will not obtain loans from any other institutional creditor.

6. The borrower will not consolidate or merge with or into any other business.

7. The borrower will not make capital purchases in excess of a stated annual limit.

8. The borrower will not grant or allow to exist any other encumbrance upon the collateral in which the lender has perfected a security interest.

Financial covenants

This section of the loan agreement usually contains requirements for the maintenance of specific financial ratios and sets other criteria, such as the maintenance of a given amount of dollar equity. For example:

1. The borrower will maintain a stated current ratio.

2. The borrower will maintain a stated equity ratio and equity of no less than a specified dollar amount.

3. The borrower will maintain a sales-to-receivables ratio and a cost-of-sales-to-inventory ratio of at least a specified percentage.

Default provisions

Default provisions are important, since they determine what events create a default and, thereby, enable a bank to pursue its legal remedies. The note and security agreement also often contain default provisions; if so, the default provisions in the loan agreement should conform to those in the note and security agreement. Typical events of default listed among the loan agreement's default provisions would be:

1. Nonpayment.

2. Failure to comply with the other provisions of the note, security agreement, and loan agreement.

3. The death of the borrower or any guarantor.

4. The bankruptcy of the borrower or any guarantor.

5. Another creditor securing a judgment or lien against the debtor or any guarantor.

6. The bank deeming itself insecure.

Special conditions

The loan agreement may also contain provisions especially tailored to a specific situation. For example:

1. The borrower agrees to sell, within the next twelve months, at public auction, or by any other commercially reasonable means, commercial property owned by the borrower located at the corner of Oak and Spring Streets in Center City.

2. The borrower agrees, within 180 days, to divest itself of its interest in a partnership known as Tucker Freight Lines, and to apply any and all proceeds thereof to its loans.

3. The borrower agrees to obtain, as soon as possible, and assign to the bank, $100,000 of term life insurance upon the life of its chief executive officer.

Precautions

Although a well-drafted loan agreement is extremely useful to the lender, avoid "overkill" in drafting the provisions of the agreement. Provisions necessary to protect the lender's position should certainly be included, but provisions that are so restrictive that they prevent the debtor from operating the business in its normal course can cause serious problems for the lender. In such a case, management, stockholders, and other creditors may accuse the bank of having undue control and influence over the operation of the business. If the business fails, legal action may be initiated alleging that the bank is responsible for the failure of the business due to its relationship with the borrower.

The bank should also not include loan agreement provisions that it does not intend to enforce. Most loan agreements provide that the lender's failure to enforce a specific provision on a given occasion does not waive its right to do so in the future. If the bank repeatedly fails to enforce the provisions of the agreement, however, it may establish a "course of dealing" that will prohibit it from enforcing those provisions in the future.

In summary, a loan agreement is a useful tool for the commercial lender which will enable it to exert some control over the borrower's activities. This may be of significant value in enabling the lender to maintain and protect its position. The lender must exercise care, however, to avoid making the provisions too stringent, and be prepared to enforce the provisions contained in the agreement.

Dealing with Guarantors: Problems Galore!

When dealing with a borrower whose financial status is insufficient to meet the standards of the lender, the lender often requires that a loan be guaranteed by a third party or parties. As a policy matter the bank may also require that the principals of a closely held corporation or partnership guarantee the loans of the corporation or partnership. The guarantor usually becomes obligated to pay on a particular note or line of credit by executing a separate instrument, commonly called a "guaranty agreement" (GA). In the past, lenders often felt that both the guarantor and the GA could be ignored once the guarantor's signature was affixed. Not true!

103

Lenders are learning, to their dismay, that there can be many problems in their relationships with guarantors. As soon as a guaranty is involved, a unique three-way relationship arises between the borrower, guarantor, and lender. This relationship is generally uneventful—and even pleasant—until a default occurs and the lender demands payment from the guarantor. At that point, the guarantor expresses shock and indignation that the lender actually expects payment. The guarantor will often raise a multitude of objections to the enforceability of the guaranty. These will typically involve issues of consideration, fraud, or impairment which may invalidate the guaranty or reduce the guarantor's liability.

The ten most common defenses being used by guarantors are:

1. **LACK OF CONSIDERATION.** The GA is a contract supported by consideration to be enforceable. If the guaranty is executed prior to or simultaneously with the underlying note, the loan proceeds furnish sufficient consideration for both the note and the GA. When a guaranty is obtained subsequent to the original transaction, however, it must be supported by new consideration which exists at that particular time. A guarantor who admits executing a GA may still have an enforcement defense based on lack of consideration. Therefore, lenders need to be aware that a "new" GA must always be supported by "new" consideration, such as a loan disbursement, renewal, extension, or term adjustment. A lender who does otherwise should anticipate significant difficulties in collecting from the guarantor.

2. **MISLEADING THE GUARANTOR.** If the lender misinforms the guarantor about the status of the loan or any material aspect of the transaction, the guarantor may have a defense to payment. The lender has a duty to act in "good faith." He should not, for example, misrepre-

sent the financial strength of the primary obligor or the value of the collateral pledged to secure the loan. A guarantor who has been fraudulently induced to become involved may actually be no guarantor at all.

3. FAILING TO KEEP THE GUARANTOR INFORMED. The guarantor should be kept generally informed about the status of the loan. The lender is not required to send the guarantor a copy of every routine communication, but, in situations where a problem appears to be developing, the guarantor should fully and promptly be informed. If the lender is sending the borrower a delinquency or default notice, or demanding payment or additional collateral, it is essential that the guarantor be notified. There is no substitute for an informed guarantor.

4. FAILING TO PERFECT A SECURITY INTEREST IN COLLATERAL. If the parties to the transaction (including the guarantor) have agreed that the loan is to be secured and the lender subsequently fails to obtain and perfect a security interest in the collateral, the guarantor may have a defense to payment. In these situations, the collateral is often lost to a competing creditor—the tax collector or a trustee in bankruptcy. This is an occurrence guaranteed to create an unhappy guarantor.

5. FAILING TO MAINTAIN A PERFECTED SECURITY INTEREST IN COLLATERAL. Although initially perfected, there are many ways a lender's security interest can subsequently become unperfected. Such an occurrence may impair the guarantor's position for the reason stated above. To maintain its perfected status, the lender must file a continuation statement (UCC-3) when required and supervise the collateral to avoid other situations in which perfection may lapse, such as the removal of the collateral to another state.

105

6. **RELEASE OF COLLATERAL WITHOUT GUARANTOR'S CONSENT.** If the loan has been secured by collateral, the guarantor will always be relying on the liquidation value of the collateral to reduce his financial exposure. To avoid impairing the guarantor's position, the lender should always consider obtaining the guarantor's consent prior to the release or substitution of any collateral.

7. **FAILURE TO NOTIFY THE GUARANTOR OF THE SALE OF COLLATERAL.** According to the Uniform Commercial Code, a "debtor" is any person who owes payment or other performance of an obligation or who is an owner of the collateral. The Code requires that all "debtors" be given reasonable notice of the sale of collateral, if not otherwise specified in the applicable security agreement. Therefore, a guarantor who has not been properly notified of the proposed sale of collateral may have a defense to paying any deficiency arising after the sale.

8. **FAILURE TO MAINTAIN CASUALTY INSURANCE.** The terms of most security agreements require the borrower to maintain adequate casualty insurance on the collateral. The lender often fails to actually procure evidence of insurance, however, and often has not even been designated as an additional insured on the policy. In the latter situation, the lender will not be notified if the coverage is terminated and will not have an opportunity to pay the required premium, obtain new insurance, or repossess. Obviously, the guarantor will feel his position has been impaired if the lender's conduct has created a situation which results in an uninsured casualty loss.

9. **RELEASE OF CO-GUARANTOR.** Many loans involve multiple guarantors who are jointly and severally obligated: Each is obligated for the full amount of the loan. Even though a guarantor may in fact be jointly and severally obligated, he usually perceives that the guaranty is

106

proportionate. If one guarantor is released, the proportionate share of the other guarantors is increased. Consequently, the release of any guarantor without the consent of the others may create an impairment problem—at least in the view of those still obligated.

10. INVALID UNDERLYING OBLIGATION. When lending to a corporation or partnership, the lender must be cognizant of the terms of the "resolution to borrow" presented by the borrower. If for example, the lender loans a larger amount than authorized in the resolution, loans to a dissolved corporation, or fails to require proper execution of documents, the underlying debt may be invalid or unenforceable. If so, the obligation of the guarantor may be equally difficult to enforce.

Lender-guarantor relationships are unique and can sometimes be perilous for the lender. In most cases, many of the impairment defenses discussed above

---

How to avoid problems with guarantors

1. Always support a "new" guaranty agreement with "new" consideration.

2. Do not mislead the guarantor about any aspects of the loan.

3. Keep the guarantor informed about the status of the loan.

4. Perfect and maintain a security interest in the collateral, and do not release or substitute collateral without the guarantor's consent.

5. Be sure that adequate casualty insurance is maintained.

6. Get the consent of all co-guarantors before releasing one.

7. Be sure you've made a proper loan in the first place.

will have been specifically waived by the guarantor if a properly drafted GA is involved. Guarantors will often allege fraud or duress on the part of the lender in an attempt to nullify the legal effect of their previous waiver. The lender must always proceed with caution and should remain constantly alert to the pitfalls that exist in dealing with any guarantor.

Loan Participations: A Perspective

Although many bankers routinely handle transactions involving loan participations, misconceptions abound. Some bankers fail to recognize that since there is generally no recourse to the selling bank, the purchase of a participation is an extension of credit which involves as much risk as a similar direct loan—and in some cases significantly more. This article will examine the basic concepts involved in the sale or purchase of loan participations and outline certain precautions for handling them.

A participation represents a proportionate interest in a loan which may range from one to 100 percent of the loan. From the borrower's standpoint, the sale of a participation has no effect on the underlying loan; the borrower will usually not be aware that the participation has been sold. All the borrower's dealings will generally continue to be with the originating bank, since that bank will still service the loan.

The participation certificate is the document that evidences the sale of the participation. The purchasing bank treats the participation certificate in much the same manner as it would a promissory note for a direct loan. Although the participation may not be for a greater amount or for a longer term than the underlying promissory note, the other terms of the participation may vary from the terms of the underlying loan.

For example, even though the promissory note calls for the payment of interest at an annual rate of 10 percent, the interest rate on the participation may be negotiated by the selling and purchasing banks and may be higher or lower than the rate shown on the note. If the participation rate is lower, the selling bank will then have an "override" on the interest; if the participation rate is higher, the selling bank must subsidize the interest payments.

The manner in which loan payments are shared will also be negotiated. In some instances all repayment will be shared on a proportionate basis. In others, the purchasing bank may be on a "last in, first out" basis, and receive all principal payments while interest payments are shared on a proportionate basis. Generally, the purchasing bank obtains a proportionate interest in both the collateral and any guaranties pertaining to the loan.

A bank may wish to sell a loan participation for a number of reasons. If the bank's loan–deposit ratio is higher than normal, it may sell participations to reduce the ratio and to gain liquidity, since the effect of the sale is to reduce the bank's loans and increase cash reserves. A small bank with a relatively low legal lending limit may sell a loan participation to avoid violating those limits. For example, a bank with a legal lending limit of $2 million will be able to make a $3 million loan to one of its customers, provided it can find another bank willing to purchase a $1 million participation in the loan.

In some instances, participations may be sold to diversify risk. For example, in a community with a number of emerging high-tech businesses, several banks may enter into an informal agreement to share in any substantial loan made by any one of them to a high-tech business, provided, of course, that the credit is of acceptable quality. Many banks have an informal agreement for the exchange of participations with other local or regional banks when the need arises. Therefore, in some instances, a bank may purchase a participation simply to accommodate the needs of another bank with which it has a working arrangement.

A bank might wish to purchase participations for several reasons. If the bank's loan demand is weak, it may wish to purchase participations simply to increase its loan-deposit ratio, resulting in a higher yield on its assets. It may also want to buy participations from another bank to encourage the selling bank to accommodate its own future need to place participations.

Possible pitfalls

Making a credit decision on a participation is often more difficult than making a decision on a direct loan. The purchasing bank usually has little direct knowledge of the borrower, and in many cases will not have had the opportunity to participate directly in loan negotiations. It is therefore much more dependent on the quality and completeness of the selling bank's information. Since the selling bank generally prepares all loan documentation, the buyer is much more dependent upon the quality of the selling bank's documentation.

In many cases the selling bank will use forms and procedures that differ from those of the participating bank. Therefore, the purchasing bank must be careful to ensure that it obtains adequate information and that the loan documentation complies with its own standards. Under the provisions of most standard loan participation certificates, the selling bank will represent that it has exercised due diligence in connection with the granting and the disbursement of the loan, but will generally make no further representations or other warranties with respect to the loan.

Problems may also arise from the fact that the selling bank is usually in charge of servicing the loan; in some cases, the selling bank may be less attentive to the servicing needs of the loan than the participating bank desires. The participation certificate will generally contain a statement like the following: "We will undertake to service the loan, in which connection we will use the same degree of care and diligence as we would if said loan were made entirely for our account, and it is agreed that we may use our sole discretion with respect to exercising or refraining from exercising our rights with respect thereto. If having used such degree of care and diligence, a loss should occur, we will not be responsible therefore."

When problems with the underlying loan occur, such as delinquency or other default, the participating bank must usually rely on the selling bank to take appropriate action to solve the problem. Such action may be less timely and less aggressive than the participating bank wishes, and a controversy may arise between the banks regarding the proper course of action. Unless the banks have specifically agreed otherwise, the selling bank is in charge of any collection action; as long as the selling bank exercises due prudence and diligence, the participating bank may be able to do little except protest.

To handle these problems, some banks will enter into a participation agreement that specifically establishes the rights and duties of the banks involved prior to the time that any participation certificates are bought or sold. Such an agreement is especially important if there are a number of participating banks. Unless specifically agreed otherwise, the participating bank is obligated to reimburse the selling bank for its proportionate share of any legal costs, attorney's fees, or other expenses incurred by the selling bank in forcing collection of the loan.

Precautions for prudent buyers

In view of the potential problems that exist in the purchase of loan participations, we recommend that bankers heed the following precautions:

1. Request a copy of the selling bank's credit policy to determine that its lending philosophy is similar to that of

your bank. Significant variance in philosophy, policy, and procedures will almost invariably create problems.

2. Perform your own complete credit analysis, which should be as thorough as your analysis of a similar direct loan request. Don't rely on the analysis of the selling bank.

3. If you are dissatisfied with the information submitted by the selling bank, don't hesitate to ask for more information.

4. Although from an ethical standpoint the purchasing bank should not make direct contact with the borrower, it is acceptable to request permission from the selling bank to visit the borrower's business. Ideally, this visit should be made by representatives of both the selling and participating banks.

5. Request an opportunity to inspect copies of the proposed loan documentation. If it does not meet your bank's standards, request changes in the documentation.

6. If the underlying loan doesn't meet your bank's credit quality standards, don't hesitate to decline the participation, even if you have an excellent working relationship with the selling bank. No bank has the right to expect another bank to purchase a participation with which it is not comfortable.

7. Before accepting the participation, learn how the selling bank handles a default or other nonperformance. If this varies significantly from your bank's procedures, a specific agreement regarding collection procedures may be required.

8. Your bank should have written policies and procedures for the handling of loan participations, and your lending staff should be familiar with them.

In summary, it is often advantageous for a commercial bank to either sell or buy participations. In many instances, however, banks have been confused about the nature of participation transactions and have handled them too casually. If handled prudently, the bank's portfolio of participations can be just as profitable as the bank's portfolio of direct loans.

Eight ways to avoid loan participation problems

1. Be sure the selling bank's credit policy is similar to your bank's.

2. Perform your own credit analysis—don't rely on the selling bank's analysis.

3. If you need it, request more information from the selling bank.

4. Request permission from the selling bank to visit the borrower's business.

5. If the proposed loan documentation doesn't meet your bank's standards, ask for changes.

6. Don't purchase a participation that fails to meet your bank's credit quality standards.

7. Find out how the selling bank will handle nonperformance on the loan—and request a specific collection agreement if necessary.

8. Have written policies and procedures for handling loan participations—and make sure your lending staff is familiar with them.

Domestic Letters of Credit

Although international letters of credit—time-honored and highly developed documents used to facilitate international commercial transactions—remain the exclusive purview of the larger city banks, most community banks will occasionally issue a domestic letter of credit in response to a customer's request. In some instances, neither the bank nor its customer fully understands the obligations and duties of each party involved in a letter of credit. The bank may view the issuance of a letter of credit more as an accommodation to its customer and as a source of fee income than as an extension of credit. Unless the full amount of the letter of credit is covered by a cash deposit, however, the bank generally has the same exposure on a letter of credit that it does on a loan—a fact which some banks fail to recognize. Therefore, the issuance of most letters of credit must be treated as an extension of credit which requires a loan decision. This article will discuss the basic issues involved in both commercial and standby letters of credit.

Applicable law

The rules and regulations governing letters of credit have been established through two sources. The first of these is Article 5 of the Uniform Commercial Code, "Letters of Credit." Since the Code has been adopted throughout the United States as the basic body of commercial law, Article 5 represents statutory law. The second source of regulations governing the issuance of letters of credit is International Chamber of Commerce Publication No. 400, *Uniform Customs and Practice for Documentary Credits.* Publication No. 400 will invariably govern any international letter of credit; in most cases involving a domestic letter of credit, it will also be designated as the governing document. In those rare instances when the provisions of the letter of credit fail to specify which set of regula-

114

tions are being used, Article 5 of the Code governs. Every banker involved in letter of credit transactions must be familiar with both Article 5 of the Code and ICC Publication No. 400. A copy of each of these publications should be a basic part of every bank's legal library.

Parties involved

Every letter of credit involves at least three parties: the issuer, the customer, and the beneficiary. The issuer is defined as the bank or other party issuing a letter of credit. The customer (or account party) is the buyer or other person who causes an issuer to issue a letter of credit. The beneficiary is the party who is entitled, under the terms of the letter, to draw or demand payment. In some cases, an advising bank—defined as a bank which gives notification of the issuance of a letter of credit by another bank—may be involved. In still other instances, a confirming bank may also be involved. This is the bank which agrees either that it will itself honor a credit issued by another bank, or that such a credit will be honored by the issuer or a third bank.

Revocable or irrevocable

A letter of credit may be either revocable or irrevocable. A revocable letter of credit may be amended or canceled by the issuing bank at any time without prior notice to, or the consent of, the beneficiary. Beneficiaries are usually quite reluctant to accept a revocable letter, since they have no assurances that it will not be canceled or amended without their consent. The issuing bank may, however, be obligated to reimburse any other bank for any payment, acceptance, or negotiation made by such bank prior to receipt of a notice of the amendment or the cancellation. An irrevocable letter of credit binds the issuing bank with a noncancelable obligation to pay any

115

sight draft presented against the letter, provided that the documents required by the letter are presented, and that the terms and conditions of the letter are complied with. To be irrevocable, the letter must so state, and failure to do so will result in a revocable letter of credit.

A letter of credit may also be transferable to another beneficiary, but only if the provisions of the letter so provide. Every letter of credit includes an expiration date indicating when the bank's obligation to pay ceases.

Commercial letters of credit

A commercial letter of credit is issued for the purpose of facilitating a sales transaction. The parties involved almost always contemplate that funds will be drawn against the letter. Suppose that Harry's Sporting Goods Company of Indianapolis, Indiana, wishes to purchase 400 bicycles at $140 each from East Asia Imports, located in Olympia, Washington. Since these two businesses have not engaged in previous transactions, Harry's Sporting Goods is unwilling to send the purchase price of $56,000 to East Asia for fear that it will not receive the bicycles in return. East Asia, on its part, is unwilling to ship the bicycles unless Harry's Sporting Goods pays in advance. This is a common dilemma in the commercial world which is easily solved by the use of an irrevocable letter of credit. Through use of the letter, the issuing bank's "full faith and credit" is substituted for the full faith and credit of Harry's Sporting Goods, and East Asia is assured that it will receive its money if it provides the documentation required by the letter of credit.

For example, Harry's Sporting Goods asks its bank to issue a letter of credit with East Asia as the beneficiary, which requires the bank to pay the $56,000 purchase price upon receipt of a sight draft accompanied by any documents specified in the letter of credit. In this instance, the letter of credit

116

requires that a bill of lading for the bicycles be attached to the sight draft. A bill of lading is a document of title which verifies that the goods have been delivered into the possession of a common carrier for delivery to the purchaser. Upon receipt of the sight draft, bill of lading, insurance certificate, and any other required documents, the bank is then obligated to pay the funds to the beneficiary.

All parties must understand that the letter of credit, by its nature, is a separate transaction from the sales or other contract on which it is based, and the paying bank is not concerned with or bound by such contract, even if a reference to the contract is included in the credit. Neither is the bank concerned with the goods themselves or their condition. When a letter of credit is issued, all parties involved deal in *documents*, and not in goods, services, or any other performances to which the documents may relate.

Standby letters of credit

A standby letter of credit is one issued for entirely different reasons than a commercial letter of credit. Rather than facilitating a commercial transaction, a standby letter guarantees the payment or performance of an obligation. Contrary to a commercial letter of credit, under which funds are almost always drawn, a draw on a standby letter of credit is usually not contemplated unless a problem of payment or performance arises. By its very nature, a standby letter of credit is more likely to be subject to controversy than a commercial letter of credit.

Suppose, for example, that Dr. Andrews, a successful physician, wishes to invest in Forest View Estates, a limited partnership which is purchasing an apartment complex. As a limited partner, Dr. Andrews is required to invest $50,000. To make the investment more attractive, the general partner agrees that the physician may invest $10,000 cash now and sign a $40,000 note to the partnership, which will require an annual payment of $10,000 for each of the next four years. The general partner also requests that this obligation be covered by a standby letter of credit.

Dr. Andrews approaches his bank and arranges for the issuance of a standby letter of credit in which Forest View Estates is the beneficiary and in which Dr. Andrews is the customer for whose account the letter is issued. To draw funds under the provisions of the letter of credit, Forest View Estates is required only to provide an affidavit verifying that Dr. Andrews is delinquent in making the required $10,000 annual payment. Upon receipt of a sight draft and an affidavit to that effect, the bank is required to disburse funds against the letter of credit.

Two years later, Dr. Andrews is completely disillusioned with his investment in the limited partnership. The apartment project in which the partnership invested is in financial trouble, and the Internal Revenue Service has disallowed its tax shelter aspects. Dr. Andrews, now highly indignant at having been fraudulently induced to invest in such a shoddy project, instructs the bank not to honor any sight draft against the letter of credit. Can he do this?

The answer is no, since the bank has made an irrevocable commitment to pay the partnership if all the provisions of the credit are met. This kind of situation can cause significant problems for the bank, since, on the one hand, it may have a good customer irately demanding that the bank not honor the letter of credit; and, on the other hand, it may have the beneficiary threatening legal action if the bank fails to comply with the terms of the letter. A temporary solution to this problem may be for the bank to advise its customer to obtain a court injunction prohibiting the bank from paying against the letter. Unless fraud is involved, however, the bank may ultimately be required to honor the letter of credit. Because such situations are fraught with legal peril, the bank should proceed only upon advice of its legal counsel.

Policy and procedures

Every bank should have a written policy regarding the issuance of letters of credit, addressing factors such as eligibility criteria, procedures, fees, and record-keeping requirements. In every case, except one where the letter of credit is covered by a cash deposit, the bank must make a credit decision based on the same criteria it uses for making loan decisions. If the bank does not obtain a cash deposit, it should obtain a promissory note from the customer to ensure that it has a source of funds if a draw is made against the letter. Such a promissory note, although undisbursed, should be secured in the same manner as a loan if the circumstances require. Since a letter of credit is a contingent liability of the bank, a register of all letters outstanding and other adequate records must be maintained.

In summary, the issuance of letters of credit can be both a source of income and a service which the bank can provide for its good customers. The bank must be cognizant of the exposure involved, however, and should be careful to ensure that all letters of credit are handled in a prudent manner.

4

Dealing with Collateral

Collateral is the lender's second line of defense. If the repayment that was anticipated from the normal cash flow of the borrower's business fails to materialize, the lender may then take possession of the collateral, liquidate it, and utilize its proceeds to repay the loan. This process, although simple in concept, is often fraught with difficulties.

The first article discusses the many problems that a lender may encounter in dealing with collateral. The lender must be able to identify the collateral and properly describe it in the security documentation. In some instances, the lender, having failed to inspect the collateral or otherwise verify its description, may simply not know enough about the collateral to either identify it or adequately describe it in the security documentation. Banks also often encounter problems with the valuation of collateral. In some instances, even though every other aspect of the loan is adequately documented, the bank's information concerning the liquidation value of its collateral may be minimal. Relying on the borrower's estimate of the value of the collateral, or utilizing other unverified information, the bank may assume that it is "fully collateralized" when in actuality the liquidation value of the collateral is far less than the balance of the loan. It is in this kind of situation, where the bank fails to recognize its exposure, that the probability of a loan loss is greatest. It is therefore essential that every commercial lender develop procedures for the realistic evaluation of collateral. The manner in which a bank's security documentation is completed may also cause problems. Although the rules for establishing and perfecting a security interest under Article 9 of the Uniform Commercial

Code are clear, some bankers fail to fully understand these provisions, and therefore may fail to establish and maintain an enforceable interest in the collateral. An example of such a problem would be where the bank attempts to perfect its security interest without having first established an enforceable security interest by having the debtor execute a written security agreement. Lenders often also encounter problems during the repossession and sale of collateral. This process can be perilous for the lender, and failure to comply with all the rules established by Article 9 for repossession and resale may result in the lender being unable to collect a deficiency and being sued for damages by the borrower. Therefore, if the lender is to avoid a loss, it must deal carefully with collateral to ensure that these potential problems are avoided.

The second article stresses the importance of obtaining credible appraisals of collateral. This is especially essential if the lender is making an asset-based loan. Although lenders have historically obtained outside independent appraisals of real estate which is to secure a mortgage loan, and are, in fact, now required to do so by banking regulations, bankers have been much less oriented toward professional appraisals of other types of collateral. Choosing a competent appraiser is essential, and in some smaller communities, finding an appraiser who is qualified to appraise such collateral as equipment and inventory may be difficult. However, with some diligent research, and with assistance from its city correspondent, even a small community bank can usually locate a qualified appraiser. The article also points out that an appraisal is valid for a limited period of time, and will eventually become inaccurate as the condition of the collateral and market factors change. Therefore, if the bank is considering a liquidation of the collateral several years after the original appraisal was made, a new appraisal will be required to provide the bank with current information regarding its collateral coverage. Generally, bankers have been much too

122

willing to accept unverified information provided by borrowers concerning the value of collateral. It is obvious that if lenders were more demanding of professional appraisals at the time a loan is made, many loan losses could be avoided.

The final article discusses the value of life insurance as collateral. Life insurance on the life of the borrower or on the life of a principal in a business is often overlooked as collateral. The bank may benefit from the assignment of such life insurance in several ways. If the borrower or a key management person in the business dies, the death benefits will be paid to the bank and may be utilized to reduce the balance of the loan. In addition, if the borrower defaults, the bank may be able to liquidate the insurance policy and obtain its cash value. Consumer loan departments in most banks are strongly oriented toward the sale of credit life insurance. However, commercial lenders are often much less sensitive to the value of life insurance as loan collateral. This article outlines the various types of policies and discusses the four or five parties involved in every insurance contract. It also includes a detailed discussion of the procedures for the assignment of a life insurance policy. Lastly, it discusses the importance of life insurance in many workout situations.

Dealing with Collateral: Avoiding the Problems

When a loan is made, the lender normally anticipates that it will be repaid on or before maturity with funds generated by the borrower. The source of this payment will ordinarily be cash flow from the normal operation of a business, or from an individual's salary or wages. In some cases, the cash flow may result from the planned sale of specific assets or a return on investments.

Far too often, the best laid plans go awry. A business may be unable to sell its inventory as quickly or for as high a price as anticipated. Its operating expenses may be higher than ex-

123

pected or it may have difficulty collecting its receivables. As a result, there may be little or no net cash flow available to repay the loan. An individual may lose a job, incur unexpected medical expenses or experience other adversity which prevents him or her from making required loan payments.

In many cases, financial mismanagement is a significant factor in the borrower's failure to repay the loan. When repayment fails to materialize from the anticipated sources, the unsecured creditor usually has few alternatives for collecting the loan. The secured creditor, however, has a second line of defense: repossessing the collateral, converting it to cash, and using those proceeds to pay off the loan.

Unfortunately for the lender, there are many pitfalls along the road to realizing on collateral. Generally speaking, problems with collateral fall into the following five basic categories: identification, description, valuation, security documentation, and repossession and sale.

1. IDENTIFICATION

   If a lender cannot actually identify its collateral, it will be impossible to describe it adequately in the security documentation, ascertain its value, or locate it when repossession is attempted. Lenders generally obtain information about collateral from the borrower, using such records as depreciation schedules. However, lenders have learned from experience that it is often beneficial to verify this information by inspecting the collateral. Such an inspection also provides useful information regarding the location, condition, and probable value of the collateral. Periodic collateral inspections are usually required if the lender is to . maintain adequate supervision and control of the collateral during the term of the loan.

2. DESCRIPTION

   Collateral descriptions cause more problems and

124

litigation than almost any other aspect of secured lending. A description of personal property or real estate is sufficient whether or not it is specific, if it *reasonably* identifies what is described (UCC 9-110). What is meant by "reasonable" is a subject of discussion among lenders and legal scholars. A generic description such as "all assets of the borrower" is unacceptable since the courts have generally rejected such descriptions as being too broad in scope. A preferable description is probably one that is neither overly specific nor overly broad. Since judicial views concerning collateral descriptions vary considerably, the lender should consult with legal counsel regarding what is acceptable in a given transaction.

A defective description can cause severe problems for the lender and an incorrect description will usually invalidate a security interest. Despite the obvious necessity of having adequate descriptions, many banks approach the subject quite casually and exhibit little concern as to the adequacy of the descriptions used in their collateral documents.

3. VALUATION

When a secured loan becomes a problem and the lender is forced to liquidate the collateral, there will often be a deficiency: The proceeds of the collateral will be insufficient to pay the loan in full. This is because lenders often grossly overestimate the liquidation value of collateral. Collateral valuations may be obtained from such sources as the debtor's financial statements, published price guides, a dealer, or a formal appraisal of the collateral by a qualified appraiser. A formal appraisal is the most credible information source, but due to the cost and time involved and the scarcity of qualified appraisers in some areas, many banks seldom rely on this source of information when dealing with collateral such as equipment or inventory. It is risky for a banker to rely on the representations of the borrower without any attempt to verify the value of collateral.

The lender must also be aware that many factors affect the liquidation value of collateral. In the case of inventory, factors such as obsolescence, damage, perishability, and market demand may affect value. The age, average size, concentration, and type of account debtor will affect the secured lender's ability to collect on receivables. The value of equipment will be affected by its age, condition, and whether it is state of the art or obsolete. Collateral that is unique, custom built or one of a kind will almost always be difficult to sell if ultimately repossessed by the lender.

Although many lenders do an excellent job of identifying and describing their collateral, they often devote insufficient time and effort to determining its value. Many lenders do not recognize that collateral usually fails to bring its full market price in a foreclosure sale. They also forget that the cost of repossessing, reconditioning, and reselling collateral can be prohibitive.

4. SECURITY DOCUMENTATION

In most cases, the requirements for perfecting a security interest in collateral are found in Article 9 of the UCC. The secured party must establish and perfect a security interest in collateral covered under Article 9. A written security agreement is generally required when dealing with business-related assets. However, one may not be required in instances in which the collateral is in the possession of the secured party. To perfect its interest, the secured party generally must either take possession of the collateral or file a financing statement in the appropriate filing office.

126

Filing is generally required in the case of business assets and an improper filing can cause significant problems for the secured lender. In addition, incorrectly listing the debtor's name or address or failing to file a continuation statement in a timely manner may leave the secured lender in an unperfected position. A frequent error is not filing in the jurisdiction where the company's principal place of business is located, as well as filing in the jurisdiction in which the collateral is located. An unperfected status may result in the secured party losing the collateral to a third-party claimant who has a perfected position, such as a bankruptcy trustee, the Internal Revenue Service, or another financial institution.

5. REPOSSESSION AND SALE

When the debtor defaults on a secured loan, the lender will often use a "self-help" repossession of the collateral, with the intent of selling it and using the proceeds to pay off the loan. Although the rules vary by state, a self-help repossession is usually permissible in commercial transactions as long as the lender or its agent does not commit a "breach of the peace." What constitutes a breach of the peace is open to some debate, but generally, a verbal threat directed at the debtor, entering the debtor's premises after being forbidden to do so, forcing entry by breaking a lock, and similar actions may violate the debtor's rights and result in a legal problem for the lender.

The lender must comply with two additional rules when it proceeds to sell the repossessed goods. First, *all* debtors involved must be given reasonable notification of the proposed sale. In this context, the term *debtor* includes the principal debtor, a co-maker or guarantor and any owner of the collateral even though not obli-

127

gated on the debt. "Reasonable notice" is generally defined either by statute or by provisions in the loan documents. The second rule requires the sale to be conducted in a "commercially reasonable" manner. Both private sales and public auctions are permissible if conducted in such a manner. The sale of repossessed collateral to an "insider" such as an officer, employee, director, or major stockholder of the bank is almost always subject to challenge and should be avoided. There are several penalties for failure to comply with these rules, including loss of the right to pursue the debtor for a deficiency and the possibility of being sued for damages by the debtor.

In summary, the mere fact that a loan is collateralized will not prevent a loss. The lender must be able to locate and identify the collateral, take possession of it, and then be able to liquidate it for sufficient proceeds to pay off the loan. There are many pitfalls in the process of realizing on collateral, and lenders must be more aware of these potential problems in their secured lending transactions.

Appraising Collateral

A good collateral appraisal is crucial to making a good asset-based loan. How does a lender find a good appraisal firm and what are the elements of a good appraisal?

"The loan officer's dilemma used to be, 'What's it really worth?' Now, the concern is, 'Who can give me the answer?'" says David Levy, of Levy Associates, a Southfield, MI, firm offering auction, appraisal, and liquidation services. "Some firms provide appraisals that are not based on market data and the latest auction figures. Past performance and the ability to back up an appraisal are what the loan officer should look at when deciding which firm to trust to do the appraisal. The appraisal is the insurance policy for the loan. If the appraisal isn't right, it can jeopardize the whole loan. A banker has to know the value of the collateral so he can properly structure the loan. A banker must have a good security agreement with a comprehensive listing of the assets, or he can't do the proper UCC filings and can't perfect the bank's secured position.

"The banking industry has changed in the last 25 years, especially in terms of its relationships with customers," says Levy. "When banks used to lend to big corporations, they had no problem placing their funds. But then corporations discovered they could issue commercial paper, and banks needed another place to put their money—hence the growth of asset-based lending and the need for valuations. Banks could turn to traditional valuation firms, who do a good job appraising for insurance and depreciation purposes. But such firms are not as good at appraising something in terms of the marketplace, and that's where the growth of forced liquidation appraisals comes in. When banks started getting hurt by nonmarket-based appraisals, they realized that the firms best able to provide information were the ones with a database of information from auctions."

Choosing an appraiser

"The most important measure of an appraiser is past performance," says Leslie H. Miles, Jr., senior appraiser with the Dallas-based appraisal firm, MB Valuation Services, Inc. "Ask the appraiser what he did before and how it came out. Investigate the appraiser's proven past history. This may not be a complete measure, but it can make you feel more comfortable about working with the appraiser. Some kinds of value concepts are difficult to prove. Since the majority of asset-based lenders tend to ask for the most dependable value of a liquidation appraisal, there's an historical record. Also, who is the individual within the firm who will handle the appraisal? What are his qualifications—including background, education, and experience within the profession?"

Miles suggests the following as questions for lenders to ask a prospective appraisal firm:

- Have you ever sold/auctioned equipment?

- Have you attended auctions? How many? For what kind of equipment? Were they bankruptcy auctions?

- What is your approach to value, the first thing to look for? "If they say cost, you can hang up the phone, because you can't get cost at an auction," notes Miles.

- What is your firm's appraisal record?

- Do you need to sell [conduct auctions and liquidations] to do a good appraisal? "A firm can argue either way, so it's important to listen to how they argue the point."

- What method would you use for a specific piece of equipment?

- Does the appraiser have membership in various professional societies? "Credentials show the appraiser is involved in the profession, but where they really become important is in court testimony."

Appraisal myths

"The seminars we offer for lenders focus on the steps to performing a good appraisal and the interrelationship of the appraisal company and the data from auction sales," says Levy. "We try to explode some of the myths surrounding appraisals, one of which is that you can look at new cost and arrive at present value. It can't be done. Another myth is that you can lend on fair market value. However, fair market value is not indicative of value recoverable on the market, especially under stressed circumstances. You must look at the forced liquidation value. To do that effectively, you must have auction data and must be an auctioneer. There are some other firms out there with this approach, but they're not running an average of 100 auctions per year. Many firms do appraisals on the basis of depreciation, cost, or engineering data, and that's just not safe for a lender. It's important to look at the marketplace and know what the numbers are and have been in other cases."

"Liquidation value is the most commonly used concept," says Miles, whose firm also provides seminars for lenders. "Asset-based financing is changing—it's focusing more on cash flow. In equipment, there's a trend toward asking for orderly liquidation value (instead of liquidation/auction value), but this is somewhat dangerous. It assumes that there will be an orderly liquidation. Fair market value could be used for a collateral appraisal, but it isn't used too often for asset-based lending—it's used more often for allocation of purchase price."

"Besides being careful about who does your appraisals, get as much information as possible," Levy recommends. "An appraisal has a limited lifetime. Sooner or later, it will become inaccurate, whether because of market changes, the addition of new equipment, or the need for more capital. It's smart to deal with an appraisal firm that can perform a re-appraisal and back it up. In general, any time you're lending on the value of the collateral, it's foolish not to talk to someone about it. Appraisal is a prerequisite to a good asset-based loan."

Elements of the appraisal report

"Most banks tend to categorize types of collateral as 'special' or 'standard,'" says Miles. "Items that are highly volatile in price when you sell them or that bring low numbers compared to cost fall into the special or conditional category. Standard types of collateral are those on which you can rely to be within a certain range without much volatility. Examples of industries with that kind of equipment would be plastics and metal- and wood-working. Also in the standard category would be inventory like sporting goods—things that could be sold easily. When you get to real estate, which is volatile in itself, you find that it has a reasonable type of stability. There are, however, pieces of real estate which would be difficult to sell—such as a one-million-square-foot property in a small town."

According to Miles, the following is the absolute minimum a lender should find in an appraisal report:

1. letter of transmittal;

2. definition of value concepts being applied;

3. statement of limiting conditions;

4. the subject of the appraisal (proper listing and description);

5. qualifications of the appraiser, and

6. certification of the appraiser.

Miles also believes a good appraisal report should contain a cover page identifying the value concepts, the effective date of the study, the type or name of company being appraised, and the name of the senior appraiser in charge of the study.

"There should also be a recapitulation sheet that specifies the derived value in aggregate and an index of the report's contents," Miles says. "The report should include a 'special consideration' page, in addition to incorporating 'statements of limiting conditions,' when there is the possibility of an unusual or special area being overlooked and yet significant to the formulation of the overall value indicator of the study. It's also helpful if there is a general overview of the method of appraisal, as well as photographs and maps, if appropriate."

132

According to Levy, factors that help determine value include market conditions, geographic location of assets, uses of equipment (specialized or general purpose), physical condition of assets, and expenses for removal, reinstallation and/or transportation of assets. Research is also a key to a good appraisal; the appraiser should have access to data about comparable assets and past auction sales, as well as contacts with dealers and manufacturers.

Miles suggests that lenders understand how a particular appraisal firm defines terms. "Be sure you know what the firm means when it says 'forced liquidation value,' because there is not an industry wide standard definition. Get the definition ahead of time, because once you get the report it's too late. Lenders should also communicate with their clients more about what type of appraisal is needed and define the value concepts ahead of time. Lenders shouldn't just say, 'Get an appraisal,' but should also recommend three or four appraisal firms they're familiar with and whose work they will approve."

Life Insurance: Overlooked Collateral?

When a bank makes a substantial loan to a business or an individual, it usually seeks to perfect a security interest in virtually all of the business assets of the debtor. This is standard banking practice, and such an approach is generally referred to as taking a "broad form" or "blanket" security interest. In this process, however, one significant asset is often overlooked: life insurance owned by the business itself or the principals involved. This may be a serious oversight on the lender's part, since life insurance often has considerable collateral value.

The bank may benefit from an assignment of life insurance in two different ways. First, if the insured, who is usually the proprietor or key person in the business, dies, the death benefits will be paid to the bank and may be used to reduce the outstanding balance of the loan. Second, if there is a default, and the assigned policy is a whole life policy, it will probably have cash value, which the bank may obtain by surrendering the policy. Some life insurance companies may hesitate to do this, however, and may require the policy owner's signature before canceling the policy and paying the cash value to the bank. Unfortunately, in such a situation, the debtor may either be uncooperative or unavailable and legal action may be needed to compel the debtor to execute the required documents or to force the insurance company to pay over the cash value without the debtor's signature. The lender may encounter this problem despite clear language to the contrary in the assignment form.

Types of policies

A whole life policy is one that remains in effect until the death of the insured, provided that the required periodic premiums are paid. Whole life may be characterized as "permanent" insurance and will accumulate cash value, which in most instances the owner can borrow against. Such policy loans are usually available at low interest rates and are an attractive source of borrowed funds for the owner. If the policy owner fails to make required premium payments, cash value may be used by the insurance company to make premium payments.

Term life insurance is often characterized as "temporary" coverage that is purchased for a specific purpose, such as mortgage insurance, which enables the debtor's estate to pay off a mortgage loan. A term policy is generally effective for a given time period; upon its expiration, the insured must purchase a new term policy if continued coverage is desired. Term policies do not accumulate cash value and therefore have no loan value. Consequently, the premium for term insurance is significantly less than that for a comparable amount of whole life coverage.

Lenders are familiar with term life insurance since most banks offer a credit life insurance program to their borrowers. In many banks, credit life insurance is aggressively marketed by consumer lenders, but is often unavailable for commercial loan customers. The banks that do successfully market credit life insurance to both consumer and commercial loan customers have found it to be a valuable service to their customers and an excellent source of commission income.

Parties involved

There are always four or five parties involved in the process of assigning a life insurance policy. They include the following:

1. THE INSURANCE COMPANY. This is the entity issuing the policy, which entitles it to receive specified premium payments.

2. THE OWNER OF THE POLICY. This is the person or "entity" who has "rights" in the policy—who may designate the beneficiary, borrow the cash value, surrender the policy, or allow it to lapse. The owner is the only party with the power to assign the policy to the bank.

3. THE INSURED. This may or may not be the same party as the owner. The policy's death benefits only become payable upon the death of the insured.

4. THE BENEFICIARY. This is the party designated by the owner who is entitled to receive the death benefits under the policy. The beneficiary, however, has no rights in the policy. The owner may designate a new beneficiary without notification to or consent of the previous beneficiary.

5. THE ASSIGNEE. Upon proper completion of the assignment process, the assignee acquires rights in the policy,

135

which are specified by the form of assignment utilized. At this point, the owner is barred from exercising most rights under the policy, but cannot be compelled to pay any future premiums.

Assignment procedures

The Uniform Commercial Code (UCC 9-104[g]) specifically exempts assignments of life insurance policies from Article 9 coverage. Therefore, a security agreement and financing statement are not required to establish a secured party's rights to an insurance policy, and would in fact be ineffective if used. Instead, a fairly standard assignment form is used by most banks. This form has also been approved by the insurance industry and is readily accepted by almost all insurance companies. It is generally executed in triplicate—the bank retains one copy and forwards two copies to the life insurance company. The insurance company keeps one copy for its files and returns an acknowledged copy to the bank as the assignee.

It is crucially important for the policy owner to execute the assignment, since the owner is the only person authorized to assign the policy to the lender. Most standard assignment forms also have a signature line for the beneficiary. It is advisable to obtain the beneficiary's signature, if possible; however, the assignment is valid and enforceable without it.

The legal effect of the standard assignment form is clearly stated in its first paragraph: "The undersigned, by executing this document, hereby assigns and transfers to the bank all claims, options, privileges, proceeds, rights, title, and interest which the undersigned or the undersigned's heirs, representatives, or successors might have in the policy, subject to the terms of this assignment and all superior liens, if any, which insurer may have against the policy, and the terms and conditions of the policy." The "superior liens" mentioned

136

above refer to preexisting liens or prior assignments that may exist with respect to the policy. Included among these will be the insurance company's right to use cash value to pay off any preexisting policy loans or fund any unpaid premiums.

It is crucial that the executed assignment be forwarded to the insurance company for acknowledgement at the earliest opportunity, since the assignment is ineffective against the insurance company until such acknowledgement has occurred. Once the assignment is acknowledged, the assignee has rights similar to those of the policy owner. These generally include the right to be notified of nonpayment of premium or cancellation of the policy, although state law varies and some jurisdictions may not actually require the insurer to give such notification to the assignee. Consequently, lenders need to develop some system for monitoring premium payments and should not rely solely on notification from the insurer.

In addition to obtaining the assignment and having it acknowledged by the insurer, the bank should also physically obtain and hold the actual insurance policy. This prevents the debtor, or anyone else, from delivering it to another creditor for the purpose of assignment, although this will not automatically prevent a subsequent assignment. More importantly, the original policy must be surrendered to the insurance company in order to obtain the cash value or death benefits. Retaining custody of the policy facilitates delivery to the insurer, if necessary. It does not relate to "perfection by possession," since Article 9 does not apply to this procedure.

The life insurance assignment questionnaire

The mere fact that the bank is an assignee of a life insurance policy does not provide the bank with information about the status of the policy or its value as collateral. To obtain pertinent details, most banks submit a questionnaire to the insurer along with the executed assignment. If the inquirer is an acknowledged assignee, the insurance company will generally provide information regarding the status of the policy. Many standard questionnaire forms, however, have an authorization section, which the policy owner must sign. The use of such a form, which may be presigned by the owner, is recommended to expedite the process.

The following questions are generally contained in the questionnaire:

1. Are there preexisting assignments? The insurance company will generally accept any number of assignments, which will have priority in the order in which they are acknowledged. The bank may be either the first assignee or the fifth, depending on the circumstances.

2. What is the cash value of the policy? The higher the cash value, the greater the immediate collateral value of the policy.

3. What is the amount of any policy loan? A policy loan will be a potential setoff against the cash value, or any death benefits, and will also require periodic interest payments.

4. What is the amount of the premium, and to what date is the premium paid? The bank obviously needs to monitor the situation to ensure that premiums are paid when due. The bank should ask the insurance company to send it duplicate copies of the premium payment notices. The bank should also ascertain whether the insurer will send a notice prior to cancellation if premiums are not paid.

Life insurance in a workout

When attempting to improve its collateral position with a problem loan, the bank may find that a life insurance policy

138

is the only unencumbered asset of the debtor—one often overlooked not only by the bank, but by other creditors as well. In such a situation, the bank should act immediately to obtain assignment of the policy, since the policy may have cash value, and will provide death benefits at a future date.

As an example, consider the following case: Community Bank had a $600,000 loan with Ted Slick, owner of an automobile dealership and various other business enterprises. Due to poor business practices and the failure of some subsidiary business ventures, Slick's primary business also failed. The bank then learned, to its dismay, that it had failed to perfect its security interest and therefore lost a major portion of its collateral to other creditors and the trustee in bankruptcy. As a result, the bank suffered a $400,000 loss. The bank did, however, have a valid assignment of a $150,000 life insurance policy on Mr. Slick's life. At the time of Mr. Slick's bankruptcy, the bank could have surrendered the policy and received its $10,000 cash value. Because of Mr. Slick's age and lifestyle (which was not conducive to longevity), the bank decided to keep the policy in force by continuing to pay the annual premium of approximately $3,000. Seven years later, as a result of its foresight and an additional investment of $21,000, the bank collected death benefits in the amount of $150,000, and had a net recovery in the amount of $129,000.

In summary, it is obvious that an assignment of life insurance may have considerable collateral value. This is especially true in a situation where the success of a business primarily depends on one person, as is the case with many small companies. In such instances, the bank should insist that the key individual be covered by adequate life insurance that is assigned to the bank. The assignment of life insurance is a relatively simple procedure, which may produce significant benefits to the bank and is often a critical factor in avoiding loan losses.

139

5

Article 9 of the Uniform Commercial Code

Article 9 of the Uniform Commercial Code governs the great majority of non-real estate-secured transactions. With a few relatively minor exceptions, almost every commercial and consumer secured loan transaction is subject to Article 9 rules. It is therefore imperative that every lender understand the rather complex rules established by Article 9 for creating and perfecting a security interest in collateral. Some lenders, baffled by its somewhat complicated rules, dislike Article 9. Because they do not fully understand its provisions, these people fail to recognize that Article 9 is good law for lenders. Its flexibility gives lenders a number of options that did not exist under previous law, including the ability to cover after-acquired property and the ability to secure future loans or advances readily. Article 9 also automatically extends the security interest to the proceeds of collateral, thereby enabling the lender to pursue proceeds if the collateral has been sold or otherwise disposed of. Also, in a commercial transaction, the lender is not required to relate specific items of collateral to a specific note as was required under the old chattel mortgage laws. All of these basic Code concepts are discussed in the first article in this section, which stresses Article 9's great flexibility for the lender.

The second article discusses the Code's collateral classification system, which is the basis for all collateral descriptions, and which also determines the procedure required for perfection. The Code establishes six general classifications, and all collateral (except for real estate, which is excluded from

Article 9 coverage), no matter how unique it is, will fit into one of these classifications. All tangible property will fit into the first category, called "goods." Intangibles fall into the other five categories, which are instruments, documents, chattel paper, accounts, and general intangibles. In the original 1962 version of Article 9, there was an additional category called contract rights, which has now been merged into the accounts classification. Therefore, when a lender uses the term *accounts* in a collateral description, it will cover both accounts receivable and contract rights. This article discusses the specific definitions of the various categories of collateral. Since all of the terms used in the Code's classification system are specifically defined, they should be used by a lender constructing a collateral description. For example, the term *accounts* should be used rather than *receivables*, and the term *inventory* should be used rather than the term *merchandise* or *stock in trade.*

The third article discusses perfection, which is the process by which a secured party establishes its priority as to competing third-party creditors who have a claim against the same collateral. Therefore, to avoid losing its collateral to such competing third parties as the judgment creditor and the bankruptcy trustee, it is essential that the lender perfect its interest. This article discusses the four methods by which a security interest may be perfected—by attachment alone, by taking possession of the collateral, by filing a financing statement, or by complying with a statutory scheme. By allowing perfection by taking possession of the collateral in some instances, Article 9 recognizes the ancient pledge concept, which has existed for thousands of years. Recognizing that it is impossible or inconvenient for a secured party to perfect by taking possession of some types of collateral, the Code has established a filing system under which a secured party may perfect by filing a financing statement (usually called a form UCC-1) in an appropriate filing office. Depending on the type of collateral involved and on the specific filing rules of the state in which the debtor and/or the collateral is located, either a central filing, a local filing, or a dual filing both centrally and locally may be required. Obviously, it is crucially important that a lender perfect its position, and it is therefore essential that the lender understand all of the Article 9 rules pertaining to perfection.

A separate article discusses maintaining perfection. This article points out that, although the filing of a financing statement is generally valid to perfect for a period of five years, certain events may occur, which will cause the secured party to become unperfected. These events include the debtor changing its location, the removal of collateral to another jurisdiction, a change in the debtor's name, or, in some instances, a change in the use of collateral. If such a change occurs, the secured party may be required to refile a financing statement to maintain its perfected position. Constant vigilance and adequate supervision of the loan is required to alert the secured party to the occurrence of any event that may jeopardize its secured position.

There is considerable confusion among commercial lenders regarding the extent to which future advances may be secured by a preexisting security interest. The fifth article deals with the Article 9 rules pertaining to future advances. Generally, the secured lender has great flexibility in securing future advances with a preexisting security interest, and in most instances the security interest covering these future advances will have the same priority established by the filing of the original financing statement. This, of course, makes it very easy for a secured lender to deal with a revolving loan, in which there is a constant turnover of collateral, and a constant stream of future advances. There are, however, limitations to the secured party's ability to maintain its priority position as to future advances in some instances, and the problems and concerns to which a secured lender should be alert are discussed in detail. The article also discusses the effect of an intervening lien creditor such as a judgment creditor or the Internal Revenue Service. The point is made that the secured lender must be familiar with Section 6323 of the Internal Revenue Code, which establishes the rights of the Internal Revenue Service versus the creditor who has a previously perfected security interest.

The secured creditor's right to proceeds is the topic of the sixth article. The Code in most states provides that proceeds are automatically covered by the security interest without any specific reference to proceeds in the security documentation. However, many conservative lenders continue to specifically describe proceeds in their collateral description. This article points out that the secured lender has an enforceable right to proceeds and discusses the alternatives available to the secured party if conversion (unauthorized disposition) of the collateral takes place. The article also discusses the special rules which apply to sales in the ordinary course of business. The Code specifically provides for the protection of buyers in the ordinary course of business, and in such an instance, the secured party's right to pursue proceeds of inventory may be effectively cut off. There are, however, exceptions to the general rule with which the lender must be familiar. Finally, the article discusses special rules that apply to the sale of farm products, which generally require that the secured party must take additional steps, such as prenotification to a prospective buyer, if it is to retain the right to pursue the collateral or its proceeds into the hands of a third party.

Financing inventory and receivables is also specifically discussed in the following article. As indicated previously, the Code rules allowing a secured party to cover after-acquired property and future advances with a preexisting security interest facilitate the establishment of a revolving loan to finance inventory and receivables. This article makes suggestions for monitoring collateral and for assessing the quality

144

of a debtor's accounts receivable. It also discusses the use of a borrowing base certificate to monitor collateral margin, and the use of a lock box to control cash collections.

Still another article discusses the use of titled vehicles as collateral. Secured transactions involving titled vehicles are often mishandled by bankers because the normal Code rules for perfection generally do not apply. Rather, if the titled vehicle is classified as consumer goods or equipment, the procedure for perfection is usually established by a statute outside of Article 9, such as a state motor vehicle statute. Therefore, in most instances, the secured party's interest is perfected by registering a lien on the vehicle title rather than by filing a financing statement. However, if the titled vehicle is classified as inventory, then normal Code perfection rules will apply, and the filing of a financing statement describing inventory in the appropriate filing office is required. Many bankers fail to recognize this distinction and will attempt to perfect their security interest in inventory consisting of titled vehicles by holding certificates of title or certificates of origin. Even though the bank may have registered its lien on these titles, this is ineffective, since the Code specifically requires the filing of a financing statement. Failing to understand this distinction in the rules, some bankers have suffered a loss that could easily have been avoided if they had understood the procedures established by Article 9.

Although most bankers are somewhat familiar with the "purchase money security interest," which is one kind of super-priority security interest, most fail to understand the super-priority concept and the Code rules that govern this special category of security interest. Super-priority security interests fall outside of the general Code priority rule, which is "first to file or perfect, first in priority." Compliance with the rather complex rules for establishing a super-priority by the secured party will always result in a first priority security interest, even though under the ordinary Code priority rules

145

another creditor who had filed previously might have first priority. The ninth article discusses the various types of super-priority interests, and the special rules that govern the creation of these interests.

The final article discusses secret liens. Most lenders are unaware of the fact that in some instances the operation of the Code will result in a secret lien that is enforceable, but that will be undiscoverable in a normal UCC search. The various types of secret liens include non-UCC-recorded liens, unrecorded perfected security interests, and hidden liens. Failing to recognize that a secret lien may exist, a lender may perform a Code search and erroneously conclude that the security interest which it is about to perfect will have first priority. To avoid this kind of problem, lenders must be familiar with the various kinds of secret liens. This article discusses the circumstances under which a secret lien may exist and makes suggestions as to how the bank may protect itself from this problem.

The Advantage of Article 9: Its Flexibility

When Article 9 of the Uniform Commercial Code was adopted by most states during the 1960s, it replaced a large number of previous state statutes covering chattel mortgages, conditional sales, installment loans, trust receipts, etc. It also introduced the concept of the security interest, which replaced such pre-Code security devices as the chattel mortgage, factor's lien, trust receipt, and conditional sales contract.

The adoption of Article 9 also introduced a number of revolutionary concepts, which lenders who deal with secured transactions must fully understand. Although commercial lenders are often frustrated by the workings of Article 9, it has proved to be vastly superior to pre-Code law because of the inherent flexibility it provides the secured lender.

146

For instance, in a commercial transaction, the lender is no longer required to relate specific items of collateral to a specific note as was required under the old chattel mortgage laws. This pre-Code requirement often resulted in a collateral surplus on one note and a collateral deficiency on another, but the lender was precluded from applying surplus from one note to the deficiency on the second. In addition, the secured lender now has several other options available that did not exist under previous law. These pertain to the concepts of after-acquired property, future advances, and the proceeds of collateral.

After-acquired property

Under Section 9-204(1) of the Code, a security agreement may provide that any obligations covered by it are also to be secured by after-acquired collateral. In other words, the debtor may give the lender or secured party a security interest not only in property owned now, but also in property of the same general nature or type, which may be acquired by the debtor at some future date.

This security interest in after-acquired property attaches even though the debtor may have paid for the newly acquired assets from cash on hand or received the property as an inheritance or gift. It will also attach if some other lender has advanced the funds for the purchase of the after-acquired property, even though that third-party creditor has properly perfected a purchase money security interest (PMSI). In such an instance, the PMSI lender will have a security interest superior to that of the previously perfected lender who has an after-acquired clause in his/her documentation. Since vendors and other purchase money financers are often quite lax in complying with the Code's purchase money rules, the previously perfected lender with an after-acquired property clause in its documentation may obtain a prior security interest in the newly purchased asset by technical default.

147

Consider the following example: Curtis Construction Company purchases a new Caterpillar earthmover from its local dealer, and the dealer agrees to finance the purchase. Curtis executes a note, security ageement, and financing statement (form UCC-1). However, the dealer fails to file the form UCC-1 within the required time period (this varies from state to state, but is ordinarily either 10, 15, or 20 days from the date the debtor receives possession) and therefore fails to achieve a PMSI. Second National Bank, which has previously filed a financing statement covering all construction and earthmoving equipment and which has a security agreement containing an after-acquired property clause, now has a first priority position as to the earthmover under the Code's "first to file, first in priority" rule, even though it may be unaware that Curtis has purchased the earthmover.

If the secured party intends to cover after-acquired property, that fact must be clearly stated in an after-acquired property clause included in the security agreement and should preferably also be disclosed in the financing statement. A typical after-acquired property clause will usually refer to a category of assets "now owned or hereafte acquired."

Future advances

Another Code option that provides flexibility to the lender involves the possibility of having future loan advances covered by a pre-existing security interest. The Code (Section 9-204[3]) states that obligations covered by a security agreement may include future advances, whether or not the advances are given pursuant to a commitment. Therefore, the security interest created at the time of an initial loan transaction may cover not only that transaction, but any number of future loan transactions, even though no future loans were actually committed or contemplated at the time of the initial transaction.

148

This coverage of future advances is not automatic. Rather, a future advances clause must be contained in the security agreement. Most standard security agreement forms cover future advances and contain language such as "all present and future debts" or "all indebtedness and obligations whatsoever of the debtor to the secured party, whether now existing or hereafter arising." In addition, some conservative lenders are now also disclosing in the financing statement that the security interest covers future advances, although this is not specifically required by the Code.

Suppose, for example, that the bank's customer, Cutter Corporation, obtained a $200,000 working capital loan in August 1989 secured by equipment, inventory, and receivables. The security agreement contained a future advance clause. Therefore, when the company requested an additional $100,000 loan in December, the new loan was automatically covered by the security interest established in August. Neither the execution of a new security agreement nor the filing of an additional financing statement was required. The bank will have a prior security interest with respect to the $100,000 loan made in December, even though another creditor had filed a financing statement covering the same collateral in October 1989.

Obviously, the lender who uses both the after-acquired property clause and future advances clause in loan documentation greatly enhances its collateral position. These two clauses also enable the lender to establish and maintain a "floating lien" on both inventory and receivables. Since a loan secured by inventory and receivables ordinarily involves multiple disbursements, it is revolving in nature, with inventory and receivables constantly turning over. Without these key Code provisions, the secured lender would have severe problems in maintaining its security position due to the revolving nature of the collateral. By utilizing these Code provisions, the lender is able to secure successive disbursements with a continuing security interest in inventory and receivables, even though they are in a constant state of flux.

Proceeds

Article 9 also provides the lender with increased protection and flexibility in dealing with proceeds of collateral. The Code (Section 9-306) indicates that proceeds are whatever is received from the sale, exchange, collection, or other disposition of collateral, including money, checks, and deposit accounts—all of which are referred to as cash proceeds. All other proceeds, such as accounts receivable, negotiable instruments, or property taken in trade, are noncash proceeds. Under the provisions of the Code, the security interest automatically extends to proceeds even though it is not specifically included in the collateral description in either the security agreement or the financing statement.

However, to avoid problems, many conservative bankers continue to refer to proceeds in the collateral descriptions in both the security agreement and the form UCC-1. In the case of a loan secured by inventory and receivables, the collateral is constantly being converted to proceeds, and the extension of the security interest to proceeds is usually contemplated by everyone involved. However, when the debtor is converting or liquidating collateral without the consent of the lender, the existence of this automatic proceeds provision facilitates recovery by the lender, so long as the proceeds, regardless of their form, can be traced and identified.

In summary, it is obvious that the great flexibility provided by Article 9 is advantageous to the secured lender, if the lender understands these concepts and utilizes them properly. Lenders should view Article 9 as an extremely valuable working tool and apply its provisions to their advantage in both structuring and enforcing loan provisions.

Collateral Classifications: The Crucial Issue

A tremendous variety of personal assets may be used as collateral under the provisions of Article 9 of the Uniform Commercial Code. To deal with this great diversity in the kinds of collateral that can be used to establish a security interest, the Code specifies six basic categories into which all collateral is classified. These include the following: goods, instruments, documents, chattel paper, accounts and contract rights, and general intangibles. Unfortunately, many bankers neither understand nor recognize the importance of this collateral classification system. A secured lender, however, must understand these six collateral categories, because the procedure for establishing and perfecting a security interest will vary depending upon the category into which the collateral fits.

To understand the classification system, the secured lender must be familiar with three basic rules:

1. At any given time, an item of collateral must belong in one, and only one, classification.
2. The classification of an item is based upon its primary use by its owner, *not* upon its innate nature or character.
3. The classification of an item of collateral may change repeatedly as its use changes.

The six categories of collateral classification are described below with examples provided to help clarify the distinctions among them.

Goods

The Code (Section 9-105[h]) describes goods as including "all things which are moveable at the time the security interest attaches or which are fixtures, but does not include

151

money, documents, instruments, accounts, chattel paper, general intangibles or minerals or the like before extraction. Goods also include standing timber which is to be cut and removed under a conveyance or contract for sale, the unborn young of animals, and growing crops." All tangible collateral falls into this category, which is divided into the following four subcategories:

a. **consumer goods:** These are goods used or bought primarily for personal, family, or household purposes.

b. **equipment:** Equipment includes goods used or bought for use primarily in business (including farming or a profession) or by a debtor who is a nonprofit organization or a governmental subdivision or agency; or if the goods are not included in the definitions of inventory, farm products, or consumer goods.

c. **inventory:** Inventory includes goods held by a person who holds them for sale, lease, or to be furnished under contracts of service (or if he has so furnished them), as well as raw materials, work in process, or materials used or consumed in a business. Equipment which is held for the purpose of being leased is classified as "inventory," not "equipment."

d. **farm products:** Farm products are crops, livestock, or supplies used or produced in farming operations, or products of crops or livestock in their unmanufactured states (such as ginned cotton, wool clip, maple syrup, milk, or eggs) and if they are in possession of a debtor engaged in raising, fattening, grazing, or other farm operations. If goods are farm products they are neither inventory nor equipment. Crops, livestock, or other farm commodities are classified as "farm products" only as long as they are held by a producer. When the producer sells these items to a middleman or processor, they become "inventory."

As noted earlier, the category into which goods fall is determined by the manner in which the debtor will use them. Therefore, identical goods used for different purposes may fall into different categories. As a result, the procedures for establishing and perfecting a security interest in these goods may vary depending on how the collateral is classified. Suppose, for example, that Jerry Smith purchases a used 1986 Oldsmobile Delta 88 automobile which is financed by First National Bank. Since the vehicle will be used as a family car by the Smiths, it is "consumer goods." In this instance, the bank must establish its security interest by having Smith execute a security agreement. In most states, it must then perfect by registering its lien on the title to the automobile as required by various state statutes pertaining to motor vehicles.

For the sake of this example, assume that a second identical 1986 Oldsmobile Delta 88 is purchased by Perfection Printing Company to be used as a delivery vehicle. In this case, the automobile is classified as "equipment," but the procedure for establishing and perfecting a security interest remains the same as described above. Now suppose that a third 1986 Oldsmobile is purchased by Harry's Motor Sales, a used car retailer. Since this vehicle is held for resale, it falls into the Code classification of "inventory"; as a result there is a significant change in the procedure for perfecting a security interest. The bank must still have the debtor execute a security agreement, but in order to perfect its interest in the inventory of used cars it is financing, the bank must file a financing statement in the appropriate filing office, usually that of the Secretary of State.

The bank may wish to hold the titles to the used automobiles it is financing to control and monitor its collateral; but in this case, holding the vehicle title (even with the bank's lien registered on the title) generally neither perfects the bank's security interest nor establishes its priority among competing creditors. Interestingly, if the vehicle is the inventory of a retailer, and a competing bank has attempted to perfect by holding the vehicle title and registering its lien, the bank that has filed a financing statement in the proper filing office will ordinarily prevail if a conflict arises.

Instruments

This category covers both negotiable instruments and securities and any other writing that evidences a right to the payment of money and is not itself a security agreement or lease, and is of a type which, in the ordinary course of business, is transferred by delivery with any necessary endorsement or assignment. The term *negotiable instrument* includes drafts, checks, certificates of deposit, promissory notes, and the like. The term *security* includes stocks, bonds, or other instruments that are commonly traded on securities exchanges or markets. To perfect against an instrument, the secured party must generally take possession.

Documents

A document of title is a bill of lading, dock warrant, dock receipt, warehouse receipt, or order for the delivery of goods. This category also includes any other document which, in a normal course of business or financing, is treated as adequate evidence that the person in possession is entitled to receive, hold, and dispose of the document and the goods it covers. To be a document of title, a document must purport to be issued by, or addressed to, a bailee and purport to cover goods in the bailee's possession, which are either identified or are fungible portions of an identified mass. A distinction must be made between documents of title, which are covered by this category, and the certficates of title to motor vehicles with which all bankers are familiar. A certificate of title to a motor vehicle is merely evidence of ownership and does not involve a bailee, and therefore, does not fall into this category.

154

Chattel paper

Chattel paper is a writing (or writings) that evidences both a monetary obligation and a security agreement in, or a lease of specific goods. The agreements generally referred to as dealer paper fall into this category.

Accounts

These are rights that differ from other categories of collateral in that they are neither tangible nor physically represented by a document or instrument. The Code defines an account as any right to payment for goods sold or leased, or for services rendered, which is not evidenced by an instrument or chattel paper. This is what bankers commonly refer to as a "receivable." Note that the proper Code term for what is often called a receivable is an *account*. Therefore, in completing a security agreement or financing statement, the terms *accounts* or *accounts receivable* should be used, rather than referring to this type of asset as a receivable. A contract right, being any right to payment under a contract not yet earned by performance and not evidenced by an instrument or chattel paper, has been eliminated as a separate category in the 1972 version of the Code and is now included in the definition of accounts.

General intangibles

Without a doubt, this is the category of collateral that creates the greatest confusion in a banker's mind. The Code (Section 9-106) defines general intangibles as "any personal property (including things in action) other than goods, accounts, chattel paper, documents, instruments, and money." This catchall category covers any item of collateral that does not readily fit into any of the other categories. Royalties, liquor licenses, trademarks, patents, copyrights, blueprints, tax refunds, or the proceeds from a pending lawsuit are all examples of assets that might be classified as general intangibles. Obviously, some intangibles, such as a seat on a stock exchange, may have considerable cash value. If a business is to be sold as a going concern in a liquidation, it is usually necessary for the secured party to have control of such intangibles as licenses and trademarks.

Agricultural lenders should note that the courts have generally held government entitlements or payments from any government farm program to be either contract rights or general intangibles. Since government entitlements may constitute a substantial portion of a grain farmer's total income, lenders must understand the proper procedures for perfecting against government entitlement payments. Contrary to some bankers' perceptions, entitlement payments are *not* proceeds of a crop. Therefore, a reference to "crops, farm products, and the proceeds thereof" in the security agreement and financing statement does not cover government entitlement payments. Rather, if the secured party intends to cover government entitlement payments, a broader description, such as "all accounts, and general intangibles now owned or hereafter acquired and all entitlements and payments from state or federal farm programs," should be included in both the security agreement and financing statement. In addition, since accounts and general intangibles are not closely related to the assets normally owned and used by a farming operation, a central filing in the Office of the Secretary of State generally should be made to perfect against this type of collateral, even in states where the Code requires a local filing to perfect against assets closely related to a farming operation.

156

Perfection: Protection against Third Parties

Although the lender may have enforceable rights in collateral because attachment has occurred, those rights will be ineffective against competing third-party creditors unless the lender's security interest has been perfected. The probable existence of third-party creditors—such as the trustee in bankruptcy, the Internal Revenue Service, and judgment creditors—makes perfection absolutely essential if the lender is to establish priority and avoid losing the collateral to a competing claimant.

The Uniform Commercial Code states that a security interest is perfected when it is attached and when all applicable steps required for perfection have been taken. Just as the terms of the security agreement determine the relationship between the debtor and the secured party, so perfection establishes the legal relationship between the secured party and any third-party creditor who may have a claim against the same collateral. Although many lenders believe that there are two ways to perfect a security interest, there are actually four: attachment alone; taking possession of the collateral; filing a financing statement; or by complying with a statuary scheme established by state law outside the Code. A security interest in a titled vehicle, which must be established under the Code, but which is perfected by registering a lien on the vehicle title in compliance with a state motor vehicle act, is the best example of this filing alternative. Which of these four methods should be used to perfect depends on the category of collateral involved.

Perfection by attachment alone

Perfection may occur upon attachment when certain categories of collateral are involved. The secured party need not take possession or make a public filing to protect its interest. This creates a "secret lien," and third parties may have no way

157

of determining that the security interest exists. The following are examples of transactions where perfection occurs by attachment alone:

1. *A purchase money security interest in consumer goods* (except for fixtures and titled vehicles) is probably the most notable example, since the Code exempts this kind of transaction from the filing requirement. The drafters of the Code apparently established this exemption to avoid cluttering the public records with filings covering numerous small transactions.

   For example, if Mr. Jones purchases a $1200 barbell set from Sears, Roebuck & Company on credit, he will be asked to sign various documents, including an installment note and a security agreement—but not a financing statement. Since this transaction is exempt from filing requirements, Sears will have a perfected security interest in the barbell set even though nothing has been filed in the public records. If Jones subsequently approaches another lender and requests a loan secured by the barbell set, a UCC search by the prospective lender will obviously not reveal Sears' perfected security interest. Hence, the "secret lien."

2. *In some states* an assignment of the debtor's beneficial interest in a trust or a [decedent's] estate is exempted from the filing rule. This is especially significant in states like Illinois and Florida, where there is widespread use of land trusts.

3. *A filing is not required* to perfect a security interest in instruments or documents of title for 21 days from the time of attachment, to the extent that it arises for new value given under a written security agreement. This exemption covers those situations where the debtor must have temporary possession of the collateral to arrange proper transfer and delivery. In addition, a

security interest remains perfected for 21 days in an instrument or document of title when the secured party turns the collateral over to the debtor for the purpose of shipment, sale, or exchange.

Perfection by possession

The second method for perfecting a security interest is to take possession of the collateral. According to Article 9 of the Code, a security interest in letters and advices of credit, goods, instruments, money, negotiable documents, or chattel paper may be perfected by the secured party taking possession of the collateral. In the case of some collateral, such as money, securities, or instruments other than those constituting part of chattel paper, possession is the only acceptable means of perfecting. Some categories of collateral, such as goods and chattel paper, can be perfected either by taking possession or by filing.

A security interest in accounts receivable and general intangibles cannot be perfected by possession; in these cases, a filing must be made to perfect. It is not absolutely necessary for the secured party to have possession. If collateral other than goods covered by a negotiable document is held by a bailee—such as a warehouseman or escrow agent—the secured party is deemed to have possession from the time the bailee or escrow agent receives proper notification of the secured party's interest. The basic concept involved here is that the debtor must lose control of the collateral in order for the secured party to perfect by possession.

The case of the gold coins as collateral

Note that a secured party may perfect against goods either by taking possession or filing. Obviously, a bank will not be inclined to take possession of an earthmover or drill press, and will perfect against such goods by filing. However, in the case of some other types of goods, the best alternative for perfecting may be less clear cut. Consider the experience of two banks, both of which attempted to perfect a security interest in a gold coin collection. In June 1986, Bank A was approached by Mr. Smith, a depositor, with a request for a $25,000 loan. When the bank requested security for the loan, Smith offered his gold coin collection. An appraisal done at the bank's request indicated the collection was worth approximately $35,000. The bank took possession of the collection, issued Mr. Smith its collateral receipt, and stored the collection in its collateral vault.

Subsequently, without Bank A's knowledge, Smith approached Bank B, where he also had a deposit account. Smith requested another $25,000 loan, and Bank B, like Bank A, requested that the loan be secured. Smith then offered to pledge to Bank B his gold coin collection. When Bank B asked to see the collection, Smith explained that this would be quite troublesome, since the coins were stored in a safe deposit box in another bank 200 miles away. He produced a recent appraisal that showed an itemized listing of the coins, which indicated that the collection was worth approximately $35,000. He asked the bank's indulgence in not requiring him to drive 200 miles round-trip to produce the collection. Bank B called the appraiser and received his assurances that he had recently examined the collection and was confident of its value. The bank then proceeded to make the loan. It had Smith sign a note, security agreement, and financing statement, and then filed the financing statement in the proper filing office.

When Smith's loans at both banks became seriously delinquent, Smith finally confessed to Bank B that the coin collection was actually in Bank A's possession. The banks then became embroiled in a heated argument over which had priority to the coin collection. Bank A stoutly maintained that it had become perfected first by taking possession and therefore had first priority to the collateral. Bank B, just as staunchly, maintained that since it had filed first—and since in fact Bank A had not filed at all—that *it* had first priority. After months of legal controversy, Bank A prevailed and received payment in full from the proceeds of the coin collection, which was sold at public auction for approximately $31,000. The surplus proceeds of the foreclosure sale were delivered to Bank B. It therefore had a partial recovery, but still incurred a loss of almost $20,000, since Smith had become insolvent. In this case, both banks were perfected, but Bank A prevailed because it became perfected *first.*

Perfection by filing

The third method of perfecting the secured party's interest in collateral is by filing a financing statement—the method most familiar to commercial lenders. The filing may be made either centrally or locally. Central filings are generally made in a state office, usually that of the Secretary of State. Local filings are usually made in the office of the County Registrar, Recorder of Deeds, or County Clerk. Where the secured party is required to file depends on the type of collateral, on the version of UCC 9-401 the state involved has adopted, and on specific rules adopted by that state. Variations in filing requirements abound, so lenders must be completely familiar with the filing requirements of the state in which the filing will be made.

The drafters of the Code offered states three alternative versions of Section 9-401. The first alternative requires central filing in all cases except those involving property closely related to real estate, such as fixtures, timber, or minerals. When property closely related to real estate is involved, a filing is required in the local office where a mortgage would be recorded. Approximately ten states have adopted this alternative.

161

The second alternative requires central filing for all categories of property with four notable exceptions:

(a) equipment used in farming operations, farm products, or accounts or general intangibles arising from or relating to the sale of farm products by a farmer;

(b) consumer goods;

(c) timber to be cut, or minerals or the like (including oil and gas); or

(d) fixtures.

This alternative has been adopted by approximately half the states.

The third alternative is similar to the second, except that a dual filing is sometimes required. Generally, an additional local filing is required if the debtor has a place of business in only one county. An additional local filing may also be required if the debtor has no place of business in the state but resides in that state. The remaining states have adopted this alternative except for Louisiana (which is still in the process of adopting Article 9 of the Code), Nebraska, and the District of Columbia (which have, to some extent, unique filing requirements).

When and where to file

When should a financing statement be filed? Generally, from the lender's viewpoint, the sooner the better. Many lenders are surprised to learn that a financing statement may be filed before a loan is made or even committed. A financing statement may also be filed before a security agreement is signed or security interest otherwise attaches. Under the "first to file or perfect, first in priority" rule, it is obviously to the lender's advantage to file as early as possible, even though a loan has not actually been made.

162

A lender should be aware that filing in one, two, or even three places may not suffice in perfecting the security interest. The general rule is that the filing must be made in the jurisdiction in which the collateral is kept; if it is different, then also in the jurisdiction where the debtor resides. In the case of a business, the filing must be made in the jurisdiction in which the chief executive offices of the business are located. So, if a business has facilities in Michigan, Indiana, and Illinois, but its home office is in Michigan, then a central filing should be made in Michigan. If collateral is kept in all three states, the lender should file in all three.

Think of an additional filing as cheap insurance. If there is any doubt that another filing is necessary in an additional jurisdiction, always make the filing. If a local filing is necessary, a filing should be made in the county of the debtor's residence or in the county where the business's principal offices are located. In addition, if collateral is kept in another county, a filing generally should also be made there. The Code specifically requires that a filing be made in any county in which crops, timber, minerals, or fixtures used as collateral are located.

Follow up

A lender should also be aware that even though it initially properly perfected its interest, it may subsequently become unperfected under certain circumstances. The Code provides that where a debtor changes his name, or an organization changes its name, identity, or corporate structure so that a filed financing statement becomes seriously misleading, the filing is not effective to perfect a security interest in collateral acquired by the debtor more than four months after the change, unless a new appropriate financing statement is filed before that time expires. This is especially significant in the case of collateral such as inventory and receivables, which turn over rapidly, since perfection would last four months after the name change unless an amended filing was made.

The Code also provides that a security interest perfected in one state continues to be perfected four months after the debtor removes the collateral to another state in which the security interest has not been perfected. At the end of the four-month period, the security interest becomes unperfected unless the secured party files in the state to which the collateral has been moved. This rule is applicable even though the collateral has been moved without the knowledge of the secured party and in violation of the provisions of the security agreement. Therefore, even after the secured party has made its initial filings, it must remain alert to any changes in the debtor's situation.

In summary, perfection is crucially important to protect the secured party's position against third-party creditors. When a loan becomes a problem loan, there will invariably be third-party claimants who will challenge the lender's position. The secured lender will prevail only if it has handled the perfection process in a proper manner.

Maintaining Perfection in an Imperfect World

Every lender knows that the provisions of Article 9 of the Uniform Commercial Code require that a security interest be perfected. Perfection is the process by which the secured party protects the collateral against the claims of competing third parties. In most cases the lender files a financing statement in the proper filing office and then heaves a sigh of relief, knowing that the exalted state of perfection has been achieved and will endure for the five-year period prescribed by Article 9. Every secured lender also knows that to prevent the lapse of perfection at the end of the five years, a continuation statement must be filed where the original financing statement was filed. This must be done during a six-

"window," meaning anytime within the six months before the expiration date of the original filing.

Some secured lenders, however, fail to recognize that, in this ever-changing world, events may significantly alter, or even destroy, the secured lender's perfected status. The lender must continually monitor both the status of the loan and the collateral to ascertain that certain events have not occurred that may be detrimental to its perfected status. Such events may include the debtor moving its principal business offices or the collateral to another jurisdiction, changing the use of the collateral, or changing its name. Each of these events may have a detrimental effect on the secured party's perfected status. This article will examine the significance of each of these events and recommend procedures that will enable the secured party to maintain its perfection.

When the debtor changes location

To perfect a security interest in the assets of a commercial business, Article 9 generally requires that the lender make a central filing in the state in which the debtor's principal business offices are located. For example, if Custom Container Corporation has its principal business offices in Moline, Illinois when it obtains a secured loan from a bank, the bank is required to file centrally in Illinois. Suppose that several months after obtaining the loan, the debtor decides to move its business offices across the Mississippi River to Davenport, Iowa. What is the effect on the bank's perfected status?

The answer lies in Code Section 9-103(3)(e), which states that "a security interest perfected under the law of jurisdiction of the location of the debtor is perfected until the expiration of four months after a change of the debtor's location to another jurisdiction, or until perfection would have ceased by the law of the first jurisdiction, whichever period first expires. Unless perfected in the new jurisdiction before the end of that period it becomes unperfected thereafter and is deemed to have been unperfected as against a person who became a purchaser after the change."

In this situation one of the Code's familiar "four-month" rules comes into play. Under this rule, the bank which filed in Illinois remains perfected for four months after Customer Container Corporation moves its principal offices to Iowa. Unless it refiles in Iowa during that four-month period, it will become unperfected at the end of the fourth month, and therefore will be subordinate to any other creditor who has perfected in Iowa. It is crucial for the bank to not only understand how the four-month rule works in this case, but also to monitor the debtor's activities closely enough to know when its principal offices have been moved to Iowa.

In those states requiring a local filing, the four-month rule also applies when a business moves its principal offices to another county, or a farmer moves his residence to another county. To avoid becoming unperfected, the secured party has four months to refile in the county in which the business or farmer is now located.

What if the debtor merely moves to a different address in the same state or county? Generally, a change in the mailing address or place of residence, or debtor's place of business within the same state or county subsequent to the filing has no effect on the original filing. It is usually prudent, however, for the secured party to file an amendment to the original financing statement noting the new address. Code requirements vary from state to state in this regard, so the lender must be familiar with the Code's specific requirements in the state or states in which filings must be made.

Removal of collateral to another jurisdiction

To perfect against collateral, Article 9 requires the lender to file not only in the state in which the debtor's principal business offices are located, but also in any state where *collateral* is located. If ABC Corporation has its principal offices in Chicago, Illinois, but also has facilities in Indianapolis, Indiana, and Madison, Wisconsin, where collateral is located, then Code filings will be required in all three states. Suppose that ABC receives a contract for a sizable job in Jefferson City, Missouri. To complete that job, some of the company's equipment will be moved to that city for 30 days and then returned to its former location. Is an additional filing in Missouri required? The answer is no. As long as the removal of collateral to another jurisdiction is strictly temporary, no additional filing is required.

Suppose, however, that ABC decides to open a permanent facility in Jefferson City—meaning that collateral that was moved to that location will remain there permanently. To remain perfected, the secured party is now required to file in Missouri, and must do so within four months of the date on which the collateral was moved to that state. Failure to do so means the secured party becomes unperfected as to the collateral that was moved.

The Code's four-month rule can become a trap for the unwary lender who makes a new loan to a business that has recently relocated from another state. For example, a Jefferson City bank receives a new loan application from ABC Corporation. If the bank believes that ABC has always been solely located in Missouri, it will perform a Code search in Missouri only, and finding no previous filings, will make a new loan based on its assumption that it has a first security interest in the company's assets. If ABC has been in Missouri for less than four months, and if a previously secured party was properly filed in another state, that creditor will have a prior perfected security interest, which can be discovered only by doing a UCC search in the other state. Therefore, whenever a bank receives a loan request from a new applicant that has recently moved to its community, it behooves the bank to seek information about the business's previous location. If the business has recently moved from another jurisdiction, the bank must then do a UCC search in that jurisdiction.

Note that the four-month rule is applicable even though the collateral has been moved without the knowledge of the secured party and in violation of the security agreement. Obviously, it is to the secured party's advantage to know the location of its collateral at all times, and not to rely solely on the debtor's representations. There is no substitute for on-site inspections of collateral conducted at regular intervals, even if they are conducted without the debtor's knowledge.

Change in use of collateral

The majority of states have a filing system that requires a central filing for all categories of collateral, except for collateral utilized in a farming operation, consumer goods, or collateral closely related to real estate (in which case a local filing is required). If the collateral is business equipment, a central filing is usually required; if it is consumer goods, a local filing is necessary. For example, if a borrower purchases a personal computer for home or personal use, it is considered to be "consumer goods," which requires a local filing. If the debtor, however, removes the computer to his or her business office and begins to use it as business equipment, it is then classified as "equipment," which requires a central filing. As a result of this change in usage (of which the lender is probably unaware), the lender may have become unperfected because the required central filing has not been made. To avoid this problem, many banks make it a practice to double-file both centrally and locally. (Please note that in some states, double-filing is mandatory.) Also, some states have specific Code provisions stating that the secured party will remain perfected despite a change in the use of the collateral.

Debtor name changes

Let us assume that ABC Corporation changes its name subsequent to a filing under its original name by a secured party. What was formerly ABC Corporation is now XYZ Corporation. This is not unusual, since it is relatively easy for a corporation to change its name. Another instance in which the name change often occurs is when a partnership becomes incorporated. The Code (Section 9-402[7]) requires a tracking of the debtor's name. When a name change renders the originally filed financing statement "seriously misleading," the original filing will be insufficient for perfecting a security interest in collateral acquired by the debtor more than four months after the name change. To cover such after-acquired collateral, a new filing will have to be made under the new name prior to the expiration of that period. To enable the secured party to stay perfected with the least difficulty, this new filing generally does not require the debtor's signature.

Note that for collateral that does not turn over, such as equipment, a name change does not affect the original filing. In the case of collateral such as inventory and accounts receivable, however, which do turn over relatively rapidly, perfection will last only four months after the name change unless an amended filing is made.

In summary, maintaining its perfected position requires the secured party's constant vigilance. If one of the above events does occur, the secured party should take immediate steps to comply with the Code requirements for maintaining its perfection. Failure to do so may lead to disastrous consequences for the lender.

Future Advances: Are You Really Secure?

For lenders, one of the great advantages of Article 9 of the Uniform Commercial Code is the efficiency and flexibility it

169

allows in securing future advances. If the security agreement contains a future advances clause—often called a "dragnet" clause—the security interest that is created may collateralize not only the current loan, but also future loans to the debtor. Section 9-204(3) of the Code provides that "obligations covered by a security agreement may include future advances or other value whether or not the advances or value are given pursuant to a commitment." Interestingly, the security interest covering these future advances, whether optional or mandatory, may have the same priority as that of the original loan since priority is generally established on the date the initial financing statement (UCC-1) is filed, rather than when future loans are disbursed. Section 9-312(7) of the Code provides, in part, that "If future advances are made while a security interest is perfected by filing or the taking of possession, the security interest has the same priority . . . with respect to the future advances as it does with respect to the first advance."

Establishing priority: An example

Suppose, for example, that on September 1, 1988, Sutherland Manufacturing Company obtains a $100,000 working capital loan from First National Bank. The loan is collateralized by a security interest in the company's equipment, which is appraised at $150,000. The security agreement executed by Sutherland provides that the security interest covers not only the original loan, but also "any and all other liabilities of the debtor to the bank, direct or indirect, absolute or contingent, due or to become due, now existing or hereafter arising, whether or not contemplated by the parties"—a typical future advances clause.

Later, on October 1, Sutherland approaches Second State Bank and negotiates a $30,000 working capital loan. For this discussion, assume that Sutherland has no significant assets other than its equipment. Therefore, to secure this new loan, it offers Second State Bank a security interest in the same equipment, citing the fact that $50,000 equity still remained after the first lien. Having solicited Sutherland's business on several occasions, Second State Bank decides to make the $30,000 loan secured by a second lien on the equipment. Prior to disbursing the loan, Second State Bank verifies by a telephone call to First National that the outstanding balance owed it by Sutherland is indeed $100,000.

On November 1, 1988, Sutherland returns to First National and obtains an additional $30,000 working capital loan. Although the borrower executes a new promissory note, the bank does not require the execution of either a new security agreement or an additional financing statement, since it was already perfected as to the equipment pursuant to a security agreement with a dragnet clause. Unfortunately, as often happens, Sutherland Manufacturing Company fails, and the only remaining asset is its equipment, which is sold at public auction for $140,000. Obviously, the liquidation proceeds are insufficient, and one of the banks will have a $20,000 loss.

To a lender unfamiliar with the Code, it might appear "fair" for First National to receive the initial $100,000 of proceeds and Second State the next $30,000, with First National then receiving the remaining $10,000—leaving a $20,000 balance to be charged off by First National. That is not how the Code works, however. Since priority is established by the date of filing (as opposed to disbursement), First National has first priority to the collateral for the entire $130,000 owed it. State Bank, having filed its UCC-1 after First National's filing, has a junior interest in the collateral. Consequently, Second State only has a right to the remaining $10,000 and will incur the $20,000 loss.

Obviously, Second State Bank could have done a number of things to avoid this type of loss, which is often foreseeable. First, Second State should have ascertained whether First National had a future advances clause and, if so, whether a subordination agreement would be provided. If not, Second State had the option of paying off First's loan or simply not making the loan at all. Because Second State failed to address the future advances question, it made a loan which eventually had no underlying collateral value to support it, even though a security interest had been properly perfected.

Basic concepts and problem areas

In recent years, there has been an ongoing legal dispute over the exact type of advances that may be covered by a future advances clause in a security agreement. The legal question is whether the future advance must be related or similar in purpose to the original loan. Suppose the original loan was short-term financing to pay operating expenses and the future advance was a four-year term loan for the purchase of new equipment. Does this dissimilarity of purpose invalidate the future advances clause? Unfortunately, some courts say "yes" and adhere to the so-called "relatedness rule," arguing that a future advance must be of the same class as the original loan in order to retain its priority. These decisions focus on whether the parties actually contemplated the future advance, despite generic language to that effect. Although the better view is that the future advance need not be similar to the original loan, lenders should be aware of this potential problem when structuring additional advances. At minimum, the new note (if one is used for the advance) should contain a specific cross-reference to the preexisting security agreement containing the future advances clause. If some reasonable relationship exists between the original loan and the future advance, most courts should uphold the priority position of the original lender.

Another question concerns whether a future advance must be made within a certain time period after the original loan transaction. For instance, is a future advance made three months after the initial loan closing still entitled to the priority of the original perfected security interest, while one made three years later is not? Both may be covered, as long as the original security interest remains perfected. Also, as indicated by Section 9-204(3), it is unnecessary for the advance to be either committed or contemplated at the time the original loan is made. It appears, therefore, that a future advance made two or even five or more years later may still be covered by the original security interest if perfection has been maintained.

What if the original loan was paid in full prior to the future advance? Assume that Acme Hardware Stores obtains a $50,000 working capital loan from Community Bank. The loan is collateralized by a security interest in the business's assets, and the security agreement contains a standard "dragnet" clause. Ninety days later, Acme repays the loan in full and has no outstanding obligation to the bank. Is the security interest automatically extinguished as a result of the full repayment of the loan? The answer is no. In commercial transactions, unless specifically terminated, the bank's security interest remains legally viable even though the debtor has no outstanding obligations. Therefore, when Acme returns to the bank six months later to obtain a new working capital loan, it could be automatically collateralized as a future advance under the previously perfected security interest.

Traditionally, a revolving loan inherently involves future advances. Here, it is the clear intention of both the debtor and lender that periodic additional disbursements be made. Often, these disbursements are mandatory advances pursuant to the terms of a loan agreement, as opposed to optional advances at the discretion of the lender. Such loans are usually secured by a "floating lien" on both accounts receivable and inventory. It is the combination of both the after-acquired property clause and the future advances clause in the lender's loan documentation that makes this type of loan workable for the secured party. Obviously, any future advances will be directly related to the primary loan and are clearly contemplated by the parties. Despite these facts, a problem may still arise if the lender erroneously assumes that the future advances priority can be extended to cover either an advance inadvertently designated as being unsecured, or an overdraft by the debtor.

Intervening lien creditors

Often an intervening lien creditor will appear on the scene after the original loan transaction, but prior to a future advance. Sometimes, the creditor is the holder of a junior security interest in the same collateral. More often, the intervening lienor is a judgment creditor or the Internal Revenue Service with a lien for unpaid federal taxes. The legal issue here is whether the lien of an intervening creditor cuts off the ongoing priority of the lender who continues to make future advances. In other words, is the postlien advance of the lender subordinate or superior to the intervening lien?

Regarding the junior security interest, Section 9-312(7) of the Code allows the original lender to retain priority for future advances as long as perfection was achieved by filing or possession. This rule applies whether the future advance is optional or mandatory and regardless of the lender's awareness of the existence of any competing liens. This was the legal rule enforced to the detriment of Second State Bank in the earlier example of Sutherland Manufacturing Company.

As to intervening judicial liens, Section 9-301(4) of the Code provides that "a person who becomes a lien creditor while a security interest is perfected takes subject to the security interest only to the extent that it secures advances made before he becomes a lien creditor or within 45 days thereafter or made without knowledge of the lien or pursuant to a commitment entered into without knowledge of the lien." The net effect of this rule is that the original lender retains priority as to any postlien advances made within 45 days of the lien's inception. Beyond 45 days, the original lender's priority will continue only if the future advance was made without knowledge of the intervening judicial lien or was made pursuant to a prior commitment. Clearly, a lender with no knowledge of an intervening judicial lien could fund future advances indefinitely and retain absolute priority as to the new debt being created. Since most judicial liens, however, are filed in public court records, a lender may find it difficult to assert it had no knowledge of the lien.

Regarding a federal tax lien, Section 6323 of the Internal Revenue Code provides some limited protection for lenders making future advances. Basically, the IRC subordinates the intervening tax lien to advances made within 45 days following the filing of the tax lien if the lender was unaware of the lien's existence. In contrast to judicial liens, however, any advances made after 45 days *will* be subordinate to the tax lien, regardless of knowledge by the lender. Similarly, Section 6323(c) of the IRC places additional limitations on the extent to which collateral acquired after the tax lien filing can be used to secure either preexisting loans or advances made within the 45 day period. As a result of these rules, the existence of a federal tax lien significantly diminishes the priority rights of a lender making future advances.

Summary

The ability to cover future advances with a preexisting security interest is a powerful tool for the commercial lender. Any lender contemplating a future advance, however, needs to be aware that the process is not foolproof and that various problems can arise. Most importantly, lenders need to be sensitive to the existence of intervening lien creditors and take appropriate actions, such as periodic record searches, to protect their collateral position.

The Secured Creditor's Right to Proceeds

Under Article 9 of the Uniform Commercial Code, a security interest generally continues in collateral notwithstanding sale, exchange, or other disposition by the debtor unless the disposition was authorized by the secured party in the security agreement or otherwise. The security interest also continues in any identifiable proceeds from the sale or disposition. While bankers generally perceive "proceeds" to be cash received from the sale of the collateral, the term has a broader definition under the Code. If the sale is made on credit, the proceeds may be an account receivable or a promissory note. If a "trade-in" is involved, the proceeds may then be goods received in trade. If the collateral is destroyed by fire, payment received from the insurance company may be proceeds.

In most states, proceeds are automatically covered by the security interest without any specific reference to proceeds in the lender's security documentation. However, many conservative lenders continue to include a reference to proceeds in the collateral description in both the security agreement and the financing statement. Part of such a reference might read, "all machine shop equipment now owned or hereafter acquired, and all proceeds from the sale or disposition thereof."

Conversion

The legal term "conversion" refers to the unauthorized disposition of the collateral by the debtor, a criminal and civil offense in most states. In situations involving conversion, the lender may proceed against both the debtor and the third-party purchaser to recover the collateral, the proceeds from the disposition or conversion, or both. Note that the debtor and the third-party purchaser may be liable to the lender for punitive damages and attorney's fees that arise from the conversion of the collateral. In addition, the debtor who converts collateral may be unable to obtain a bankruptcy discharge for

176

that particular debt—at least to the extent of the value of the converted collateral.

Consider the following example: Suppose that contractor Jones owns a Caterpillar tractor in which First National Bank has a perfected security interest to secure a $50,000 working capital loan. Without authorization from the bank, Jones sells the Caterpillar tractor to another contractor, Commercial Builders. As proceeds of the sale he receives $30,000 cash and a used International tractor with a value of approximately $10,000. Jones in turn sells the International tractor to James Moore, a local farmer, for $7,000. Jones deposits the cash into his account at Second National Bank and subsequently uses $15,000 of these funds to purchase a used Chevrolet two-ton truck. In this case, Jones, Commercial Builders, and Moore are all guilty of conversion.

Upon learning of Jones' unauthorized disposition of the Caterpillar tractor, First National Bank may institute legal action to recover the remaining identifiable proceeds of approximately $22,000 from Jones's account at Second National Bank. It may also institute legal action to recover the International tractor from James Moore—even though Moore had no knowledge of the underlying facts. First National may repossess the truck from Jones, and may also proceed to sue Jones, Commercial Builders and Moore for punitive damages and attorney's fees. Whether this is unfair to Commercial Builders, and James Moore depends upon the perspective from which the overall transaction is viewed. However, that is how the Code operates as to proceeds, proof indeed of the old adage, "Buyer beware."

Sales in the ordinary course of business

An exception to the usual conversion situation involves a buyer in the "ordinary course of business." Such a buyer is defined by the Code as a person who, in good faith and

177

without knowledge that the sale to him or her is a violation of the ownership rights or security interest of a third party in the goods, buys in ordinary course from a person in the business of selling goods of that kind—that is, a dealer. The Code specifically provides for the protection of buyers in the ordinary course of business in order to facilitate normal sales transactions. As a result, an individual who buys a new television set from an appliance dealer, or a contractor who buys an item of new construction equipment from a dealer, may take possession of those goods without fear that the lender who financed the dealer's inventory may ultimately repossess the goods.

The Code (Section 9-307[1]) further states that a buyer in the ordinary course of business (other than a person buying farm products from a person engaged in farming operations) takes possession free of a security interest created by his or her seller even though the security interest is perfected and even though the buyer knows of its existence. Therefore, when a dealer sells inventory in the normal course of business, any security interest held by an inventory lender is cut off at the point of sale, and the lender has no recourse against the purchaser.

It is essential, however, to realize that the only security interest that is cut off by a sale in the ordinary course of business is one created by the seller. Therefore, if a dealer has granted a security interest to an inventory financier, that security interest is clearly cut off. However, if the dealer is selling an item of equipment which is subject to a security interest created by a former owner, that security interest will remain intact despite a sale in the ordinary course of business. Obviously, this situation usually arises where a debtor sells or trades an item of used equipment to a dealer in violation of the lender's security agreement and the dealer subsequently re-sells that item to an innocent third party. Since this sale does not cut off the original security interest, the lender may repossess the equipment and initiate legal action for conversion against both the dealer and the third-party purchaser.

Therefore, if ABC Hardware purchases a new Mita copier from its local Mita dealer, it can be assured that it is receiving clear title to the copier, even though State Bank financed the dealer's inventory of copiers. In this case State Bank's security interest is cut off at the point of sale, and its security interest transfers to the proceeds of the sale. However, if ABC Hardware buys from the dealer a used copier that was previously owned by Jones Trucking and in which Jones had granted its bank, Second National Bank, a security interest, then ABC Hardware takes title to the used copier subject to Second National's security interest, even though neither it nor the dealer may have any knowledge of such a security interest.

Sales of farm products

Historically, the sale of farm products by a producer has not been considered a sale in the ordinary course of business, and therefore, the purchaser took title to the farm products subject to any existing security interest. Needless to say, this exception caused considerable discontent among buyers, especially those in the grain and livestock trade. Responding to pressure from these industry groups, many agricultural states have amended Code Section 9-307 in recent years to provide some relief to the purchaser confronted with the risk inherent in the farm production exception. All this state legislation was superseded by the provisions of the Food Security Act of 1985, which became effective December 24, 1986. The section of that act entitled "Protection of Purchasers of Farm Products" preempted certain provisions of the Code as they previously existed in the various states. Although it does not eliminate the farm products exception as set forth in Code Section 9-307(1), it severely restricts its operation and requires compliance with new procedures described in the statute.

Essentially, each state is required to set up a central filing system for recording security interests in farm products and a registration of buyers engaged in the business of purchasing farm products. As an alternative, the states were given the option of adopting a "prenotification procedure" which is prescribed in the statute. To date, some of the agricultural states have adopted the central filing system, but most have elected to use the prenotification process. The prenotification procedure requires an annual notice of any security interest to prospective purchasers of farm products owned by the debtor. Failure to comply with the provisions of the new law prevents the lender from instituting legal action for conversion of collateral against the purchaser of farm products.

In summary, the Code provisions that transfer the security interest from the collateral to its proceeds provide se-cured lenders with a useful tool in ensuring that the proceeds of collateral are actually delivered to the secured party. Every bank lender should understand the operation of these important Code rules.

Financing Inventory and Receivables

Commercial lenders have traditionally been concerned about loans secured by inventory and receivables due to the revolving nature of the collateral. Unlike collateral such as real estate or equipment, which generally remains unchanged over a period of time, inventory and receivables are constantly turning over. The borrower may be continually purchasing and/or manufacturing new inventory while selling inventory. Therefore, goods which made up the borrower's inventory in May will have been replaced by an entirely new but similar set of goods in August.

Proceeds of the sale of inventory will take the form of accounts receivable in most businesses. Like inventory, accounts receivable will be turning over constantly, with accounts being collected while new accounts are being generated. A loan secured by inventory and receivables usually takes the form of an ongoing line of credit characterized by periodic payments as proceeds of the collateral are applied to the loan, and periodic additional advances of funds for the acquisition of new inventory. This situation creates three distinct problems for the lender financing inventory and receivables: maintaining a continuing lien, controlling the collateral and its proceeds, and monitoring collateral margin.

Maintaining the liens

Article 9 of the Uniform Commercial Code contains three basic concepts that enable the lender to establish a "floating lien," which automatically attaches to new inventory and new receivables as they are acquired. The Code also enables the second party to automatically secure future advances made subsequent to the date of the original secured transaction. UCC 9-204 broadly validates security agreements that cover property presently owned by the debtor, as well as property of the same type or category to be acquired in the future. This clearly establishes the principle of a continuing general lien, which automatically attaches to after-acquired inventory and receivables. There is no requirement for the execution of new security agreements from time to time or for the lender to obtain confirmatory schedules.

The second Code concept that makes the floating lien possible relates to future advances. UCC 9-204(3) states that obligations covered by a security agreement may include future advances or other value, whether or not the advances or value are given pursuant to a commitment. Therefore, the security interest created at the time of the initial loan transaction may

181

cover not only that transaction, but any number of future loan transactions, even though no future loans are committed or contemplated at the time of the original trans-action. Because coverage of future advances only occurs if the secured party's documentation so provides, the security agreement must contain a "future advances clause."

The third Code concept related to floating liens concerns proceeds. The security interest, upon the sale or other disposition of the collateral, automatically extends to the proceeds received, without the necessity of mentioning proceeds either in the security agreement or the financing statement.

Controlling collateral

Article 9 of the Code also establishes a procedure under which a lender or supplier may establish a purchase money security interest in inventory that takes priority over the holder of a previously perfected competing security interest in after-acquired inventory. The financer of inventory must comply with the following rules to establish its purchase money status. First, it must file a financing statement in the proper filing office *before* the debtor receives delivery of the inventory. Second, the supplier or lender must also give notification *in writing* to the holder of a previously perfected competing security interest in after-acquired inventory. The holder of the competing security interest must have received written notification within five years before the debtor receives possession of the inventory. Finally, the notification must state that the holder of the purchase money security interest in the inventory has, or expects to acquire, a purchase money security interest in the inventory of the debtor, describing it by item or type. Since the notification to competing secured parties is effective for five years, the lender should establish a tickler file to insure the proper notification is given at least every five years.

182

The suppliers of inventory on consignment must comply with rules similar to those for the supplier or financer of inventory. In fact, the consignment seller is treated by the Code in exactly the same manner as the inventory financer. The consigner must file a financing statement before delivering the goods and give written notification to any competing inventory financer who has previous filings on record. As in the case of purchased inventory, the holder of the security interest must receive the notification within five years before the consignee receives possession of the goods.

There is always a potential conflict between the inventory financer and the financer of accounts receivable, because accounts are generally the proceeds of inventory. The receivables financer, relying on his perfected security interest in the receivables, will stoutly maintain that he has first priority. Meanwhile, the financer of inventory will maintain that his perfected security interest in inventory transferred to the proceeds of inventory, which may in fact be the same receivables claimed by the receivables financer. Banks should avoid a situation in which such a potential conflict exists. One possible remedy, if obtainable, is to sign a triparty agreement between the borrower and the receivables and inventory financers that clearly defines the priority of the interests of the two lenders.

Due to the revolving nature of inventory and receivables, collateral valuations are also constantly changing. Therefore, the inventory and receivables lender must set up a system for monitoring the value of those assets. At the very least, this will involve obtaining quarterly or monthly financial statements from the borrower. In many instances, the lender may require the submission of weekly or monthly aged lists of all accounts receivable as well as schedules showing the quantity of inventory by category.

Even though inventory amounts are known, it may still be difficult to realistically evaluate inventory. Raw materials,

183

especially bulk commodities, are usually relatively easy to value and liquidate. Finished goods, especially staple products with established markets, may also be fairly easy to value. Work in process, however, may be very difficult to evaluate and market in a liquidation. Many commercial lenders consider a loan secured by work in process to be an unse- cured loan. In evaluating work in process, a cautious lender may assign it a liquidation factor of zero percent.

Evaluating the quality of accounts receivable also often presents problems. In assessing the probable quality of a company's receivables, the lender should ask the following questions:

1. What is the company's credit policy?

2. How good is the company's credit department?

3. How effective are the company's collection efforts?

4. What is the company's policy for charging off bad accounts?

5. What is the company's bad debt experience?

6. How concentrated are the company's receivables?

Concentration in a few very good customers is not a credit problem, but is a business risk. On the other hand, a large number of small accounts receivable can be a real problem if the bank has to collect them. Accounts receivable are also often subject to dispute, especially if the receivable is generated from services performed instead of goods sold. A lender should also raise the question as to how agings are calculated. The age of an account should always be determined from billing date, not from due date.

Monitoring collateral margin

Many commercial lenders use a borrowing base certificate to monitor collateral margin. First the amount of eligible inventory and receivables is calculated, and then a percentage

184

factor is applied. (The percentage is determined by what percent of the value of inventory and receivables the lender is willing to loan.) The maximum loan amount for which the borrower is eligible is calculated and is then compared with the amount of the loan outstanding or requested by the borrower. A borrowing base certificate is usually completed monthly, but may be done weekly, depending on the nature of the agreement between the borrower and the lender.

A system often used by lenders to control the cash generated by the collection of receivables involves a lock box. This is generally a post office box rented by the borrower that is under the lender's control. Statements mailed to the account debtors include an envelope addressed to the post office box. As payments are mailed to the lock box, the bank picks them up and deposits them in a remittance account. Depending on the agreement with the debtor, the proceeds from the remittance account may either be applied against the loan or deposited to the borrower's account on a daily, weekly, or monthly basis.

In summary, loans secured by inventory and receivables can be an excellent source of income for a bank and can provide a valuable service needed by many of its customers. However, if a bank is to be a successful lender in this field, it must understand the rules of the game and establish proper controls and safeguards.

Titled Vehicles as Collateral: A Closer Look

Although lenders are routinely involved in numerous transactions involving titled vehicles, a multitude of misconceptions exist concerning the appropriate procedures for dealing with this kind of collateral. At first glance, a casual observer might ask what could possibly be so difficult or complicated in dealing with motor vehicles and the certificates of title issued for them. However, there are a number of reasons this area of lending continues to be difficult for both lenders and, to some extent, the legal system. Some of these reasons are readily apparent and others are not quite so clear.

Documents of title

Contrary to popular belief, a certificate of title for a motor vehicle is *not* a "document of title" as defined in the Uniform Commercial Code (Section 1-201 [15]). In the Code, the term *document* or *document of title* refers to bills of lading, dock warrants, and warehouse receipts. These types of documents represent goods in the possession of a third-party bailee, usually in transit or storage. In general, a document of title is viewed as representing specific goods and, if it is negotiable, it actually takes the place of the goods described. As a result, documents of title usually have an intrinsic value and can be pledged as collateral for a loan.

On the other hand, a certificate of title for a motor vehicle is merely evidence of ownership. It is not a substitute for the motor vehicle and, standing alone, has no inherent value. The real collateral value exists only in the motor vehicle—not in the title itself. If the certificate is lost, it is quite simple to have a substitute or duplicate issued without regard to whether the motor vehicle has any value or is even in existence. As a result, the lender must recognize that while a "document of title" may be adequate collateral in its own right, a motor vehicle title has no similar value. A "certificate of title" is not necessarily good collateral simply because it is in the lender's possession.

The underlying security interest

A second source of difficulty concerns the creation and perfection of a security interest in the motor vehicle involved. Unfortunately, many lenders focus on the second phase of this process—perfection—and lose sight of the fact that a security

186

interest must always exist before perfection of any lien can occur. Since a motor vehicle is a form of "goods" under the Code (9-105[h]), a security interest must always be established pursuant to its terms. This will usually involve the execution of a note and security agreement by the debtor in exchange for the loan (consideration) being granted by the lender. This procedure creates the required security interest, which is then enforceable by the lender against both the debtor and the motor vehicle. As between the debtor and the lender, the security interest need not be perfected, although perfection is required to protect the collateral from competing creditors, including a trustee in bankruptcy.

In many situations, the lender concentrates exclusively on having its lien registered on the certificate of title, which is then placed in the loan file. Once accomplished, any subsequent examination of the file will always indicate that the lien has been properly inserted on the certificate being retained by the lender. Ironically, this cursory analysis usually omits a more detailed examination to ascertain the existence of an executed security agreement and, therefore, a security interest that is enforceable against both the debtor and third-party claimants. Without an underlying security interest having been created, the lender's lien will not be enforceable, even though it has been appropriately registered on the certificate of title.

Perfecting the lien

An additional area of confusion arises from the fact that the Code, for the most part, does not directly mandate the procedure for perfecting a lien on a motor vehicle. In most cases, the Code is rather explicit in dictating the exact process by which the lender perfects its security interest, usually requiring that it file a financing statement (UCC-1) in a particular location. In cases involving purchase money security interests in consumer goods, the Code dispenses with any possession or filing requirement and simply provides that the lender's lien is automatically perfected.

None of these customary rules for perfection apply to motor vehicles, even if a purchase money consumer transaction is involved. When a motor vehicle is involved, the Code (9-302[3]) indicates that the lender can only perfect by complying with the certificate of title statute or title registration law of the state involved, except when the motor vehicle constitutes inventory. Since most states have now adopted certificate of title laws, which include lien registration provisions, perfection will usually be accomplished by notation of the lien on the certificate of title. However, there is no real degree of uniformity among the states, and some jurisdictions require both a lien registration and the filing of a financing statement. In states requiring both steps to achieve perfection, visual inspection of the certificate of title will not suffice to assure the lender that its lien has been perfected.

The inventory problem

Since motor vehicles are usually movable at the time the security interest attaches, they are generically defined as "goods" under the Code. This general category of collateral is further divided into four distinct classifications: Consumer goods, equipment, farm products, and inventory. The primary use of the collateral by the debtor determines the applicable classification. In turn, the collateral classification controls the exact procedure for perfection.

As suggested above, "inventory" is a specific exception to the standard lien registration procedure. When a motor vehicle is classified as inventory, due to its use by the debtor, perfection can only be accomplished by the appropriate filing of a financing state- ment (not by taking possession). The insertion or registration of the lender's lien on the certificate of title is legally ineffective and will not protect the new or used car inventory from the claims of third parties. Physical possession of title certificates containing a lien may provide some comfort to the lender who is using this technique as an inventory control device. However, no lien is perfected by this process, and the lender risks losing all of the collateral.

The theory in practice

To illustrate the foregoing concepts, consider the following examples:

Suppose that Robert Jones applies to First National Bank for an $8,000 loan and tenders the title to his 1987 Mercury automobile as collateral. The bank has Jones execute a promissory note, which contains a security agreement specifically describing the vehicle involved. Since Jones uses this automobile as a family car, the Code classifies it as a "consumer good," and the bank is required to perfect its security interest by registering a lien on the certificate of title. The bank is not required to file a financing statement, and the fact that the vehicle is a consumer good in the debtor's hands does not change the application of the perfection rules.

Now, suppose that ABC Printing Company applies to First National Bank for financing to purchase a similar 1987 Mercury automobile, intending to use it as a delivery vehicle. Since the vehicle will be used in the operation of the business, the Code classifies it as "equipment." In this case, the bank should have the debtor execute a note and security agreement in which the vehicle is specifically described as "equipment." To perfect its security interest, the bank will cause its lien to be inserted upon the certificate of title to the vehicle. Even though this is a business transaction, no financing statement is filed because the collateral involved is subject to a certificate of title law, and perfection can only be accomplished by compliance with that law— usually a lien registration provision.

189

In our final example, Fred Carter, doing business as Carter's Quality Used Cars, purchases a similar 1987 Mercury automobile for the purpose of placing it upon his lot for resale. Obviously, the vehicle will be classified as "inventory" under the Code, and the bank should have Carter execute a security agreement utilizing that precise term, without describing any particular automobile. In this case, the bank will also file a financing statement covering "inventory" in the appropriate filing office. Although the bank may want to retain the certificate of title as part of its procedure for monitoring collateral, mere possession of the certificate is of no particular significance. Similarly, the registration of the bank's lien on the certificate of title is of no legal effect, so long as the vehicle is being held for resale by the debtor.

In these situations, the existence of a misunderstanding by the lender will not be apparent until it is too late and the collateral is lost to the Internal Revenue Service or a bankruptcy trustee. The preceding discussion is an attempt to eliminate some of the confusion that exists in this area and to help lenders avoid unnecessary loan losses when motor vehicles are involved.

Super-Priority Security Interests: Exceptions to the Rules

When dealing with most categories of collateral, the Uniform Commercial Code (the Code) generally requires the lender to perfect its security interest by filing a financing statement in the appropriate local or central filing office. The filing notifies any third party of the secured party's interest. It also establishes the secured party's priority against any other party claiming a security interest in the same collateral. Because the general priority rule is "first to file or perfect, first in priority," several parties with conflicting claims in the same collateral may literally engage in a race to the filing office.

190

However, Article 9 of the Code establishes several exceptions to the general priority rule, most of which pertain to "purchase money" transactions. In most situations, superpriority status is not achieved automatically but is the result of the lender's strict compliance with a number of special rules that govern the creation of purchase money security interests (PMSI). The rules described in this article vary depend-ing on whether the collateral involved is inventory, fixtures, accessions, or other goods.

1. PURCHASE MONEY SECURITY INTEREST IN COLLATERAL OTHER THAN INVENTORY
   To perfect a PMSI in compliance with the Code
   (Sec. 9-312[4]) the lender must not only provide the purchase funds, but must also file within ten days of the date the debtor receives possession of the goods. Some states have adopted nonconforming amendments to Article 9 that extend this deadline to 15 or 20 days. Note that the time clock begins to run on the date the debtor receives possession, and *not* on the date the purchase order is signed or the loan is made.

   In many instances, the date on which the debtor actually receives possession may be difficult to identify, which has resulted in considerable litigation. The cautious lender should file at the earliest opportunity to avoid any unnecessary problems with timing. The lender should also issue a joint check payable to both the borrower and the supplier of the goods.

2. PURCHASE MONEY SECURITY INTEREST IN INVENTORY
   A lender or supplier must take additional steps to perfect a PMSI in inventory (Sec. 9-312[3]). The financer of inventory does not have the ten-day period in which to perfect, but must perfect by filing prior to the time the debtor receives possession of the goods. The supplier or lender must also give written notifica-

tion to the holder of a previously perfected security interest in after-acquired inventory. This written notification is effective for a five-year period. It must state that the sender has or expects to acquire a PMSI in the inventory of the debtor and describe that inventory by item or type. Suppliers of inventory on consignment are required to comply with similar rules. Unfortunately, lenders often fail to recognize the legal significance of these notification letters when they are received and do not develop a concern about the likely erosion of their collateral position.

3. PURCHASE MONEY SECURITY INTEREST IN FIXTURES
The Code defines fixtures as personal property that becomes permanently affixed to real estate. If a lender fully complies with the special rules for fixtures (Sec. 9-313), he may achieve priority over an existing mortgage or other encumbrance on the real estate to which the fixture becomes attached. The rules are as follows:

(a) The security interest must be a purchase money interest; i.e., the lender must have furnished the funds for the acquisition of the fixtures.

(b) A financing statement covering the goods which are to become fixtures must be filed in the office where a mortgage on real estate would be filed or recorded. This is usually the Recorder or Registrar of Deeds.

(c) The financing statement must include a legal description of the real estate to which the fixture is to become attached. In a number of states, the financing statement must also show the name of the record owner of the real estate, if that is different from the debtor. In most states, the filing officer must also cross-index the fixture, filing under the name of the debtor as if he or she were the mortgager in a real estate mortgage.

(d) The financing statement generally must show clearly upon its face that it is a "fixture filing."

(e) The filing must be made prior to the time that the fixture becomes attached to the real estate.

4. ACCESSIONS

An accession is an item of personal property that becomes permanently attached to other personal property. A security interest in an accession usually takes priority over claimants to the whole if the security interest in the accession attaches before installation. However, there are major exceptions to this rule (Sec. 9-314). A security interest in an accession does not take priority over a subsequent purchaser for value of any interest in the whole. Nor will it take priority over a creditor with a lien on the whole subsequently obtained by judicial proceedings, if accomplished without knowledge of the security interest and prior to its perfection.

Similarly, the same rule will protect a lender with a prior perfected security interest in the whole to the extent that subsequent advances are made. The rules for perfecting a security interest in accessions may vary by state, and lenders need to be familiar with the rules that may apply to each transaction.

5. CROP IN-PUT LIEN

Another section of the Code (Sec. 9-312[2]) creates a unique type of security interest intended to permit heavily indebted farmers to finance production costs for the current year's crop. By complying with the rules, the so-called "seed money" lender may in some instances achieve a super-prority in the new crop to the extent that funds are used for current crop production costs. In other words, the holder of a previously per-fected security interest in crops will have its lien rights subordinated to the rights of the in-put lender. This provision of the Code tends to confuse agricultural lenders and suppliers who fail to realize that this super-priority is quite limited in application. Lenders must comply with the following rules:

(a) The lender must give "new value," that is, disburse new funds as opposed to a renewal.

(b) The funds must be advanced for the specific purpose of producing the new crop and used accordingly.

(c) The funds must be advanced within three months prior to planting—a crucial date if litigation occurs.

(d) The lender prevails only to the extent that the obligation secured by any competing security interest in crops was "past due" more than six months before the new crop is planted.

This final requirement is especially significant and, from a practical standpoint, it appears that few transactions would fit the factual circumstances required by the Code. Although most lenders will probably avoid situations of this nature, a competing creditor or supplier may erroneously assume com-pliance with the Code and assert an unenforceable claim as to the crops being produced. It is essential that all lenders be fa-miliar with this section of the Code and any nonconforming amendments to it.

The concept of the PMSI was devised by the Code's drafters to facilitate sales transactions. It enables the seller or lender to acquire a first priority position in the goods being purchased, even though the Code rules would normally favor the holder of a previously perfected security interest with an after-acquired property clause. So, the smart seller on credit or financer of goods will properly perfect a PMSI if he is relying on the collateral as a source of repayment.

Secret Liens: Lender Beware

Commercial lenders generally rely on a Uniform Commercial Code search to reveal prior Code filings indicative of a third party's perfected security interest. If the search reveals that the collateral is "clean," the lender usually proceeds on the assumption that the security interest which it is about to perfect will have first priority. Many lenders have learned to their dismay that, although a Code search has not revealed any prior perfected interests, these may in fact exist. Rather than having the first priority which it assumed it had, the lender may in fact have a second, or even third, priority to the collateral.

There can be a number of reasons for this problem. Due to the type of collateral involved, the normal Code filing procedures may have been preempted by either federal or state law. In such a case, the lender is required to follow either a federally prescribed procedure, or, if a titled vehicle is involved, a special filing procedure established by a state statute. Perfection may have been by attachment alone. In other cases, a financing statement may indeed have been filed in the proper filing office to perfect the security interest, but for a variety of reasons, this filing may be quite difficult to discover during a routine UCC search.

Non-UCC-recorded liens

Federal legislation requires that all liens covering aircraft be recorded with the Federal Aviation Administration Aircraft Registry Office in Oklahoma City. Therefore, the lender intending to make a loan secured by an aircraft must check the FAA registry to discover any prior liens, instead of doing a UCC search. Similarly, ship mortgages must be recorded in a regional office of the United States Coast Guard and will not be revealed by a routine UCC search. Federal statutes also provide for the recording of security interests in copyrights, trademarks, and patents, all of which generally must be recorded with a federal agency. The bank should consult its legal counsel when dealing with these categories of collateral.

Most states have statutes covering titled vehicles such as automobiles, trucks, trailers, mobile homes, and motorcycles. To perfect a lien against such a titled vehicle, a lien usually must be registered on the certificate of title. This is ordinarily done by following procedures established by the Motor Vehicle Division of the Secretary of State's Office in each of the states. Except in those relatively few states that require the filing of a financing statement to perfect a lien in a titled vehicle, a UCC search will not reveal such a lien.

Unrecorded perfected security interests

In some instances a security interest is automatically perfected by attachment alone, and there is no need for the secured party to either file a financing statement or take possession of the collateral. In most states a purchase money security interest in consumer goods is the most notable example of a transaction where perfection is by attachment alone. For example, if Jones purchases a $600 exercise bicycle from his local sporting goods store and the vendor finances the purchase, Jones signs a promissory note and security agreement, but no financing statement will be filed. So, when Jones approaches another lender and offers the exercise bicycle as security for a new consumer loan, the prospective lender will not discover the sporting goods store's purchase money security interest by doing a UCC search.

In a number of states an assignment of a debtor's beneficial interest in a trust or in a decedent's estate is usually exempted from the filing rule. Therefore, in such an instance, an interested party conducting a record search will not discover the existence of a perfected security interest.

Taking possession of the collateral is another alternative for perfecting a security interest in the case of some categories of collateral. The Code (UCC 9-305) states that a security interest in letters of credit and advices of credit, goods, instruments, money, negotiable documents, or chattel paper may be perfected by the secured party taking possession of the collateral. In the case of some collateral (such as securities, instruments, or money), taking possession is the only acceptable means of perfecting. Some categories of collateral, such as negotiable documents, goods, and chattel paper, can be perfected either by taking possession or by filing.

It is interesting to note that in the case of goods, the secured party may perfect either by filing or by taking possession. Suppose that Simon Carter obtains a $25,000 loan from Bank A and offers the bank his gold ingot as collateral. The bank agrees, has Carter execute a note and security agreement, takes possession of the ingot, issues a collateral receipt to Carter, and disburses the loan proceeds. Thirty days later, Carter approaches Bank B and requests a loan, again offering the gold ingot as collateral. Bank B does a UCC search, which fails to disclose any previously perfected security interest. It therefore has Carter sign a note, security agreement, and financing statement and proceeds to file the financing statement in the proper filing office. In such a case, Bank A would have a first security interest perfected by possession, and Bank B would have a second security interest perfected by filing.

Another type of unrecorded security interest may exist when the collateral is of a type excluded from the coverage by the Code, such as an assignment of a life insurance policy. Since assignments of life insurance policies are excluded from the coverage of Article 9, an interest in a policy is not perfected by filing, but rather by taking possession of the policy, filing an assignment with the insurance company, and having the insurer acknowledge the assignment. Obviously, such an assignment will not be disclosed by a UCC search.

Effect of the PMSI grace period

A secured lender must be aware that another type of unrecorded perfected security interest arises from the fact that a secured party may have a grace period in which to make a filing. If the filing is made during that grace period, the secured party automatically achieves a first priority. This is true in the case of a purchase money security interest in goods other than inventory. In this instance, the secured party has a grace period of either 10, 15, or 20 days (depending on the state) in which to make a filing to perfect its interest. This grace period begins on the date on which the debtor receives constructive possession of the collateral.

Suppose, for example, that on August 13, ABC Machine Shop purchases a new drill press costing $17,000 from Larson Industries and receives possession of the press on that date. Larson accepts a $3,000 down-payment and agrees to finance the remaining balance of $14,000 over a three-year term. Larson has ABC execute a note, security agreement, and financing statement. On August 23, ABC approaches its local banker and requests a $10,000 loan. The bank agrees to make the loan provided that ABC will grant it a security interest in its equipment, and proceeds to do a UCC search, which fails to disclose any previous filings. The bank agrees to make the loan based on the assumption that it will have a first security interest in all of ABC's equipment—including its most valuable asset, the new drill press. The bank files a financing statement in the proper filing office on August 25. Two days later, Larson files a financing statement covering the new drill press. Since the Code in that particular state allows a 20-day grace period, Larson has filed in a timely manner to perfect its purchase money interest and therefore now has a first security interest in the drill press, *despite* the fact that the bank filed two days earlier.

Hidden liens

In some instances a financing statement may have been properly filed but, for various reasons, may be very difficult to locate during a routine record search. One such instance is where the financing statement has been misfiled by the filing officer. The Code (UCC 9-403[1]) states that a secured party becomes perfected when a properly completed financing statement is delivered to the proper filing office accompanied by the correct filing fee. A secured party meeting these requirements becomes perfected even though the filing is misindexed by the filing officer. For example, if the debtor's name is Trans-American Industries, Inc., and an absent-minded clerk in the filing office indexes this filing under "A" instead of "T," the secured party is perfected, even though a third party searching the records might have great difficulty locating this filing.

Another reason a previous filing may be difficult to locate is a recent name change by the debtor. It is relatively simple for a business entity to change its name, generally requiring an amendment to its charter, which must be approved by the issuing agency in the case of a corporation. If a proprietorship or partnership is involved, a name change may require only a notification filing in a local public office.

Suppose that DEF Corporation applies for a loan at First National Bank. The bank, unaware that the company changed its name from ABC Corporation several months ago, performs a UCC search, which fails to reveal any previous Code filings. There may, however, be valid filings under the old

199

name of which the bank is unaware. Article 9 provides that when a debtor so changes its name that a previous filing becomes seriously misleading, the secured party must refile under the new name in order to perfect with respect to collateral acquired more than four months after such a name change. However, the previous filing under the original name remains effective as to collateral owned by the debtor prior to the name change or acquired within four months of the name change.

A hidden lien may also result when a debtor moves the collateral from one state to another. To avoid becoming unperfected in such a case, the secured party has a four-month grace period to refile in the state to which the debtor has moved. So, when Jones Industries, Inc., moves to Indiana from Pennsylvania, Bank A remains perfected for four months after the move, even though it has not yet filed in Indiana. When Jones approaches Bank B in Indianapolis, it may fail to disclose that it moved to Indiana less than four months ago. Therefore, Bank B may do a UCC search only in Indiana and be misled by its results.

Another type of hidden lien may result if the loan applicant has purchased the collateral from a third party who has granted a security interest in the assets being purchased and who is converting collateral. Carlson Construction has asked Bank A for a working capital loan to be secured by its Caterpillar earthmover. The bank does a record search on Carlson that fails to disclose any Code filings covering this equipment. However, Carlson purchased the machine several months earlier from Bogus Construction Company, which sold it in violation of its security agreement with Commercial Credit, and to which it failed to deliver the proceeds. Commercial Credit's security interest is still effective, and, to both Carlson's and Bank A's surprise, it may repossess the earthmover. For Bank A to protect itself, it would have needed to perform a UCC search not only on its customer (Carlson), but also on the former owner (Bogus), even though it was unaware of the circumstances.

In summary, although a UCC search is beneficial and should always be performed—especially in the case of a new borrower—commercial lenders should be aware that security interests may exist which will not be disclosed by a search, and that further inquiry concerning the status of the collateral may be necessary.

6

Lending to Small Businesses

Of approximately sixteen million businesses in the United States, some fourteen million are small. These small businesses account for more than 40 percent of the gross national product (GNP). Utilizing Small Business Administration (SBA) standards, about 97 percent of all nonfarm businesses are categorized as small businesses.

It is therefore evident that the great majority of bank commercial accounts and loans involve small businesses. This is especially true for small- and middle-market banks. While the large city and regional banks deal with the larger national and regional business corporations, community banks must rely on small businesses for their commercial deposits and loans. Therefore, middle-market bankers must develop an understanding of small businesses and become adept at serving their needs, which often differ from the needs of larger businesses. This may involve working with poorer quality financial information, less sophisticated management, more restricted markets, and fewer financial resources. This section explores several aspects of dealing with small businesses, such as assessing and meeting the needs of such a business and evaluating its strengths and weaknesses.

The first article in this section deals with assessing and meeting the needs of small businesses. The bank's relationship with a small business customer will be different than its relationship with a large corporate business, as small businesses generally look for a closer, one-on-one relationship with the banker. The small business manager prefers a banker who takes a personal interest in the business, who takes the time to visit the business, and who has a sincere desire to meet its needs. The author emphasizes the "walkaround" method of learning about the operations of the business and also discusses the five stages of the business life cycle. This article also provides suggestions for developing a successful program for dealing with small businesses, and suggests that quality of service, rather than pricing, is of greatest importance.

A second article stresses the importance of a comprehensive strategic operating plan for a business customer. Such a plan, which should define strategic objectives to be achieved in the next several years, is an important ingredient for the future success of a business. It is important for the bank dealing with the business customer to evaluate properly the viability of such a plan based on economic, industry, and competitive environments. Judging the prospects of success for a business also involves a judgment of the adequacy of physical, financial, and human resources. This should include a critical assessment of the capability of management, which is generally the principal factor affecting the success or failure of a business. Another article provides suggestions for analyzing the closely held company. This involves becoming familiar not only with the financial statements of the business, but also involves becoming familiar with the capacity of management and the ability of the business to compete within its industry.

The fourth article discusses the stages of small business development. It discusses the problems and challenges facing the business in each of these stages of its development. In its initial stage, the business will struggle to obtain adequate financing, develop competent management, develop a product or service, and penetrate its market. At this stage the banker will have to deal with low equity, unproven performance, significant borrowing needs, and inadequate sales volume. In the second stage of the business's development, the banker will need to deal with the business's desire for growth before profits and cash flow justify the further extension of credit. Although now somewhat profitable, the business will still have a weak balance sheet and significant borrowing needs. In the third stage, which is reached by only about 15 percent of small businesses, the business will be quite profitable, will be securely established in its market, and will become a very good customer of the bank. In its final stages, the business has matured, owners and managers are aging, and the business may become a candidate for sale or merger. Recognizing these distinct stages in the business's life cycle, the banker will be better able to understand and anticipate its banking needs.

Another article deals with the topic of meeting a small business's basic needs. This involves identifying not only the needs of the business, but also those of its owners. This article discusses the question of why businesses are inclined to bank with a number of institutions, and why businesses switch their accounts from one institution to another. The article points out that calling on customers is crucial and that failure to do so on a consistent basis will make that customer a ripe target for a competing institution.

The sixth article discusses the ways in which a lender may help turn a small business around. The article points out that many companies having tremendous growth potential fail due to lack of financial sophistication. Many such companies are undercapitalized, and due to their lack of expertise, do not fully understand their financing needs. In many instances, such companies receive little help from their banker, either because the banker lacks the time to work with them or due to the banker's concern about lender liability if he becomes too involved in the management of the company. The article further discusses various techniques for solving the problems of businesses that are in financial difficulty. It also suggests that the bank not become too involved in the management of the business, but that it develop a list of reasonably priced consultants who may be able to assist the company in solving its problems.

Another article in this section discusses financing high-tech entrepreneurs, and the problems involved in doing so. Such a business often produces a unique and highly sophisticated product, but its owners and managers may lack financial sophistication. The business may require a significant amount of funds for research and development, and this need should ordinarily be financed by equity investors. However, once a product is perfected, a bank financing may be requested to enable the business to manufacture and market its product. With low equity and unproven performance, and in many instances, a product that is unique, it may be very difficult for the bank to finance such a venture unless it can obtain an injection of venture capital and/or government guarantees of its loans. This article provides a comprehensive check list which will be of assistance to a prospective lender in judging the viability of a loan request from a high-tech entrepreneur.

The final article considers the benefits that a business incubator may provide to an infant business. A business incubator is a facility established specifically to nurture the growth of small young companies by providing various services at a reasonable cost. Incubators receive their funding from a wide variety of sources including government agencies, not-for-profit organizations, and venture capital groups. The article points out that a business incubator can be a tremendous asset to a community by providing an environment that will promote the growth of new small businesses. It also discusses the manner in which a business incubator may be formed and the problems and challenges involved in financing this type of business.

206

Assessing and Meeting the Needs of Small Business

How can your bank discover what its small-business customers want and develop a program to meet those needs? David A. Enger, senior partner with the Seattle-based consulting firm Management Advisory Services, Inc., spoke on this topic at a small-business banking conference sponsored by the American Bankers Association.

"Only three percent of the 16 million businesses in America have over $5 million in sales," says Enger. "Seventy percent of households with a net worth greater than $1 million are headed by small-business owners. But the failure rate of small businesses is high, so of course there's risk. But the wrong way to build a relationship with small business is using high-tech in what is essentially a high-touch market. Many banks send a customer 'downtown' once his business reaches a certain size. This tends to upset the customer, who can't understand why his original loan officer and bank can't continue to serve him. There's a niche for full-service, local banks." Enger is an admirer of the "hub" system of banking because it gets the loan officers out in the field, close to their customers.

Appreciating customer attitudes

Enger describes what he terms "small business attitudes—savvy lenders take note! First the small-business owner wants a banker who's able to make a decision. Second, small businesses are not price-sensitive; they care more about a relationship. Third, credit is the major product they want. About 40 percent of the companies we surveyed didn't want the bank to call on them at all trying to sell them junk they don't need. Fourth, small-business owners think all banks are the same—the owners form loyalties to *people* not organizations. Finally, small-business owners want to keep a local banking relationship. They don't want to go 'downtown' to the bank's main office if they're happy with their local branch."

Small-business owners have three major complaints about banks, according to Enger. "They dislike the high rate of officer turnover. They complain that the loan officer never comes to visit them at their business, and they complain that the banker doesn't understand the company's business or industry. Also, a business owner's ego doesn't always allow him, an $80,000-per-year executive, to take advice from a $20,000-per-year loan officer."

Understanding the business life cycle

"Don't depend entirely on a company's financial statements," Enger recommends. "Learn about the company during the walkaround. The first thing I look at is the parking lot—what does the owner drive? That will tell you a lot about the owner. You want to get an idea of the owner's business judgment, education, experience, and common sense. Go in and ask the broad, seemingly naive questions: "How do things run around here?"

Enger describes the five stages in the business life cycle. "In the first stage, the owner (usually a 30-to-40-year old rugged individualist) has a dream and begins the company. At this point, however, the bank is interested only in making collateral loans to the entrepreneur. During the second stage, the losers quit because they realize it's a jungle out there. The ones who decide to stick it out work hard and experience high growth. The owner takes on multiple roles and becomes the company's best employee, which often causes self-destruction as the company grows.

"Manufacturing companies tend to self-destruct when they reach $3 million in sales, wholesalers and distributors at around $5 million to $7 million," notes Enger. "Contractors get into trouble when they turn from subcontractors into general contractors, and retailers tend to self-destruct when they open another store. Service companies begin to have problems when they reach the point of having about 30 employees.

"During the third stage," Enger continues, "the owner begins to create 'myths' about his business, i.e., 'My business is different.' This is also when the bankers finally get interested in lending to the company. But then it enters the fourth stage, when the owner's age becomes a controlling factor in the business. It's time for the owner to either teach and share what he knows or destroy the business. Finally, the business either enters the fifth stage, where the owner liquidates it, or enters a sixth stage, in which the founder's successors begin the hard work of growing the company again."

Tips for successful small-business lending

To deal successfully with small-business owners, Enger recommends a ten-step program for banks:

1. Create a small-business strategy that has the support of the bank's senior management.

2. Run a focus group or two. Ask the customers what they want—and ask former customers why they left the bank.

3. Train your lenders to deal with small-business people.

4. Learn when to pay attention to the accounts—when they need it.

5. Have a career path for small-business lenders and value the small-business lenders you have. Don't tell them they have to do national accounts to be somebody within the context of the bank.

6. Segment your market, create industry specialization of lenders, and tailor products to the needs and life cycle of the businesses you serve.

7. Don't compete on price alone. Add value and service.

8. Tailor your delivery system to create loan officer stability and quick turnaround. If you ask lenders to do timesheets, you'll find them spending an inordinate amount of time on paperwork. Create efficiency by training someone else to do the paperwork.

9. Strive for continuous customer contact. Set goals for your lenders to contact so many borrowers, so many nonborrowers, and new prospects each month.

10. Get the message across that you care about your customers and their businesses.

Evaluating a Firm's Future*

Middle-market lenders analyze the future of a firm to design a loan that will be profitable for the bank. Specifically, lenders use information derived from the analysis to structure the loan, design the covenants and loan-specific monitoring procedures to protect the bank's interest; and to give the borrower enough flexibility in its operations. Lenders also use such information to price the loan so that fees and interest earned from loans and deposits will not only cover all direct and indirect costs incurred by the bank on the loan, but will also give the bank a reasonable profit.

This article will discuss suggestions for evaluating the future of a firm. To do so, a loan officer should seek answers to the following two questions:

1. Does the firm have a carefully developed, comprehensive strategic and operating plan for its future operations?

---

*This article was written by Frank C. Jen, an M & T bank professor of banking and finance at the State University of New York at Buffalo. He has been the director of the advanced commercial lending and credit analysis program offered at the University of Buffalo since 1977. The program is designed for middle-market lenders.

2. If such a plan exists, is it viable from both a business and a financial point of view?

Strategic and operating plans

For a middle-market firm to succeed, its managers must first develop a comprehensive strategic and operating plan which defines the firm's long-term business and financial goals. Second, such a plan defines the strategic objectives to be attained in the next few years and provides an intermediate-term operating plan for the managers trying to attain these strategic objectives. Third, it includes a financial plan indicating the target financial performance and the amount of funds needed to support the planned operations. Finally, the plan should indicate short-term operating specifics contemplated for the next year and projected financial results. The importance of such a comprehensive plan to the firm's future cannot be overemphasized. The success of a firm depends on the concerted and coordinated actions of all its managers and employees working together toward the strategic and financial goals.

Evaluating the plan's viability

The viability of the plan depends on whether the actions proposed in it are appropriate, considering the external environment the firm is expected to face and the firm's own internal capability. The future success of any firm depends on its ability to adapt its products and services to anticipated external environments.

Three aspects of external environments are important for a loan officer to analyze:

1. general social and economic environments
2. industry environments
3. competitive environments

General social and economic environments include changes in consumer tastes, shifts in GNP and personal income levels, and expected changes in interest rates and tax policy. These factors all affect future business opportunities and, hence, a firm's profitability.

A firm cannot escape problems facing its own industry. With this in mind, the loan officer should thoroughly analyze any special problems the borrower's industry is facing. When the competition is fierce because of imports—take semiconductors, for example—a firm must make meaningful efforts to improve its competitive position (typically through research and development). Middle-market firms often operate within a particular region, and customers in that region may have special characteristics that allow the firm to operate in a manner different from the national firms.

Finally, a loan officer must ensure that the firm's managers are correctly perceiving impending changes. The loan officer must evaluate how well the managers can handle the future because the managers determine the firm's future. Since much of this information is not included in the firm's comprehensive strategic and operating plan, a loan officer must generate these evaluations by questioning managers and verifying the answers using other materials.

Evaluating a firm's capabilities

A loan officer must also evaluate a company's internal capability to implement its plans. There are three important factors to consider. The first is the availability of adequate physical, financial, and human resources. Whether enough financial resources are either already available or soon obtainable is a question often unanswered by many managers due to a lack of financial training. A mistake often made in human resource management is overestimating the ability of managers to handle new ventures successfully, particularly when the new ventures demand handling matters beyond their immediate experience. Finally, many managers may be ignorant of recent technological changes in their industry and purchase the wrong equipment, hurting their firm's competitive ability in the long run.

A successful firm must have a strong management system to support management actions. External environments and internal resource capabilities are always changing. Managers must therefore have an appropriate management information system to keep them apprised of changes, and a supporting management process to ensure that the implications of such changes are understood and considered before key decisions are made.

Evaluating proposed management actions

The final factor for the loan officer to consider is the most important one: the appropriateness of proposed management actions and the resulting financial conditions specified in the operating and strategic plan. To evaluate whether such actions are appropriate, the loan officer should ask these three questions:

1. DO THESE ACTIONS MAKE USE OF THE COMPETITIVE STRENGTHS OF THE FIRM AND AVOID ITS COMPETITIVE WEAKNESSES? This question should be answered from the viewpoint of whether the proposed actions represent reasonable extensions of current management strengths.

2. HAVE THE PLANNED ACTIONS BEEN OBJECTIVELY AND RIGOROUSLY EVALUATED? A loan officer must be sure that cash flows from the proposed actions are realistically forecasted. If analytical methods such as net present value and internal rate of return are *not* used to evaluate the proposed actions, the investment involved

213

in preparing for future actions may not be cost-effec-tive—the cash flows earned may be lower than the cost involved, even if the proposed actions are successful.

3. **ARE THE FINANCIAL PROJECTIONS IN THE OPERATING PLAN ATTAINABLE IN THE NEXT FEW YEARS?** In the intermediate and short-term plan, management's financial projections should show what funds are needed and which funds will be internally generated. Such projections must be realistic. In performing the audit, the loan officer should rely not only on historical trends, but on facts gathered during the investigation.

The loan officer should use trade publications, regional and national economic studies, and industry analyses from the United States Department of Commerce, Standard & Poor's, etc., to evaluate answers regarding competitive positions.

Regarding a firm's projected financial strengths, a loan officer should make sure the figures submitted by managers are realistic. For example, large projected sales increases must be supported by a well-designed sales plan, which in turn is founded upon thorough and realistic market analysis. Similar attention should be paid to cost-cutting moves. A projected cut in labor costs must be supported by actual time and motion studies, the use of new production techniques, and/or new raw materials.

Many managers of middle-market firms argue that they are "too busy" to prepare a comprehensive written plan. The loan officer should ask managers if they have an unwritten plan formulated with all the appropriate factors included. Even if they do, a written plan is likely to be more thorough, internally consistent, and more useful for coordination purposes. A manager running a firm with an unwritten future plan must be viewed as a greater risk and thus be handled with care.

214

Indeed, a slightly higher risk premium may be justified on loans to a firm with such a characteristic.

Summary

The loan officer must determine whether a middle-market firm has a carefully prepared strategic and operating plan describing its long-term goals. The lender must also determine whether such a plan has taken the competitive external environments and the firm's internal capabilities into account and whether the planned actions make use of the firm's traditional strengths.

Analyzing the Closely Held Company

"Bankers lending to large firms are accustomed to looking at fully audited financial statements, but small companies don't necessarily have them available," says Janet L. Myers, president of Dearborn Business Group, Ltd., in Chicago. "So the banker must spend more time interviewing to know what the numbers do mean. At best, the RMA (Statement Studies) numbers serve as a guideline for a small company's numbers.

"One of my clients is one of two major commercial banks in a large city," says Myers, who was a commercial lender with The First National Bank of Chicago in the early 1970s. "The loan officers were spending nearly all their time trying to get financial statements from closely held companies. This left little time to get to know the owners, the operation, or the industry. When the statements did come in they would determine that the numbers weren't the kind they could lend to. If you do a good job of interviewing, the numbers shouldn't be a surprise." Prior to starting her bank consulting firm, Myers held senior marketing and sales management positions with Data Resources Inc. and opened a Chicago office for Omega, a bank consulting company. She now works with financial institutions, focusing on improving the profits, productivity,

215

and performance of both the institutions and their most costly customer contact resource, the calling officer.

"Calling officers must understand that they are the most costly resource a bank has. Once they understand that, they want to spend their time more productively. An important ingredient in being productive as a middle-market banker is building rapport so the customer will describe the management decisions that generate the financial numbers—and so the banker can educate the customer at the same time. The ultimate goal is that bankers are not surprised by the financial statements. By spending time more effectively on fewer appointments, bankers will have fewer surprises from the financial statements."

Careful interviewing is crucial

"One starting point for credit analysis is how a company recognizes revenue," Myers notes. "It says a lot about the quality of the financial statements (income and balance sheets). A company with a technically oriented leader doesn't always realize he's making a financial decision when he chooses a way to recognize revenue. A banker should also look at the company's inventory policy, timing, and valuation of purchases. What makes the inventory obsolete for the company and industry? How is cost of goods sold determined and matched to revenues? Ask management to explain the company's credit policy and accounts receivable. Inquire about any and all prepaid and accrued expenses and the related decisions. What is working capital? Be sure to interview all members of the company's management. How well do they understand their industry, markets, and competitive issues? What does management plan for the future of the company? This interview should use the open-ended type of questions covered in sales training. Open-ended questions gain more information and make a calling officer more productive.

"This type of interviewing allows the banker to set himself up as an educator instead of an adversary," says Myers. "Don't ask for the financials first. Instead, interview first, doing lots of listening to assess whether you are being told what you anticipated, *then* look at the financials. Another common pitfall is asking only for the company's business statements when you ask for the financials. Bankers should also ask to see the company and owner's individual tax returns. It's a way to have checks and balances, especially for the unaudited financial statements. Although a company may not have updated financials, it must have current tax returns.

"Some analysis pitfalls are common for any size company," Myers continues. "For example, inventory and cost of goods sold. From an accounting viewpoint, a banker thinks: Beginning inventory minus cost of goods sold equals ending inventory. The IRS views it differently: Beginning inventory minus ending inventory equals cost of goods sold. Depending on how you look at this, a seemingly simple difference affects the bottom line differently.

"Bankers are concerned about equity," Myers notes. "Because of the tax laws, an S corporation is given negative incentive to keep net worth in the company. Small-business owners read IRS Publication 334, *Tax Guide for Small Business,* but I'm surprised that many bankers don't read it—and some don't even know it exists! I suggest that bankers read it so they know how the IRS influences the financial statements that bank customers prepare."

The triangle of responsibility

"It's an opportunity and a challenge for the banker to educate the business owner. Firing closed-end questions at the customer causes the banker to be viewed as the prosecuting attorney. The banker should be able to explain the impact of various company management decisions, why he wants to know the information, and how the bank views management's decisions. The challenge is not to tell them what to do, which is the other extreme. Bankers tend to try to explain things in 'bankerese'—they must make an effort to adjust to the level of the customer's experience. I would explain things differently to a customer in engineering than to a customer with a sales background. It comes down to respecting the business owner—appreciating how difficult it is to start and run a successful business."

Industry associations are good secondary sources of information for credit analysis, according to Myers. "How many bankers are really active in industry associations for those industries they've targeted? Many bankers are involved in their local Chamber of Commerce. Bankers need to read industry and trade publications. These often have very specific information about the future of an industry. Publications which focus on closely held companies are also available (e.g., *Inc.* and *Venture*).

"One of the challenges of lending to a small business is that the banker has a large number of customers—which means it's difficult to stay in touch with changes at every small business. Small businesses, however, tend to have greater swings than large ones. How do you staff for that? The challenge is making time to call on all those customers.

"Bankers are inside a triangle of responsibility. Business development is the opportunity to sell and cross-sell. They interview to stay on top of whether the company is creditworthy, and then service the account. This connection is very tight for the small business lender. The banker is balancing three distinct responsibilities for each client. The resultant conflict can be business owners who feel they don't get enough service from the bank and bank loan officers who feel they're doing as much as they can." Effective prospect interviews as well as thorough interviews at the time of annual reviews enable the calling officer to increase productivity, assure creditworthiness, improve customer service, and further the bank's profitability.

Stages of Small-Business Development*

Most small businesses appear to follow a fairly predictable "life cycle." By pinpointing the stage a small business is in, the lender can better serve his or her customer and deal more effectively with the unique personality characteristics of the small-business owner. The four stages of small-business development are described in this article along with some tips on dealing with business owners.

The first stage: Meet basic money needs

In the first stage, small businesses are usually started by individuals between age 30 and 40. Prior to age 30 they lack technical expertise and after age 40 they usually lack nerve. Seed money comes from dipping into a small savings account, remortgaging the family home, and borrowing money from relatives and friends. The business owner begins to live a dream of freedom, independence, and wealth. The spouse, however, usually has visions of the shame of failure, unemployment, and perhaps loss of friends with more money. The typical start-up business owner is undercapitalized, overextended, undermanaged, and overworked.

Bankers quickly learn that these people survive by "RLC" (rat-like cunning). Some are stubborn and ruthless, pushing the line on what's ethical and what's not. They tend to live on withholding and pledge receivables that are really work-in-

---

*The writer of this article is Steven L. Cranfill, a partner with Management Advisory Services, Inc., a Seattle-based firm involved in management consulting, business valuation, and seminars. Mr. Cranfill was previously with Ranier National Bank.

progress. They usually don't seek or use professional advice from lawyers or accountants because they often can't afford it and may not recognize or appreciate its value. A great deal of secrecy often surrounds the business, which the owner encourages. He or she is concerned that if suppliers, employees, and the banker knew how bad things really were—they'd all quit.

Owners of businesses in the startup phase are not great prospects for buying bank products. They have low sales, low profits, low net worth, and low cash. Frequently, there is no collateral available and no primary source of repayment for debt. They are poor credit line prospects, but more money is not necessarily the answer to their problems. Liberal access to funds could promote sloppiness, a lack of urgency, and more debt than the business could handle. The banker working with a business in its first stage will probably focus on meeting basic needs with transaction accounts, and perhaps second-mortgage loans and business credit on a transaction basis.

The second stage calls for cautious lending

The odds of success are very low, but the lucky business owners who survive the first stage enter the second phase of the business life cycle. Now something wonderful happens— profits! The business begins to add sales, employees, and, unfortunately, creditors. Because sales and profits are good but cash flow is generally poor, growth businesses are difficult to finance. Owners typically feel that sales and profits are the answer to any problem they might have. They do not understand that receivables, inventory, and other assets create a greater need for funds than the company generates internally. So, while the income statement continues to look good, the balance sheet may steadily deteriorate.

Small-business owners have three concerns at this stage: convenience, cash needs, and taxes. They are therefore targets for payroll services, merchant's credit card relationships, credit lines, fixed asset loans for expansion, and even employee benefit plans for tax savings.

Sufficient collateral and a primary source of repayment now begin to make loans to the business possible. The banker, however, must ensure that growth is conducted on a controlled basis and that debt does not build excessively.

The third-stage businesses: Good loan prospects

Only about 15 percent of small businesses will survive both the first and second stages to blast into the third stage. The owners of these businesses have it made. These individuals have built secure, solid businesses that are important to the community. They create jobs, are recruited for the local United Way campaign, and join the local bank's board of directors. Their children drive company cars, and all their relatives want summer jobs. They can often be difficult customers for the banker to serve. They may be loud, opinionated, and obnoxious. They're never around when you need to see them, and they typically "know it all." Secrecy is even more important now to the business owner than it was in the first stage. He reasons that if employees know how good things are, they will all want raises or leave if they don't get them. The business owner is intent on maintaining the status quo and usually begins to take fewer risks; this sows the seeds for the eventual decline of the business.

This is the time the banker begins to pay the price if he ignored the business in its startup phase, however. The business owner really needed the bank back in the early days, but now the company's success allows him to be selective. Owners of third-stage small businesses are excellent prospects for deposit relationships, investments, credit lines, real estate loans, and trust services. They're also candidates for installment loans for the company car, boat, plane, and condominium.

221

The fourth stage: Winding down

In the fourth stage, the business owner discovers that age has become the controlling partner in the business, with no investment. The wear and tear of a 30-year business career begins to show and the owner loses his nerve for risk. He becomes a conservator of wealth rather than a builder. Owners often bring their children into the business but become an impediment because they retain control of purse strings. They are often caught between a desire for real escape via retirement and the desire to linger and enjoy the rewards of all their hard work.

At this stage the small-business owner usually has three choices. First, he can sell the business. In this case it might be important for the banker to assist in a sale in order to maintain the account relationship. Second, the business owner can begin to invest in the business again by identifying a successor and beginning a new growth phase. Third, he can do nothing and allow his executors to make a decision after his death.

At this juncture, small-business owners are excellent targets for bank services in the areas of estate planning, investment management, assistance with the sale of the company, various trust accounts, and perhaps assistance in identification of a successor to manage the company.

Seeing the small-business owner's needs and problems from his point of view via a life cycle approach can help the lender to better match potential services to the customer, and avoid the pitfalls and problems inherent in lending to the small-business owner.

Meeting Small-Businesses' Basic Banking Needs

"Small businesses are not just using commercial banks, according to our research," says Douglas R. Hanks, president of Whittle & Hanks, Inc. of Chicago. "They're also using thrifts, credit unions, and factoring companies. Savings banks in New England and the far West are getting aggressive in trying to get the small-business customer." Hanks shared some findings with us that can help your bank get a leg up on the competition.

"The research grew out of a series of studies done with focus groups," says Hanks. "We thought we had determined that the basis of the relationship between a banker and a small business was lending, but it turned out the small-businesses were more interested in deposit services."

Hanks says the research held some other surprises: "On the qualifications of calling officers, the ideal was not related as much to title, experience, age, position, or gender as it was to the officer's familiarity with the company and its unique needs. In terms of reaching the small-business market, the direct methods paid dividends. Small businesses react best to outside calls, seminars, and gatherings hosted by senior bank management.

"In this market, companies with sales under $50 million and usually under $1 million, the owner's needs are linked with the company's needs. There's a real opportunity for bankers to meet both sets of needs. Loan officers tend to be myopic and think it beneath them to be versed on other services like deposit accounts. But they need to have much broader and deeper knowledge of their bank's services if they're going to reach the small-business market." According to the Whittle & Hanks study, 6.7 million businesses may be considered the upper limit of the small-business market.

"The differences between what manufacturing companies and service companies wanted were mainly tied to the types of bank services used," Hanks continues. "Manufacturing companies tend to rely more on credit than service companies. A cash business will make frequent contact with the bank, perhaps two or three trips per day. Fast-food franchisees, for example, feel it's prudent to bank with the closest bank, from a security standpoint. Manufacturers and construction companies are most concerned with the idea of putting all their eggs in one basket. They tended to use several financial institutions, and in some cases played one against another to get favorable treatment."

Why do small businesses use multiple institutions?

Thirty percent said they used multiple financial institutions because each bank handled a particular function. Twenty-eight percent said it gives the company flexibility. Another 15 percent reported that they need banks at multiple locations. Respondents also said that it helps with community relations, gives them a stronger bargaining position for rates, was the result of personal relationships, and improves their chances of getting loans. For the bank, this means that specialization and flexibility are the keys. "Decide what your bank does best, and try for a small piece of that relationship," Hanks recommends.

An impressive 77 percent of the survey respondents said they had done business with their primary financial institution for 10 years or longer. Therefore, it is essential to do careful precall planning. Analyze the situation, anticipate objections, develop a solution, and know your competition. "You're dealing with habit, so remember the 'Three Ps': prospecting, preparation, and persistence," says Hanks. "And *never* knock the competition."

Why do small-businesses switch banks?

Small businesses will change their primary financial institution due to inconvenient locations, unmet lending needs, poor service, noncompetitive rates, or the lack of all required services. They may also simply outgrow the bank. Hanks recommends that at least half of all officer calls should be to present customers. "This insures customer satisfaction, and satisfied customers are your best prospects and a good source of referrals. Attention and followup can partially offset the convenience factor. As one banker told me, 'We'll do anything to get a new customer, but we often take existing customers for granted.' Don't make that mistake!"

What is most important about a bank's lending services?

Small businesses cited the following as the most important points about a bank's lending services: familiarity with the company, a willingness to lend at all times, competitive rates, and prompt lending decisions. A surprising 50 percent of the respondents said deposit services were more important than lending services. The following factors influenced the respondents' choice of a depository institution: location, range of deposit services, competitive rates, and accurate reporting.

Calling is crucial

Thirty percent of the respondents said their account officer visited them at least once per quarter, and 28 percent were visited at least once a year. But only 14 percent saw the account officer more than once per quarter. Fourteen percent were visited less than once a year, and a shocking 15 percent said they were *never* called upon. Calling officers should take to heart the old adage about "out of sight, out of mind," especially since 36 percent of the respondents said they obtained most of their information about banking services through bank calling personnel. Outside calling is crucial, especially among the larger companies. Banking is a "people" business, especially in the small-company market.

Calling officers should always arrange an appointment in advance, and keep it once it's been made. "It may sound obvious, but be on time and have a plausible excuse if you're late," says Hanks. "Never leave without setting up a definite appointment or at least a followup telephone call."

According to Hanks, there are pros and cons of telephoning ahead. "On the plus side, the officer can anticipate a more responsive customer and will be perceived to be aware of the value of the customer's time. Calling ahead implies that there is an important matter to discuss, and encourages better preparation and planning. On the negative side, it's often too easy to get turned down over the phone, and customers may say that what they have to discuss is not important enough to justify an in-person visit.

"Three quarters of small businesses were contacted by at least one financial institution in the past year, averaging 2.54 contacts per year. Larger companies were contacted most frequently, so you have a built-in advantage when you call on the smallest companies, those with under $1 million in sales," says Hanks.

Sixty-nine percent of the respondents said they were very satisfied with their current banking services, and 22 percent were somewhat satisfied. Only 9 percent were dissatisfied. "Business development is a continuous job, and it can't work until someone becomes dissatisfied," says Hanks. When that happens, the calling bank that has persistently contacted the dissatisfied prospect will likely gain his business.

Helping Turn Small Businesses Around

Paul Alegria, president of Business Solutions, a consulting firm based in Belmont, Massachusetts, got into the business of helping small troubled businesses turn themselves around because every time he switched jobs, he ended up in a company that had cash problems which he helped turn around. Alegria says he has assisted 30 companies in the past five years. "I liked the challenge, not the routine maintenance, so I set up my own shop in September 1985."

"Most small businesses are started by someone with an area of expertise—they're not normally businesspeople," says Alegria, whose assignments more often come through word of mouth than through referrals from bankers. "A company falls into a niche, and the niche propels them. They see the possibility for growth but not the business and financial implications of that growth. It's sad to see companies with tremendous growth potential fail to succeed due to lack of financial sophistication. What I try to do is look at the numbers—their financial statements—understand the business goals, and objectively articulate the needs of the company. For companies generating between half a million and $10 million in sales, probably half the failures are unwarranted."

Common problems

"Many of these small companies are undercapitalized, and their bankers don't spend as much time with them as they need," says Alegria. "Many of them get into trouble because they don't collect their receivables— they're always *reacting* instead of acting. In many of the companies I've helped, no one was handling the receivables correctly, and there was no system established to bill projects upon completion. When I worked as a controller for one company in Boston, 'work orders' were written out with no controls on them to tell the accounting department to send out bills for work completed. So we spent three solid days doing just that."

Alegria was formerly the vice president of finance for Century Three in Boston and for B&M Associates in Waltham. Both companies were going through a transition period and hired him to help them. With an emphasis on managerial accounting, he helps companies develop performance statements on a monthly basis. "You can't make decisions without data. Too often, managers act based on what they think, not on the data. I've boiled the process down to a six-line profit and loss statement to give them something to review. It's easy for a nonfinancial person to understand. The statement includes percentage figures on sales, cost of goods, gross profit, cost of sales, general/administrative, and net before taxes. Having a grasp on the numbers allows managers to anticipate things rather than simply react. The numbers are important for understanding the dynamics of the business.

"One of the most important things I do is analyze the financials and test the systems. In many of these companies, collecting money is the key to survival. People are afraid to get on the phone and collect. I tell them to establish a system, document all contacts, and be pleasantly persistent."

Another key to a successful business turnaround is communication. "There's always a sense of guilt on the part of the principals that they've failed, but they really shouldn't expect to be all things," says Alegria. "The relationship between the bank and the customer has often deteriorated by the time I'm called in. My job is to open up the communication channels again. Lack of communication is often the fault of the business principals, who withdraw or become defensive when things go badly. But bankers need to make an effort to open up communications. I try to articulate objectively to the client's bank what the client's situation is and I've always been able to find something good about a company."

Real-life actions

Alegria worked for Rhode Island Hospital Trust when he graduated from college, which he says provided insight into what banks expect from borrowers. One of the companies Alegria worked with is Spotwise Productions, a Boston-based advertising agency and production company. "Spotwise's lender had a well-collateralized loan. The loan officer who made the loan had a bad portfolio, however, so *all* his loans were turned over to the bank's workout department. We kept telling the bank that the company would survive and asked them not to conduct a workout on Spotwise's loan. They finally came back to us and said, 'Hey, you're right.'" [*Editor's note: See "Look Ma, I'm a Businessman" by Larry Crowley, president of Spotwise, in the July 1987 issue of* Inc.]

"I've been working with a company in Albany two days a week for eight weeks," says Alegria. "They were struggling to make payroll, but now they can do it. I've brought in a controller, and we've accomplished some refinancing. We've started a new banking relationship and have put in some collection controls.

"At one electronics company I consulted with, no one ever explained how much billing it would take to break even. Half the battle in turning around a small business is developing goals and the ability to manage them. It takes a little backslapping and encouragement, which many CPAs and bankers don't have time to do. Many bankers are so busy with new customers that they often forget about their old clients, especially the small businesses. And they're the ones who need the most support. What I do is part accounting, part goal-setting, and part psychology."

While Alegria acknowledges that it can be difficult for bankers to draw that fine line between advising and advising too much, he believes that banks should also develop a list of reasonably priced outside consultants and managerial accountants whom companies can turn to when they need advice a banker can't (or shouldn't) give. "Bankers lend money, but they also need to lend a little expertise," says Alegria. "Theres a niche that's not being served. Bankers could provide more service and be more responsive. Bankers should know when a problem is arising if they request monthly performance statements. When a loan goes bad, the effects are devastating for all the parties involved. There's a need to practice preventive maintenance in business."

Financing the High-tech Entrepreneur

"High tech" may mean different things to various people—but for the purposes of this article we will define a high-tech business as one that produces a sophisticated product or service—usually in the computer or electronics field—which is to some extent unique. Although the larger high-tech businesses have been concentrated in such areas as California's Silicon Valley, Boston's 128 region, and Austin, Texas, small high-tech businesses are now being formed in many communities, especially those having large universities. Therefore, many middle-market banks may have an opportunity to work with an emerging high-tech company.

One of the greatest challenges encountered by a commercial banker is financing a startup business—and high-tech businesses are no exception. Financing a new business presents a number of problems, for several reasons. First, there is no history of past performance on which to base predictions of future performance. New businesses often require a high degree of leverage, and the ability of management may be untested. If the product or service being offered is new or unique, it is usually difficult to assess its acceptance in the marketplace.

Problems may arise in getting a new product into production, especially if it requires a precision process or high degree of quality control. It may be difficult to accurately estimate construction costs of facilities and the acquisition cost of machinery, equipment, furnishings, and fixtures. Building a competent managerial team and adequately training production workers may be costly and time-consuming. In spite of the best planning, unforeseen problems requiring time, money, and managerial resourcefulness frequently arise in a new business. All these concerns are especially pertinent in the case of a high-tech business.

Most small high-tech businesses have common characteristics. They are generally created by one or two people who

230

originate an idea for a better product or service than is currently available in the marketplace. The founders often have excellent academic credentials and a high level of technical knowledge, but may be unsophisticated about business and finance. Another common characteristic is that the business may produce a product or service that is difficult for a potential lender to understand. For example, one of the author's customers produces a highly sophisticated electronic chip that is barely visible to the naked eye. Another produces complex computerized training programs for various government agencies. The lender may not only have difficulty understanding these products, but may also find it almost impossible to assign a realistic collateral value to them. A third common characteristic is that a business of this kind is often started on a very informal basis and may have little or no equity capital and minimal formal structure.

Factors in high-tech success

Dr. Peter A. Alsberg, a former university professor and current president of Addamax Corporation, is now developing his second successful high-tech venture and has identified four critical factors in the success of a high-tech business. First, and most important, is the management team, which must have expertise in business management, marketing, and finance, as well as the technical knowledge required to develop the desired product or service. Second, there must be a strong potential market for the product or service being developed. Third, it must be superior to what is currently available, and its cost must be such that it can be marketed on a price-competitive basis. This does not mean it must be lower in price than existing products or services, but it must be a good buy for the value received by the customer. Lastly, the emerging high-tech business must have adequate financing. For many infant high-tech businesses, this presents a significant problem.

231

Don Monteith, an experienced high-tech lender and executive vice president of First Busey Corporation in Urbana, Illinois, suggests the following analogy to illustrate the difficulties that a commercial bank may encounter in attempting to finance a high-tech business. "If a borrower wants a $1 million loan to construct a building that isn't there, the bank's initial reaction might be to say that it can't finance something that isn't there. However, through long experience banks have become clever enough to finance the construction of a building with the aid of safeguards such as a written construction contract, the services of an inspecting architect, performance bonds, contrac-tor's affdavits, and lien waivers.

"In the case of a high-tech firm," Monteith continues, "the business needs a work-in-process loan while the entrepreneur's idea is being developed into a marketable product or service. But if the idea doesn't work, or if its development is not completed, then all the work done previously has no value. In effect, how does the bank find an 'inspecting architect' to monitor this kind of work in process? How does the bank justify progress payments while the service or product is being developed? How does it obtain assurances that the project will be completed?"

This analogy explains why most banks have the attitude that research and development should be funded by equity or operating earnings rather than by bank loans. Initial research and development is usually done with funds from the entrepreneur's savings or with loans secured by personal assets. As the funding needs of the company grow, friends and relatives may invest funds in the company, a source Dr. Alsberg refers to as an "Aunt Matilda financing." If the entrepreneur is lucky, he may obtain sufficient funds from these sources to basically complete research and development and build a test model.

At this point, the company is probably also involved in a market study—which may simply be a survey of its potential

232

customer base. Dr. Alsberg points out that sometimes such a study may greatly overstate a market when people recognize a product is good and desirable, but don't actually purchase it due to greater needs elsewhere in the business. On the other hand, if the product idea requires a "conceptual leap," a survey may greatly understate the true size of the market because the market does not yet understand its use.

The role of venture capital firms

If test marketing to a few customers proves successful, the company may then decide to begin production on a commercial basis. This ordinarily requires sizeable funding, either from a private stock placement or a venture capital firm. Venture capital firms specialize in equity investments in companies that have developed and are beginning to market a new product or service. Lawyers, accountants, or commercial bankers will often help an entrepreneur find a venture capital company. Although most venture capitalists invest in only a very small percentage of the deals they are offered, they may invest a significant amount of capital in a small company if the business appears to have a capable management team and a product or service for which there is a strong market potential.

In return, the venture capitalist will receive a sizeable slice of the ownership and a certain amount of management control if the business plan is not met. Since the venture capitalist is assuming a high level of risk, its demands will generally be heavy; this source of funding is therefore a high cost alternative for a company that becomes successful. A venture capitalist usually fills two primary functions: placing the business' balance sheet in a position where it is bankable, and providing management guidance to the unsophisticated entrepreneur.

When the business has reached the stage where it is preparing to engage in commercial production, a bank loan may become feasible. The business will be acquiring tangible assets

233

such as equipment and vehicles, as well as an inventory of raw materials and supplies. Therefore, with cash flow projections in hand and collateral to offer, the entrepreneur may become a prospect for a commercial loan.

A lender's checklist

When processing an application from a high-tech firm, the prospective commercial lender should consider the following factors:

1. Is the management team well balanced, and does it have the depth to continue to manage the business well as it grows? Adequate knowledge of finance and financial planning is especially important.

2. What is the market potential of the new product or service? Has a sufficiently large market testing been done to indicate the size of the market? What kind of sales organization will be required to tap market potential?

3. How much additional research and development needs to be done, and how will it be funded? For most high-tech firms, research and development is a continuing process, and adequate resources must be allocated to this function if the business is to remain on the cutting edge of the market.

4. Does the company have sufficient equity to withstand a certain amount of adversity? Companies that are too heavily leveraged usually don't have the ability to withstand hard knocks. In addition, debt service costs will be a major factor. If equity position is weak, in some instances the bank may require an additional injection of investor capital prior to making a loan.

5. Do the company's cash projections indicate that it will

generate sufficient cash to service all debt obligations and build equity? Do the results of the company's market studies and tests make the company's projections credible? Unsophisticated entrepreneurs overestimate the rapidity with which sales will develop and tend to underestimate the cost of operating a business.

6. What hard assets will be available to collateralize the bank's loan? How much collateral margin will there be?

7. Is the business a candidate for a United States Small Business Administration (SBA) loan, and is it eligible for supplemental funding from various state programs, such as job training grants and low interest economic development loans? The lender can be of considerable assistance to a company in helping it to identify and apply for available federal and state assistance programs. In many instances the lender will need to be creative in putting together a complete package of conventional, SBA, and economic development loans, and industrial development bond issues for the borrower. In many cases it will be impossible for the lender to finance the business without the assistance of various federal and state programs.

8. Are the principals of the company willing to personally guarantee the loans, and what financial strength do these guarantees add?

9. Once the complete funding package is put together, what will be the bank's exposure? Does the potential exposure justify the benefits to be gained?

Lending to a growing high-tech business often will involve greater risk than some of the more traditional types of lending. If the business fails, the bank may suffer a loss, but if the loan is structured properly that loss should be limited to an amount the bank can readily absorb. However, if the business

235

is successful, the rewards to the bank can be substantial. A thriving high-tech business will be an excellent deposit account and is an excellent candidate for other banking services such as cash management, payroll services, and pension plans. A growing high-tech business may create a number of jobs in a community in a relatively short period of time. Once this kind of business becomes successful, it is often acquired by a larger company but remains an excellent bank customer and a good corporate citizen of the community even after its acquisition.

Business Incubators:
Where Future Bank Clients Are Growing

Savvy bankers should keep an eye on a new source of potential bank customers: the local business incubator. A business incubator is a facility operated to nurture small young companies by providing low-rent space, shared office services and management advice. Bankers in communities without incubators may even want to consider leading the drive to set up one of these valuable economic development tools.

"There are 272 incubators in the United States [as of March 1988] and many more in countries all over the world," says Carlos Morales, executive director of the National Business Incubation Association (NBIA), based in Carlisle, Pennsylvania. "Twenty-five percent of the industry is now private, where two years ago it was 9 percent private. By 1991, we estimate that 50 percent of the incubators in the U.S. will be private. Incubated firms are successful and grow. After eight years, the track record for tenants of incubators is 80 to 93 percent successful. For the incubators themselves, we've seen a 95 to 96 percent success rate. But all this success doesn't come easily or without effort. Incubators are complicated to run and difficult to put together. It takes hard work to make them successful."

236

Incubator basics

According to the NBIA, all business incubators share three characteristics: co-location, shared services, and management assistance. Being located physically near one another allows incubator tenants to benefit from each other's knowledge and experience. Shared services—such as centralized administrative and clerical services, shipping and receiving facilities, conference rooms, word processing and computer facilities—reduce the working capital needs of startup businesses. Incubator tenants often receive help from the community in developing business and strategic plans, securing financing, and marketing their products and services.

Incubators receive their funding through a variety of sources, including corporations, government agencies, not-for-profit organizations, venture capital groups, and private developers.

Public or not-for-profit incubators make up 47 percent of the industry, according to the NBIA. They are sponsored by government and nonprofit organizations and are primarily interested in creating jobs, as well as in economic diversification, tax base expansion, and building rehabilitation and reuse. Private incubators (25 percent of the industry) are run by venture and seed capital groups, or by corporations and real estate development partnerships. Their primary interest is high economic reward for investment in tenant firms, new technology applications, and added value through development of commercial and industrial real estate.

Incubators affiliated with colleges and universities (14 percent of industry) share some of the objectives of public and private incubators, but are also interested in starting projects for faculty research, providing alumni and associated groups with opportunities for starting businesses, and attracting quality researchers. A fourth type of incubator is the public/private (14 percent), created through a partnership between a government or other nonprofit agency and a private developer. This type of partnership gives the incubator access to government funding or resources and private-sector expertise and financing.

Some industry statistics

In 1987, David N. Allen, assistant professor, business administration, at Pennsylvania State University, and Mary Ann Dougherty, research project specialist with the Office of Economic Development at Southern Illinois University at Carbondale, conducted a study of the business incubation industry. The responses given by the managers of 127 incubators provided the base for the following conclusions. The average age of the incubators was 30 months, although half of all incubators were less than 22 months old. These figures indicated that this is still a relatively young and rapidly growing industry. The responding incubators were speculative ventures: On average, only 16 percent of the leasable space was rented by opening day. Within six months, about 38 percent of the space was leased, and slightly over half was leased at the end of one year. By two years, about 70 percent of the space was leased.

Nearly all incubators surveyed accepted companies in high tech, research and development, and light manufacturing. Three-quarters of the facilities would accept service-oriented companies, but few incubators allowed retail or heavy manufacturing tenants. Slightly over half the incubators had a stated "exit" or "graduation" policy. Graduation was determined by a tenant's length of occupancy and space and facility needs. Twenty percent of the incubators used an implied exit policy to encourage tenants to relocate and nearly three-quarters of these respondents used graduated rents for this purpose.

The three most frequently used shared office services were photocopying, receptionist, and conference room. The types of management assistance used most often by tenants were business plans, marketing, and accounting. Assistance with business plans was primarily offered inhouse, while marketing and accounting services were offered though external enterprise support networks. The incubators surveyed housed an average of 20 firms, although a median of 10 indicated that larger facilities tended to skew the average. The average employment was 169 per facility, but the median was 52. About half of the current jobs were created after the businesses moved into the incubator. Of the 117 incubators that reported graduated firms, the average was seven graduates per facility, although half the incubators had graduated one firm or less.

Lowering a startup's risk

"The smaller the community, the more likely the incubator will succeed," says Morales. "I know of one town with a population of 500 that has one incubator and is working on a second. Intimacy is important—if the managers of the incubators are on a first-name basis with local bankers, they can educate them about the concept. Some bankers like incubators because they let them 'cheat.' Because of competitive pressures, banks must venture into risk capital, but a lone entrepreneur will be turned down. But if an entrepreneur who's in an incubator approaches the bank, it's a different story. If a client comes in with an incubator's backing, that lowers the risk. The magic thing about incubators is that they lower the risk."

Morales notes that banks in such cities as Tulsa, Oklahoma, have told him they hold a lot of commercial real estate that they can't advertise, but could fill those buildings up with incubators. "Bankers should get involved," says Morales. "Incubators get money from various sources, including corporations and government agencies. But in smaller communities with a few banks and populations of 25,000 or 30,000, the bankers have been encouraging incubator development. In a few communities, they've been the prime force for getting them started."

Morales suggests that bankers serve on the board of the local business incubator. "Who will the entrepreneurs turn to later on but the banker who's been on the board and who's been involved? Architects and accountants have been supporting incubators to develop business for themselves. Corporate incubators are the newest wrinkle in the industry." IBM and Control Data Corporation, for example, have sponsored business incubators. Many business incubators have adopted niche strategies and serve specific industry segments. According to an April 1987 *Wall Street Journal* article, the city of Miami and Florida International University established the Biomedical Research and Innovation Center in downtown Miami, near hospitals and medical research institutes. The center's first tenants were high-tech medical companies. The Spokane Business Incubation Center in Washington established the Kitchen Center, where eight small food-processing companies share the facilities. A word of caution: If your community is planning a specialized incubator, be sure there are enough spinoffs from the local university or the community to fill it up.

Lending to incubators

Incubators can be tough loans, at least from one Philadelphia area banker's perspective. "The two incubators we lent to were fully secured by real estate," she says. "The problem with lending to a center in the formative stages is that it takes awhile for the cash flow from the tenants to support interest payments and debt service. The tenant companies in the incubators are typically unfinanceable and have a long way to go.

240

"If the incubator has done a good marketing job to attract tenants, it's not unusual for the incubator's manager to suggest banks for the tenant to call," the banker continues. "Our bank's relationship with tenant companies is primarily of the savings and checking account nature. We don't have a lending relationship until there's a product. The bank should be able to refer incubator tenants to equity players in the venture capital market. We will not sit on incubator boards because of lender liability concerns. We might have a senior banker on the board of a sponsoring nonprofit entity, but that's as close as we'd get if we have senior secured money out the door.

"Both of the incubators we've lent to have been successful in leasing space and have made their loan payments on time, but they're not highly successful in terms of profit. They're not generating the kind of excess cash flow which gives comfort to a banker. Another concern is if they're at full capacity, can they keep the waiting list healthy enough to replace a tenant who leaves? The concept has been successful in generating new business; the key is in the sponsorship its owners provide. In one incubator, the sponsorship was not so great, which was reflected in the results. In the other incubator, the level of sponsorship was much different, and several of its tenant companies have already grown up and moved out on their own."

Getting involved with incubators

Gerald R. Kunic, vice president, Mellon Bank, in Pittsburgh, believes that bankers should play a role in establishing and supporting incubators in their communities. "Incubators help banks contribute to local economic development and also allow banks to service startups from the ground up and watch them for the future," says Kunic, who has served on committees to start three different business incubators in Pennsylvania. "The incubator startup committees I've worked on generally consisted of a local banker, attorney, CPA, consultant, and perhaps a marketing person. Our purpose was to sell the concept to the officials in the community. Working through the director of a private or nonprofit organization, we put together a mission statement, obtained funds (including matching grants), and rented or purchased an incubator facility. Then we interviewed prospective tenants to screen those businesses that have the greatest potential for survival and could benefit from access to shared services and a 'champion'—an incubator manager who can help them with their business plan.

"What's most important is being involved in the community so you can find out what's going on," Kunic continues. "At Mellon, we've sponsored seminars for our small-business customers and find there's a real need for incubators. Bankers need to be educated on this idea, however, and one of the best ways to do that is to visit an incubator that's already in operation. If you get involved with incubator development, remember that the setup cannot come out of a cookie cutter; every incubator is different. Who are the prospective tenants and how will you set standards for 'graduation'? How flexible is the space—is there room for an assembly line, for example?"

In addition to helping with the initial incubator setup, Kunic notes that the incubator committee can meet on a regular basis to see how the incubator is working. "It may even want to go on and do another one if the first is successful," he says. "Ideally, after two or three years, an incubator should have some 'graduating' firms, so the committee could meet to screen the replacement tenants. Business incubators are a relatively new phenomenon, but they can enhance the economic development of a community."

7

Dealing with Problem Loans

A bank's loan portfolio usually comprises at least 50 percent of its total assets. Consequently, losses in its loan portfolio will have a significant effect on the bank's profitability, and it is therefore essential that the bank maintain the highest possible portfolio quality. Most loans are of acceptable quality at their inception. However, some loans will deteriorate subsequent to being made as a result of the borrower's nonperformance, deteriorating economic conditions, or other unforeseen adversity.

A problem loan can be defined as one in which there is a major breakdown in the repayment agreement resulting in an undue delay in collection, or one in which it appears legal action may be required to effect collection, or one in which there appears to be a potential loss. It is a loan in which the risk of loss is greater than anticipated when the loan was made, or in which the risk is greater than a lender ordinarily would willingly assume.

It is essential that a bank be able to identify deteriorating loans at an early stage. If this can be accomplished, the bank has available alternatives for correcting the problem, alternatives that will not exist after further deterioration. Therefore, the bank must develop the ability to recognize danger signals, and to respond promptly and aggressively to those developing problems.

The first article deals with the early identification of problem loans, and stresses the importance of a good loan review operation. It discusses in detail various danger signals indicative of loan deterioration. It also stresses the benefits that can be obtained if the bank can develop the ability to identify developing problems at an early stage.

The second article discusses the alternatives for collecting a loan. When a loan becomes a collection problem, it is imperative that the bank select the best alternative for collection, since this will have a significant effect on the amount of the bank's recovery. The significance of default is discussed and also the importance of adequate default provisions in the bank's loan documentation. The article then identifies eight specific alternatives that may be available in collecting the loan. These range from no action at all, which may be the best alternative if the debtor has no resources, to repossession and sale of the collateral, or forcing the debtor into involuntary bankruptcy. The best alternative for collecting a loan may not always be clear-cut, and any decision on a course of action to be pursued should be made only after careful review of the facts of the case. A proper decision will result in a maximum recovery, while a wrong decision will result in dispute and unnecessary expense and litigation.

Another article discusses when the bank should seek legal advice. Many bankers are far too hesitant to consult legal counsel either because they are concerned about the expense involved in doing so, or because they are hesitant to admit that they need assistance. This article points out that the most important times for the bank to consult its legal counsel are when loan documentation is being prepared prior to the closing of the loan and when the borrower defaults. It also stresses that the bank's legal counsel may be of assistance in negotiating the documentation required for a loan to insure that nothing is overlooked in the documentation process. Legal counsel may also be of significant assistance in a workout situation, both to assist in negotiations with the debtor, and to aid the lender in avoiding legal pitfalls which may result in a lender liability suit.

There is a disagreement among bankers as to who should handle workout loans. Some bankers believe that the workout should be handled by the officer who made the loan, since that officer is most familiar with the situation. However, the officer that made the loan may be too close to the situation to have an objective viewpoint, or may have an antagonistic attitude toward the debtor. Other bankers maintain that a problem loan should be turned over to a workout specialist, who has the experience and specialized knowledge required to deal with this kind of situation. Still others suggest that the officer who made the loan and the workout specialist should work as a team in dealing with the problem loan. The fifth article deals with this issue. It discusses the advantages and disadvantages of the account officer continuing to handle the problem loan and also discusses the advantages of turning the loan over to a workout specialist. The article recognizes that while in a large bank a separate workout department may be feasible, in a small bank workouts will generally need to be handled by the existing lending staff. In such a case, it suggests that accounts be transferred among account officers to provide for objectivity.

A challenging article entitled "How Bankers Contribute to Problem Loans" suggests ten different means by which a banker may contribute to problems in the bank's loan portfolio. These include ignoring loan policy, failing to determine the purpose of the loan, improper analysis and failure to develop a realistic repayment program. The article also stresses that failure to admit that there is a problem is always serious, since problems left unattended will only become bigger problems. Further, the article stresses that an effective loan review function is essential to the success of every lending operation.

The number of personal bankruptcy filings continues to increase, and in 1988 there was a personal bankruptcy filing for each 178 households in the United States. The seventh article discusses this escalating trend in personal bankruptcy and identifies a number of underlying causes. These include lack of job skills, medical and emotional problems, and inability to manage personal finances. In addition, many lenders believe that uncontrolled credit card debt is a major cause of personal bankruptcy. A number of danger signals for the lender are pointed out, such as a high ratio of debt to disposable income, and a heavy debt load in relation to net worth. The article also discusses bankruptcy exemptions and points out that debtors do not "lose everything" in bankruptcy. Rather, by doing even a minimal amount of prebankruptcy planning, a debtor may retain a significant amount of assets. The exemptions allowed the debtor, under either the Bankruptcy Code or various state exemption statutes, are also discussed. Finally, the point is made that bankruptcy has lost its social stigma and that today many people regard bankruptcy as an acceptable solution to their financial problems.

Identifying Loan Problems at an Early Stage

A strong loan review operation is an important factor in the success of a bank's lending activity. A loan review department performs many important functions, including keeping management informed of the overall quality of the loan portfolio, checking compliance with loan policy, evaluating file documentation, detecting deterioration in loan quality, and rating loan officer performance. The most crucial of these functions is the early identification of developing loan problems, because the earlier the bank begins to deal with the problem, the greater are its alternatives for achieving a solution. One of the hallmarks of a successful banking operation is its ability to identify problems early and deal with them aggressively.

The loan review officer cannot rely on the loan officer handling the loan to spot developing problems for a number of reasons. Loan officers are often too busy to analyze incoming information thoroughly and effectively monitor performance. In some instances, the loan officer may lack an objective perspective due to his or her close working relationship with the customer. Loan officers often tend to have too much confidence in borrowers with whom they are well acquainted. In other instances, the loan officer may be aware of the deteriorating situation and simply be so apprehensive that he not only fails to report the developing problem to management, but also fails to take any corrective action. Therefore, the loan review officer is often the person upon whom the bank must rely to ferret out developing problems. The review officer who is adept at doing so can save the bank thousands of dollars in charge-offs.

Even during the earliest stages of deterioration, there will be telltale signs that a problem is developing. An experienced review officer is always alert for these "red flags." This article will discuss some of the clues that signal developing trouble.

Lack of profitability

Although a business may absorb losses for a short period of time, in the long term it must be profitable if it is to prosper and ultimately survive as a successful business. In fact, a business's profit level is probably the major barometer of its financial health. While a downtrend in profitability can often indicate potential trouble, continuing operating losses should be of serious concern to the lender. It is often difficult to determine what level of profits is "adequate" for a given business. *RMA's Annual Statement Studies* can help the loan review officer determine whether a business's earnings are in line with the average for its industry.

Weak or decreasing equity

Adequate equity is crucial to the financial strength of a business; an increase in equity (net worth) is a principal indicator of financial progress. Many lenders underestimate the importance of equity and the role it plays in the ultimate success of a business. Adequate equity enables the business to weather adversity, survive periods of high interest rates, and take advantage of expansion opportunities. The amount of equity invested in a business is also a good measure of the commitment of its owners. Businesses that are heavily leveraged—that is, which have a weak equity position—are usually candidates for problems. Decreasing equity is almost always an indicator of potential problems.

Increasing debt load

A deteriorating debt-to-worth ratio or an increase in the total dollar amount of debt is often a red flag indicating approaching problems. The business may be using borrowed money to fund operating losses or heavy withdrawals by owners, or it may be involved in a capital expansion program of which the bank is not aware. Obviously, the greater the total amount of debt and the larger the number of creditors with which the business is involved, the more vulnerable it is in an economic downturn or if other economic problems develop.

Deteriorating cash position

A business requires cash to service its debt obligations, and the weaker its cash position, the greater the potential difficulty in meeting those obligations. A diminishing cash position, especially where overdrafts become a problem, should always be of concern to the loan review officer. Diminished account activity is also often a red flag, since this may indicate that the business has established accounts at another institution, and therefore may be involved in account transactions of which the lending bank is not aware. This situation can be especially serious when the account deposits represent the proceeds of the sale of collateral such as inventory. Banks are notoriously lax in monitoring a borrower's account activity, even though

248

this is an excellent source of information concerning the borrower's business affairs.

Increase in accounts payable

An increase in the business's accounts payable may indicate increasing sales volume, or it may indicate that the business's relationship with its suppliers is deteriorating. When an uptrend in payables is identified, the bank should immediately request an aged list of payables. If this reveals delinquent accounts with suppliers, immediate steps should be taken to determine the nature of the problem. A business's suppliers are often the first to recognize that a businesss is having difficulty and are an excellent source of information concerning the status and performance of the business.

Loans to officers and stockholders

Loans to officers and stockholders should always be closely scrutinized, since they may represent a business asset of questionable collectibility, and in some instances an improper use of loan proceeds. This kind of loan often represents an attempt by ownership to withdraw funds from the business on a tax-free basis, which may weaken the business's overall financial position and increase its need for borrowed funds. If the owners of the business are not personally obligated for the business's borrowings, it may represent an attempt to defraud the bank.

Fraudulent financial information

Receipt of incomplete or incorrect financial information should always be a cause for concern. In some instances this may indicate carelessness or lack of sophistication on the borrower's part. In other instances, the submission of fraudulent information is a deliberate attempt to defraud the lender.

249

The discovery of any information that is materially incorrect should be immediately investigated. If, in fact, the borrower is deliberately misinforming the bank, then immediate and aggressive action may be necessary to avoid a charge-off.

Delinquency or other default

Every banker considers failure to make scheduled payments a sign of developing trouble. The bank should realize, however, that other events of default such as failure to maintain and protect collateral, may also be a source of problems. While banks have procedures for following up on delinquent loans, they may overlook or ignore other events of default. The loan review officer should familiarize himself with the default provisions in the bank's loan documentation and if default occurs, immediately call this to the attention of the lending staff.

Failure to provide information

Delay or hesitancy by the borrower to provide requested financial information may be an indication that performance is deteriorating. The receipt of poorer quality information should also alert the loan review officer. If the customer has formerly provided an audited financial statement, and now sends the bank a compilation statement, this may be a red flag. Changing accounting firms, especially when this happens more than once in a relatively short period of time, may also be a clue that problems exist.

Cancellation of insurance

Many experienced lenders view the receipt of an insurance cancellation notice as the first sign of trouble. It may simply mean that management is careless, but it may also indicate that the business is cash-short, or that management is losing control of the business.

250

Judgments and tax liens

The appearance of a judgment creditor or the filing of a federal or state tax lien is always a sign of trouble. In such a case, the bank may suddenly find itself dealing with a competing creditor. If the loan is unsecured, the bank will be in a position where the lien creditor has a claim to the assets of the business superior to that of the bank. A large federal tax lien is always a serious matter, since the Internal Revenue Service will usually move aggressively to collect what is owed.

Investment in nonrelated ventures

Occasionally the bank will learn that a borrower is involved in a financial venture other than his primary business. The venture may be described only in vague terms, may be speculative in nature, or may involve undisclosed contingent liability. Involvement in such a venture may increase total indebtedness, divert management time and attention, divert cash and other resources from the primary business operation, and/or may mark the appearance of competing creditors. The loan review officer should immediately ascertain whether the bank has all the facts regarding such a situation and determine the extent to which the borrower has incurred contingent liabilities.

Family and marital problems

Experienced lenders know that financial and marital problems go hand in hand. A businessperson with marital problems will often devote less time and attention to management of the company. He or she may also increase living expenses and may deplete business income and assets to make alimony and child support payments, or to meet the terms of a property settlement. Therefore, a loan to a borrower with marital problems deserves more than normal attention from the loan review officer.

251

Rapid business expansion

A rapid expansion in the scope or size of the borrower's business, especially when it's undertaken without the consent or knowledge of the bank, is often a sign of potential trouble. Expansion is usually funded with borrowed money and will result in higher total debt and a higher leverage ratio. An expansion that outstrips management capacity can be dangerous. All experienced lenders have seen cases where a business does extremely well while it owns three stores, but fails when it is expanded to eight stores. Loans to rapidly expanding businesses should be closely watched.

Loss of key employees

The key employees of a business may recognize that the company is in trouble long before its creditors do. Any business will occasionally lose a key employee, but when a number of them leave a business in quick succession, it may be evidence of a "bailout" and may denote serious trouble.

Collateral problems

Missing collateral or collateral that is in poor condition is always a red flag that requires prompt followup. A complete inspection and appraisal of the collateral may be required. Any hesitancy on the borrower's part to provide information or to allow the lender to inspect the collateral is serious and may require immediate action by the bank to protect its collateral position.

In summary, an alert and perceptive loan review officer, utilizing information from many different sources, can often identify a developing loan problem at an early stage. This can be of tremendous benefit to the bank, since it will have available a number of alternatives for salvaging the situation that probably will not exist at a later stage. The result will be a higher quality loan portfolio and fewer loan losses.

Sixteen "red flags" to deteriorating loans

1. Lack of profitability

2. Weak or decreasing equity

3. Increasing debt load

4. Deteriorating cash position

5. Increase in accounts payable

6. Loans to officers and stockholders

7. Fraudulent financial information

8. Delinquency or other default

9. Failure to provide information

10. Cancellation of insurance

11. Judgments and tax liens

12. Investment in nonrelated ventures

13. Family and marital problems

14. Rapid business expansion

15. Loss of key employees

16. Collateral problems

Alternatives for Collecting a Loan

A loan default occurs when the debtor fails to make a payment required under the terms of the promissory note or violates some other provision of the loan documents. Although lenders usually equate default with delinquency or nonpayment, other events—including failure of the debtor to insure the collateral or bankruptcy of a guarantor—may constitute a

253

default. Interestingly, Article 9 of the Uniform Commercial Code does not define default, but instead explains the remedies available to the secured creditor when default occurs. To determine what specific events create a default, the lender must examine the promissory note, the security agreement, and other loan documents applicable to each transaction.

As a rule, the "laundry list" of events of default found in most standard promissory notes and security agreements will include an insecurity clause. This clause allows the lender to deem itself insecure and then accelerate the maturity of a note. The Code (Section 1-208) recognizes a creditor's right to do so, but requires the lender to have a "good faith belief" that the prospect of payment or performance is impaired in order to exercise that right. Reasonable evidence that the bank is insecure might include the discovery that the debtor has submitted a false financial statement, that a lawsuit has been filed by another bank, or that the debtor's business has closed. During recent years, as the courts have become more protective of commercial borrowers, the bank's right to exercise the insecurity clause has become more subject to challenge in court. For this reason, the lender should use the insecurity clause sparingly and only when there is a factual basis supporting the bank's "good faith belief" that it is insecure.

When a default occurs, the lender will usually give the debtor an opportunity to cure the default, and may go to great lengths to try to rehabilitate the loan. In cases in which curing the default and rehabilitating the borrower is not feasible, the lender ordinarily decides to collect the loan. When there is evidence of fraud, the lender must usually move quickly. However, the lender should always consult its attorney at this stage to decide what course of action to pursue in order to maximize its recovery of funds. The lender will usually have a number of alternatives from which to choose, as described below.

254

1. **VOLUNTARY LIQUIDATION**

   The lender's best course of action may be to convince
   the debtor to voluntarily liquidate the business's assets.
   Assets sold in a voluntary sale often bring a higher price
   than assets sold in a foreclosure, and the debtor avoids
   the stigma of a foreclosure sale. The lender, in turn,
   avoids the delay, expense, and legal risks involved in a
   repossession and resale of collateral. Of all the options
   available to the bank, a voluntary liquidation is probably
   the most beneficial, provided the bank obtains the full
   cooperation of the debtor. Even in a voluntary liquidation, the lender must closely monitor the sale of assets
   to ensure that the proceeds are ultimately applied to
   the loan, and are not diverted by the debtor.

2. **COMPROMISE SETTLEMENT**

   The debtor may propose a compromise settlement—
   an offer of something less than face value of the debt
   owed (perhaps 50 percent) in return for a full release
   of the indebtedness. When weighing the offer of such a
   settlement, the bank must consider the likelihood of
   collecting the loan in full through legal action as well as
   the cost involved in doing so. In some cases, the bank
   may conclude that it is advantageous to accept a settlement rather than undergo costly and time-consuming
   litigation. This is especially true in a case where it appears that the debtor actually lacks the resources to pay
   the debt in full, and the compromise settlement includes the proceeds of most of the debtor's remaining
   assets.

3. **REPOSSESSION AND SALE OF COLLATERAL**

   If the loan is secured, the lender may proceed to collect
   the loan by the sale of collateral it already holds, or by
   the repossession and sale of collateral in the debtor's
   possession. The repossession process is fraught with

legal pitfalls, so the bank should always proceed cautiously. A mishandled repossession may result in a substantial exposure for damages and even bar a deficiency claim against the debtor or co-obligor. The lender should also be sure that repossessed collateral is sold in a commercially reasonable manner, and that all interested parties—including the debtor, any other owner of collateral, and guarantors—are properly notified of the sale. Due to the legal liability which the bank may incur in the repossession process, it should never repossess collateral that has minimal value "just to prove a point." It should also avoid selling repossessed items to insiders such as employees, officers, or major stockholders of the bank.

4. LEGAL ACTION

In many instances, a creditor will simply initiate legal action to obtain a money judgment against the debtor. If the debtor disputes the claim, which is often the case, a trial will be held to determine the merits of the dispute. The debtor will often raise a variety of defenses, including the following: the lender's security interest is defective; the loan was not in default; the lender misrepresented the terms of the loan or violated the debtor's rights. If the creditor prevails, the judgment is entered, and the creditor may then proceed to enforce the judgment by means of writs of execution, citation proceedings, and garnishment. Unfortunately, the courts generally move quite slowly. Many months or years may elapse before the lender finally collects the debt through this process, if at all.

5. LEGAL ACTION AGAINST CO-OBLIGORS

The provisions of most standard promissory note and guaranty agreement forms allow the lender to proceed directly against co-obligors without taking legal action against the primary debtor. In a situation where the debtor is bankrupt or insolvent and the co-obligor has assets, action against the co-obligor is often the most attractive option available to the lender. The co-obligor, of course, is generally also liable for any deficiency that may exist after the lender has exhausted its remedies against the primary debtor and any collateral. If the obligation is "joint and several," then all co-obligors are jointly and individually obligated for the full amount of the debt, and the lender may sue all co-obligors individually or collectively as appropriate.

6. CREDITOR'S ARRANGEMENT
   In some instances, the lender may join with other creditors to form a creditor's committee. Under this arrangement, the creditors appoint a trustee to whom the debtor voluntarily assigns all or part of his assets in satisfaction of all or part of the debt due. The trustee then liquidates these assets in an orderly manner and divides the proceeds among the various creditors according to a previously agreed-upon plan. The creditor's committee approach is usually not feasible unless all the major creditors are in agreement. It often becomes necessary to buy out the interest of minority creditors who are unwilling to agree to the arrangement. In many situations, the debtor will prefer filing for bankruptcy as opposed to cooperating with a creditor's committee, due to the unique protection provided the debtor by bankruptcy laws.

7. INVOLUNTARY BANKRUPTCY
   In other cases, the lender may join with other creditors to force the debtor into involuntary bankruptcy. Because they usually prefer to collect the debt outside of a bankruptcy, many lenders do not consider this an attractive alternative for the collection of a debt.

However, this alternative may be advantageous in cases where a large number of secured creditors are involved and there are numerous disputes concerning priority to collateral. Lenders should recognize that certain debtors such as farmers cannot be forced into involuntary bankruptcy, and the petitioning creditors risk paying damages to the debtor if the involuntary bankruptcy proves unsuccessful.

8. NO ACTION

Another alternative to collection is to take no legal action at all and simply charge off the full amount of the loan. If the assets of the debtor have been completely dissipated and it appears that legal action may be fruitless, the bank may choose to take no action rather than incur substantial legal fees and court costs in a nonproductive action. The bank should not give up too easily, however. There have been instances where the debtor appeared insolvent, but once the lender commenced legal action, it was able to discover formerly undisclosed assets and to collect the loan.

In summary, the best alternative for collecting a loan may not always be clear cut. It may often consist of a combination of the options described above. Any decision on the course of action should be made only after a careful review of the facts of the case by the bank and its legal counsel. The wrong decision will often result in rancor, dispute, unnecessary expense, and a minimal recovery. Choosing the proper course of action, on the other hand, will avoid delays, controversy, and unnecessary litigation, and will result in a maximum recovery.

Setoff: Bankers' Traditional Remedy for Problem Loans

Unique to commercial banks, the right of setoff is a common-law right established by tradition and a long history of court decisions. Since setoff is a common-law right, in most states a bank may exercise it even though a setoff provision is not contained in the bank's loan documentation. Setoff involves the concept of "mutuality of debt," under which the bank may set off what it owes the debtor (the funds in the borrower's deposit account) against the amount the debtor owes the bank (the loan). When a default occurs, the bank generally may exercise the right of setoff without prior notice to the debtor.

While the courts have long upheld the right of setoff, they have also established limitations. While the bank may set off against a general deposit, it usually may not do so against special deposits—roughly defined as those made for a special purpose and to be used only for that purpose. The courts have generally held that in accepting a bona fide special deposit, the bank waives any right to use the funds for a purpose other than the one for which they were deposited. Special deposits include Individual Retirement Accounts, accounts established by court order in settlement of personal injury suits, or deposits held in escrow accounts. Before your bank decides to set off against an account that may fall in the "special" category, consult your legal counsel and proceed very cautiously.

In recent years debtors have become more inclined to challenge the bank's right of setoff; as a result, most banks use promissory note forms and deposit account signature cards that contain a specific setoff provision. This establishes the right of setoff by a written agreement between the bank and its customer. The following is a typical commercial promissory note setoff provision:

259

> The bank is authorized to appropriate and apply toward the payment of this note any indebtedness due or to become due from the bank to the undersigned, and all monies, credits or other property now or hereafter held by the bank on deposit or otherwise, and belonging to any one of the undersigned.

Note that this setoff provision covers not only money, but also "other property" belonging to the debtor in possession of the bank. "Other property" might include securities held in safekeeping, repurchase agreements, or other assets that do not specifically fall under the description of a deposit. In a number of court cases involving setoff, a considerable controversy has arisen as to what constitutes a "deposit." Most lenders now include in their setoff provisions the broader language covering deposits and other property.

The importance of default

A lender may generally not exercise its legal remedies until a default occurs. Therefore, a bank should not use the right of setoff until the loan is in default. The liability a bank may incur in doing otherwise is illustrated by a recent Midwestern court decision. In this case, Smith had a bank loan which had an outstanding balance of $3300 and which required a $300 payment on the first day of each month. When Smith's March payment became ten days deliquent, the bank became uneasy and decided action was required. While investigating the situation, a loan officer discovered that Smith had a $3500 balance in his savings account. The bank exercised its right of setoff, debited $300 from the savings account and made the past due payment on the loan.

However, apparently aware of other financial problems Smith was having, the bank was still uneasy. When Smith visited the bank later that morning and attempted to make a withdrawal from his savings account, the teller told him the account was "frozen." Late that afternoon, when the bank's loan committee met and was apprised of the situation, it instructed the bank's officers to proceed to collect the loan in full. The bank then exercised the right of setoff a second time, debiting the savings account for the full amount of principal and interest due. The bank was now quite pleased with the situation, having succeeded in removing an unwanted loan from its portfolio.

Pleasure turned to consternation, however, when Smith filed a suit alleging that the bank acted improperly in freezing his account and exercising the right of setoff to obtain the funds to pay off his note in full. To the bank's chagrin, the court ruled in Smith's favor. The court's decision indicated that the first setoff for $300 had been proper. However, it also indicated that the bank's subsequent action in freezing the account and exercising the right of setoff for the full balance of the loan was improper, since at that point *a default no longer existed*. In the court's opinion, the bank could have accelerated the maturity of the loan and exercised its right of setoff for the full amount of the loan at the time it made its original setoff for $300. However, since the bank declined to set off for the full amount of the loan at that time and subsequently cured the default by applying the $300 payment to the loan, it forfeited the right to make a subsequent setoff because a default no longer existed. Alas, the bank was a victim of its own ineptitude and poor timing!

Setoff procedures

A bank ordinarily has only one opportunity to exercise its right of setoff: Once a setoff is made, the debtor will usually decline to deposit additional funds in the account. Therefore, if the balances in an account follow a definite pattern, it may be prudent for the bank to monitor account activity and exercise its right of setoff when account balances are at a relatively high level. For instance, if a business usually makes a large deposit on Thursday, then Friday may be a better day to set off than Wednesday. Since time is usually of the essence, a loan officer (or combination of loan officers) who can act expeditiously—rather than a loan committee—should make the decision to set off against an account.

The actual setoff is made by debiting the account or accounts and then crediting the funds to the loan. The obvious result of the setoff will be that any checks presented subsequently will be returned "insufficient funds" (NSF). The courts have generally held that the bank has a distinct obligation to notify the debtor of its action as soon as possible, so that the debtor may take steps to minimize the damage done by checks returned. Many banks require that a loan officer attempt to contact the debtor by telephone when the setoff is made. In addition, a written notice should be mailed to the debtor that day, preferably by both regular and certified mail.

Perfected security interest vs. right of setoff

In some instances the claim of a bank exercising its right of setoff may conflict with the claim of a secured creditor. Consider the following situation: Becker Machine Company, a sophisticated machine shop, was a deposit customer of both Banks A and B. When Becker received a $100,000 contract to construct custom-built equipment for Morgan and Associates, he approached Bank A with a request for an $85,000 loan to fund the purchase of materials and labor costs for the project. Bank A agreed to make the loan and perfected a security interest in the inventory of materials being purchased and in the Morgan contract. Becker subsequently approached Bank B for an $85,000 loan, telling the bank that the proceeds were to be used for "working capital." Although he did use a portion of the loan proceeds for that purpose, Becker also paid a number of delinquent accounts with suppliers that were the result of a loss on a previous project. Relying on its long standing account relationship with Becker, Bank B made its loan on an unsecured basis.

Five months later Becker finished the custom-built equipment, delivered it to Morgan and collected a $100,000 check. Apparently as a matter of convenience, Becker deposited this check in his account at Bank B. At that time Becker's loan with Bank B was ten days past due. Bank B had learned of Becker's loss on his previous project and was consequently concerned about his financial condition. Since Becker's loan was in default, when Bank B realized that there was a $100,000 balance in his checking account, it exercised its right of setoff for the full amount of principal and interest due.

The same day that Bank B exercised its right of setoff, Becker visited Bank A and wrote a check on his account at Bank B for the full amount of principal and interest owed Bank A. Obviously, when that check was presented at Bank B the next day, it was returned "NSF." When Bank A learned that Becker's check was no good because Bank B had exercised its right of setoff, it objected vehemently on the grounds that those funds represented the proceeds of its collateral, and that under the provisions of the Uniform Commercial Code its security interest had been transferred to the proceeds upon the sale of the collateral. Bank B retorted rather smugly that it had the right of setoff both by common law and under the provisions of its promissory note, that it had simply exercised that right, and that it had no duty to ascertain the source of funds in the account.

Bank A subsequently filed a lawsuit against Bank B and the case is still in litigation. In examining the merits of the case, most attorneys agree that Bank A should prevail since it acted promptly, and the funds in the account were still "identifiable" proceeds of the sale of the collateral. In a case of this kind, any delay on the part of the secured creditor is usually detrimental to its position, since as time goes by, the funds in the account become intermingled to a greater extent with funds from other sources and therefore become less identifiable as the specific proceeds of the collateral.

Under the Bankruptcy Reform Act of 1978, the right of setoff has been substantially restricted, and the possibility that a setoff will be declared a preference has been greatly increased. This is especially true in cases where the funds were deposited in the debtor's account during the 90-day preferences period pre-ceding the filing of the bankruptcy petition. Thus, if a bank- ruptcy is involved, a bank may find that it is unable to retain funds taken from the debtor's account by setoff and that it will be required to deliver the funds to the trustee for distribution to the unsecured creditors.

In summary, the right of setoff is an extremely useful remedy, although there are some limitations regarding its use. Every financial institution should be sure that its legal documents contain adequate setoff provisions.

When to Seek Legal Advice

Under what circumstances should a bank automatically call its attorney? What are some of the more common mistakes lenders make that expose them to potential lender liability suits? James D. Chiafullo, attorney with the Pittsburgh law firm of Berkman, Ruslander, Pohl, Lieber & Engel, offered his advice on these questions.

When to consult an attorney

"The most important times for the bank to contact its attorney are when a loan reaches the documentation stage and when there is an actual event of default," says Chiafullo. "The bank should call its lawyers when it comes time to negotiate the loan documentation. We find, however, that we're being contacted even earlier—at the commitment letter stage. If the commitment letter says 'we're going to make the loan' without much language qualifying *when* you *won't*, you may be stuck with a commitment you have to honor.

"In the case of an industry fraught with environmental problems, we suggest a condition be placed in the commitment for an environmental audit. For example, in a plant that used X-rays to check for flaws in steel, there's residual radioactivity on the site. If the bank needs to foreclose and becomes the site's owner for a time, they need to establish that they aren't liable for any injuries that might occur on that site. Under the U.S. Environmental Protection Agency's 'Superfund' statutes, if you are an 'operator' of the property, you are as potentially liable as an 'owner.' 'Operator' is so broadly defined, however, that we advise banks to require an environmental audit before they make the loan.

"We find that our bank clients are coming to us prior to a foreclosure or an actual event of default," Chiafullo continues. "They want to know what they can do to work out a loan. It's better to work out a loan plan before a default and ask the lawyer to look at your plan. It's especially important to call your lawyer if there are indications that the loan is in trouble. If the borrower is late making payments or not paying trade credits, those are indications that something's wrong. There's no substitute for a yearly or more frequent review of the documentation to be sure that it's in order. This can help you avoid establishing an unfavorable course of dealing."

Common problem: Causing mistakes

"In several lender liability cases, the banks were simply inflexible and felt that they didn't have to give notice to the borrower prior to calling the loan," Chiafullo recalls. "However, demand loans aren't true demand loans any longer. The standard of good faith prevents banks from arbitrarily waking up one day and calling a loan. Instead, the bank should let the borrower know there's a problem, and give him or her a chance to find other sources of credit.

"Sometimes banks don't understand the borrower's business or its normal business cycles. They look at a static picture instead of a cycle, and expect unrealistic financial covenants. Overreaching in asking for collateral is another common mistake that can lead to legal problems. If a loan starts to go bad and you start hogging up the collateral and tying it up, the borrower is unable to operate freely and pay off his trade creditors and loans. This invites third-party suits. Sometimes the bank believes it can run the business better than the business owners can. In one case, a bank influenced the composition of the company's board of directors, used some coercion, and put itself in a position of trust. So, they were held accountable just as if they were management.

"Another area of potential trouble, especially in smaller banks, is when the loan officer is also the vice president, the workout officer, and a member of the loan committee," Chiafullo notes. "That's bad because the officer can't help but have an emotional involvement in the credit. He's had to sell the bank to the borrower and sell the loan committee on the loan. To be sure emotions don't cloud judgment, the loan officer should be pulled from making decisions on a loan when it starts going bad, and the loan should be assigned to an objective committee, to another loan officer, or to a workout specialist." A related problem is the bank failing to confer with its workout counsel early on.

"Another mistake is becoming intractable and adopting a 'take it or leave it' stance," warns Chiafullo. "It's a bad idea, for several reasons. First, the middle market is very competitive and inflexibility doesn't work—clients will just walk away. Second, if you force something down their throats, they will claim that your economic coercion forced the business into ruin, and that's when you get a summons on your doorstep.

"Finally, there's the problem of the loan officer failing to be objective in writing up the credit files. If there's a personality problem with a borrower, you must look at it objectively. No personal attacks should appear in the credit files—just the facts, with a certain amount of necessary conclusions."

Advising the borrower: Drawing the line

"I tell my clients, 'Remember, you are a debt lender, not an equity participant in the business,'" says Chiafullo. "Banks should try to keep their hands off, even though it's important to have relationship banking. Support the business, but remember that you run a grave risk if you're counseling them. There are plenty of consultants out there who can help businesses. You have a built-in bias in your advice because you want your loan to be paid off, and this could invite third-party suits.

"Some banks now make it standard to waive a jury trial, because juries are not very kindly to banks," Chiafullo observes. "They can identify more with the borrower and are more prone to see his side than the bank's. Borrowers are winning lender liability suits, but it's hard to say whether they're winning more than they're losing. We don't hear much about the ones that the borrowers lose and the banks win. We see considerable concern because of recent cases, which could be overreaction. The spate of suits, however, puts everyone on notice to do things right if they're not doing so already."

Who Should Handle Workout Loans?*

Even the best-managed loan portfolios contain some loans that need special attention to assure collection in full or to minimize loss of principal and/or interest. When a borrower

---

*This article is written by John McCarter, senior vice president with Ameri-Trust Company, N. A., Cleveland, Ohio.

is unable to pay according to terms, or the situation is such that the lender believes the borrower may not be able to pay in full, a workout situation exists. At this point, the objective of the lender is to reduce exposure to loss, either by collecting the loan or by restructuring the obligation to improve likelihood of future payment.

Frequently, the lender must decide whether his objective can best be accomplished by using the current account officer or by introducing a workout specialist. There are advantages and disadvantages to both approaches. The optimum approach may well vary from bank to bank and from case to case within a bank, depending on a variety of circumstances. However, it is important to move quickly. The lender should accomplish the necessary analysis of the workout situation and alternatives, then develop and implement the action plan without undue delay caused by debating over who will be responsible for managing the situation.

The account officer's role

In most cases, the account officer is closest to the situation and has a current understanding of the problems causing the borrower's inability to perform. Because the account officer has a relationship with the borrower and understands the business, he has important advantages in making the necessary analysis and developing an action plan promptly. The account officer may gain distinct benefits from the experience of working out his own problems. This experience may well lead to avoidance of similar problems in the future.

On the other hand, the relationship between the account officer and the borrower may be so close as to preclude effective analysis and communication of the bank's concern. There is a natural tendency to let time pass in expectation that the problem may go away without overt action. The account officer may not have the specific skills and knowledge necessary to successfully handle the situation. In some cases, the relationship between the account officer and the borrower may have deteriorated to the point where effective communication and cooperation cannot take place.

It takes time to analyze workout loans, to conduct negotiations with borrowers and other related parties, and to monitor ongoing activities and progress. The time devoted to these activities may detract from the account officer's ability to service his other accounts or to actively develop new business. The lender must ask: How can the time spent by the account officer make the most significant contribution to bank earnings? Many sales-oriented account officers can produce more income for the bank by bringing in new business than by working to reduce losses on specific loans.

The workout specialist

A workout specialist brings a fresh, objective perspective to the situation. Because he has no ties to the past relationship, the specialist is more likely to provide an objective analysis of the situation and the alternatives. This advantage may well offset the time required for the specialist to become familiar with the situation. By virtue of his involvement in other workout situations, the specialist can use prior experience in developing viable solutions. However, the specialist should have the analytical, negotiation, and legal skills necessary to do the job.

Calling in a specialist clearly demonstrates the bank's concern to the borrower. It is important, however, that the specialist recognize that collection in full of the loan and elimination of the borrower as a future bank customer is not always the best course of action. In many workout situations, rehabilitating the borrower and allowing him to continue as a viable bank customer is the appropriate approach. In such cases, the borrower may be returned to the original account officer when adequate workout progress has been made.

If the workout involves a bankruptcy action, a specialist is almost always desirable, either to handle the situation directly or to consult actively with the account officer. Not every account officer needs to master the large body of knowledge and expertise required to be an effective player in a bankruptcy court. Even prior to bankruptcy, current case law requires care on the part of a lender to exercise prudence in dealing with the troubled borrower to avoid potential lender liability.

The workout department

If your bank's loan portfolio is of a size and character that a significant number and dollar volume of workout loans are always on hand, consider a specialized workout department to be a worthwhile allocation of resources. The staffing and size of the department should be flexible, growing to meet needs in economic downturns and shrinking as the economy improves and workout activity declines. Temporary assignments to this department can be a valuable stage in the development of account officers.

However, a permanent workout department may not be necessary for banks with smaller loan portfolios. Workout accounts may be handled within the regular lending organization under the direction of the senior lending officer. Accounts may be transferred among account officers to provide for objectivity and application of the necessary skills to each situation. In many cases, asset-based lenders can provide much of the expertise required for loan workouts.

In the final analysis, the answer to the question of who should handle workout loans depends upon the individual situation. If the workouts are not numerous or complex, the line lending organization may well be able to provide adequate handling. If workout volume is high and substantial special expertise is required to prevent large losses, a workout specialist or department may well be mandated.

270

How Bankers Contribute to Problem Loans

The specter of problem loans haunts most lenders these days, whether in their nightmares or in real life. It's easy (and tempting) for bankers to point fingers at all sorts of culprits. Unfortunately, the banker's contribution to the problem loan is often the problem, according to Dennis McCuistion, owner of McCuistion & Associates, Irving, Texas. In a seminar, McCuistion outlined ten ways in which bankers often contribute to problem loans.

1. NOT PAYING ATTENTION TO WRITTEN LOAN POLICY. Most banks have a loan policy, but do the loan officers adhere to it?

2. HAVING NO REAL INITIATIVE TO DETERMINE THE PURPOSE OF THE LOAN. Where is the money going? What is it really going to be used for? If it's going to be used to pay off past due payables, say so.

3. DOING IMPROPER CREDIT WORK. Banks still shoot from the hip far too often. The judgment of the loan officer is important, but you must do an objective analysis so you know why you're making the judgment.

4. NOT UNDERSTANDING THE BUSINESS BEING FINANCED. Banks cannot be all things to all people. Don't do the deal if you don't understand it.

5. FAILING TO ADDRESS REPAYMENT REALISTICALLY. How is the loan going to be repaid? If you don't know, be sure to say so on your worksheet, and think long and hard before making the loan.

6. RELYING TOO HEAVILY ON COLLATERAL. Unless you're in the asset-based lending business, consider collateral a secondary source of repayment. Also, take it only after you've analyzed the prospects of getting repaid.

271

7. **REFUSING TO ADMIT THERE IS A PROBLEM.** Loan officers don't like to admit that they've got a problem in their portfolio because it will be presumed that they have made a mistake in judgment. While this may be true, many times the problem is caused by circumstances not foreseeable at the time of funding.

8. **BEING LAX WITH BORROWERS WHO ARE PAST DUE.** Delinquency is a habit that is hard to change. Bankers should start by being more strict with new customers.

9. **PROCRASTINATING.** Unpleasant jobs are easily put off, but don't postpone action. Procrastination will not help; it will only hurt. Problems left untended will only become bigger problems.

10. **FALLING INTO THE "RENEWAL/REDUCTION SYNDROME."** Here's a true story about a bank that postponed the day of reckoning. A certain bank was having problems and the examiners had classified a significant number of loans. The ones they classified weren't the bad ones. They were out-of-state loans, but they paid up when asked. The bad loans were the ones located in the bank's trade area, but they were not classified.

    This is how it happened. The loan policy stated that the bank could loan money to any customer without going to the director's committee unless the note (not the total debt) was over $20,000. A customer would ask for a $20,000 loan and the loan officer would give him $19,000 for a 90-day term. The program called for a 10 percent reduction at maturity and renewal. Then, the same customer returned in 60 days and borrowed another $10,000. When the original note was due, the loan officer would collect $1,900 plus interest and renew. In 30 days, the same customer borrowed another $5,000 in order to make the reduction on the $10,000 loan.

Soon the customer had a note maturing every two weeks. The loan officer would then package these loans with the notation "no new money" before taking it to loan committee. They would say, "This is okay, all we're doing is consolidating present debt." There were half a dozen borrowers who continued to pyramid loans in this way, borrowing money to pay due notes and interest, so they appeared to be current. A neat scheme, but not good for the bank. It was a bad loan policy, but also bad judgment on the loan officer's part. That officer did not remain at the bank after this was discovered.

The way to prevent this is loan review, a formal evaluation program for examining outstanding loans as to quality and signs of deterioration. An effective loan review function is imperative today. According to McCuistion, banks with $25 million or more in assets ought to have at least a part-time person doing it. Smaller banks would benefit from loan review as well.

Personal Bankruptcies: An Escalating Trend

Underlying aspects of bankruptcy

Generally, the immediate circumstances that trigger the filing of a bankruptcy petition are threats of legal action and fear that a creditor will repossess property. The underlying conditions that lead to bankruptcy are quite different, however. The basic problems of most bankrupts are the inability to manage their personal finances and to generate sufficient income to cover living expenses. Inability to manage personal finances usually involves overspending for nonessentials, accumulation of excessive credit card debt, and unrealistic optimism regarding ability to repay debt.

Unfortunately, there is nothing in the bankruptcy process which rehabilitates the debtor in the area of financial manage-

273

ment. Consequently, a high percentage of former bankrupts will experience subsequent financial problems because their basic inability to manage their finances still exists. Similarly, the inability to generate adequate income is usually a result of a lack of job skills, medical or emotional problems, difficulty in finding adequate child care, or lack of desire to hold gainful employment. Again, there is nothing about the bankruptcy process which enhances a debtor's job skills or improves a work situation.

Danger signals for the lender

Obviously, it is impossible for a prospective lender to identify a potential bankrupt in every instance, but consideration of certain key factors will assist the lender in avoiding most problems. Job stability is one of these factors. The applicant who makes frequent changes in employment should be avoided unless each change is clearly an advancement or promotion. An excessive amount of credit card debt is often an indication of poor financial management and overspending. A high ratio of debt to disposable income is usually an accurate indicator of potential problems, as is a heavy debt load in relation to net worth. Poor past repayment performance and delinquency on other obligations is also indicative of poor management, an overextended position, or lack of desire to honor obligations.

The owners of recently established businesses are also often potential candidates for a personal bankruptcy. If the business fails to prosper, as is often the case with a new business, its owner may be left with heavy obligations and few resources. In such a case, personal bankruptcy of the owner, in addition to a bankruptcy of the business, may be the only way for the former owner to relieve himself of the personal obligation incurred as a guarantor or cosignor of the business's obligations.

274

Bankruptcy Reform Act of 1978

Another reason for the significant increase in personal bankruptcies may be that the Bankruptcy Reform Act of 1978, which became effective on October 1, 1979, has made bankruptcy more attractive to debtors. This act introduced more liberal federal exemptions, made it more difficult for creditors to obtain a reaffirmation, and liberalized other provisions to the debtor's advantage. The significant increase in filings subsequent to 1979 and complaints from lenders that the new Act had gone too far resulted in some revisions in 1984, but these have been ineffective in stemming the increase in filings.

Bankruptcy exemptions

All bankruptcy attorneys and many debtors recognize that a debtor does not "lose everything" in a bankruptcy. Actually, with even a minimal amount of prebankruptcy planning, a debtor may retain a number of valuable assets. The exemptions available to a debtor, as set forth in the Bankruptcy Reform Act of 1978 (Section 522), are significantly more liberal than under previous law. These federal exemptions include a $7,500 exemption in real estate or personal property (such as a mobile home) used as a residence; a $1,200 interest in a motor vehicle; a $200 interest in each item of household goods; $500 of personal jewelry; $4,000 of dividends, interest, or cash value of life insurance; $750 of implements, tools, or professional books; and a $400 "wild card" exemption that may be applied as the debtor wishes. Further, the Bankruptcy Code specifies that waivers of these exemptions as to a lien arising from a nonpossessory, nonpurchase money security interest in household and personal goods can be avoided. Also, bankruptcy court rulings indicate that an exemption not fully utilized in one category may "pour over" into another category. In the case of a husband and wife filing a joint bankruptcy, each may claim the above exemptions.

275

The code authorizes state legislatures to preempt the federal exemptions by specific legislative action. Many states have taken such action, and in those states debtors are required to take the state-mandated exemptions rather than those established by the code. In the states that have not specifically preempted the federal exemptions, the debtor may choose either the state or federal exemption. In some cases, the state exemptions are less liberal than the federal exemptions; other states have exemptions that appear to be even more generous than those provided by the code. Consider-ing the fact that in the case of a joint bankruptcy, each spouse may claim the exemptions, it becomes evident that a married couple may retain net assets of $25,000 or more after a bankruptcy.

Many lenders also believe that bankruptcy filings are increasing because bankruptcy has lost its social stigma. A generation ago, a bankrupt was considered a "deadbeat" and was often ostracized. Today, most people regard bankruptcy as an acceptable solution to financial problems, with little or no stigma attached. As a result, the trend toward a greater number of bankruptcies will probably continue, especially if an economic downtrend occurs during the coming period. Bankers should adjust their credit criteria accordingly. Although every banker recognizes that a debtor's bankruptcy often results in a loan loss, the improved economy of the past several years has alleviated banker concern about business-related bankruptcies. Interestingly, despite an improving economic climate and a low rate of unemployment, there has been a significant increase in the number of personal (non-business) bankruptcies during the past several years. This phenomenon is creating concern on the part of bankers and other consumer lenders.

In 1946, there were fewer than 9,000 personal bankruptcies. By 1960, this number exceeded 100,000 filings annually, with an increase to about 190,000 in 1967. During the next 12 years, the number of personal bankruptcies fluctuated from year to year. In 1980, there were approximately 300,000 personal bankruptcies. In 1983 and 1984 there was a decline, and then in 1985, a significant uptrend began, reaching a new high of almost 500,000 cases in 1987. The statistics regarding personal bankruptcies per 1,000 persons are also eye-opening. In 1950, this ratio was 0.16 per thousand, but by 1970 had increased to 0.92, and in 1980 to 1.25. In 1987, this ratio reached a high of 2.03 personal bankruptcies per thousand, which represented more than a twelvefold increase in 27 years.

There are a number of possible reasons for this significant upward trend in personal bankruptcies. Consumer debt has increased substantially during recent years, both in absolute terms and as a percentage of disposable income. A recent article by Charles A. Luckett in the *Federal Reserve Bulletin* points out that the debt-to-income ratio of the average individual has increased consistently during the past three decades. In 1945, at the end of World War II, when a shortage of consumer goods existed, this ratio was 1.7 percent. By 1960, this ratio had increased to 12.4 percent, and in 1980 to 15.5 percent. In the following three years, there was a slight decline in the debt-to-income ratio. In 1984, however, this ratio rose to 16.6 percent, and in 1987 reached a high of 19.3 percent. Obviously, as the ratio of a debtor's debt to disposable income increases, the more likely it is that he will be unable or unwilling to service his debt, and the more attractive bankruptcy becomes as a possible solution to the problem.

Other reasons for personal bankruptcy include heavy medical bills, marital problems, and loss of employment or other job problems. Unemployment, however, may be a less significant factor than has been supposed, since a study of 1600 bankrupts by Brimmer & Company, Inc., indicated that almost 80 percent were employed. A study by Purdue University also indicated that approximately 20 percent of all bank-

277

ruptcies involve two-income families. Studies further reveal that many bankrupts are relatively young and have more than the average number of children. Also, persons not currently married who have children are twice as likely to file a bankruptcy petition as debtors in general. This should not be surprising in view of the difficulties single parents often face in earning income adequate to pay family living costs and the costs of child care.

8

Loan Review

As banks have increasingly recognized the importance of a sound loan portfolio, loan review has gained additional attention and support from bank management. Although a loan review department performs many functions, its most crucial function is that of identifying loan problems at an early stage. Loan review provides an internal, independent review of the bank's loan portfolio on an ongoing basis. It enables management to obtain an unbiased evaluation of the status of the loan portfolio, test compliance with loan policy and bank regulations, and gain valuable insights regarding the performance of the lending staff.

Bank regulators are also strongly encouraging banks to establish loan review and grading systems. The Federal Deposit Insurance Corporation, in its *Banking Letter* 27-89, strongly urges the banks it supervises to establish a loan review function that will, at a minimum,

1. provide for the grading of loans according to clearly established criteria,

2. identify loans that warrant special attention and supervision from management,

3. establish the reasons these loans require special attention and

4. require periodic reports to the bank's board of the status of each of these loans.

FDIC examiners have been instructed to assess a bank's loan review and grading system when conducting an examination. Those banks without a loan review and grading system, or with one that is inadequate, will be encouraged to establish workable systems.

A summation of the primary functions of a loan review department might be as follows:

1. To be responsible for implementing a system of credit analysis and control of quality of all loans made.

2. To examine all loan files systematically for adequacy of documentation, to report all deficiencies to the officer servicing the loan, and to be responsible for the general condition of all loan files.

3. To establish and implement a quality grading system for all loans reviewed.

4. To maintain a current, concise financial history of each loan in the form of spread sheets and other schedules.

5. To prepare written analyses and recommendations on all large, complex, or weak loans, for the benefit of the officers servicing the loans.

6. To prepare periodic studies of various portions of the loan portfolio for the benefit of management and the board of directors.

7. To maintain a current listing of delinquent loans and a loan watch list.

8. To prepare monthly loan reports for the board of directors.

9. To implement a system for checking collateral margins on secured loans and to report all deficiencies to the officer servicing the loan.

10. To keep management fully informed regarding the status of all problem loans and to make recommendations regarding the handling of those loans.

11. To evaluate compliance with bank policies and procedures and periodically report the results of this evaluation to management.

In summary, a good loan review program can contribute a
great deal to the strength of a lending operation. The best
loan review officers and loan review programs will not prevent
losses entirely, but there is no doubt that a strong loan review
program implemented by able personnel is a tremendously
significant factor in minimizing commercial loan losses and in
enabling management to assess portfolio quality and loan
officer performance. This section contains three articles stressing the importance of a loan review program and outlining
the benefits to be gained. Also included are suggestions for
setting up an effective loan review program.

The Importance of Internal Loan Review

A critical factor in loan administration is timely recognition of
problem credits, according to Michael A. Mancusi, executive
vice president, The Secura Group, a Washington, DC-based
financial institutions consulting firm. "The most serious
bank problems are caused by excessive loan losses, no matter
who finds them. The worst thing they do is diminish the value
of the shareholders' equity." A good internal loan review
program can help lenders spot problems before they become
costly, and in this article Mancusi discusses the benefits of
setting up an internal loan review program. [*Editor's note:
Mancusi's discussion of internal loan review was made as part of his
presentation at the American Bankers Association's 1988 National
Conference for Community Bankers, held at the end of February in Los
Angeles, California.*]

281

Benefits of internal loan review

"One of the most important benefits of an internal loan review program is that it provides senior management and the board of directors with an opportunity to review adherence to bank policies and procedures," says Mancusi, who was formerly an examiner with the Office of the Comptroller of the Currency. "Second, it allows them to review adherence to regulations and lending limits. Third, it's an opportunity to review the completeness of the loan files and collateral documentation. If you recognize problems early and the documentation is good, you can find ways to solve the problems. A fourth benefit is a chance to review compliance with accounting rules and the accrual status of credits. The program also gives bank management a chance to review lending staff quality and the quality of the loan portfolio."

Smaller banks may feel that it's too expensive and complicated to implement an internal loan review program. Mancusi, however, points out that parts of the process can be performed by existing staff. "For example, you could use your bank's compliance officer for checking compliance with laws and regulations. This work must be complemented, however, by work done by people versed in credit analysis. Some banks may want to appoint someone to head the loan review function, possibly someone from the lending staff. Whatever you choose to do, remember that those responsible for internal loan review must be independent from the lending function and should be adept at credit analysis. They should report to the audit committee or to the board, or at least to a nonlending officer of the bank. The cost of such a program may be less than you think. A 1986 survey done by Bank Administration Institute found that the mean base salary for a loan review officer in a community bank was nearly $2,000 less than the salary for a loan officer.

"Once your bank decides on an approach, identify the individuals who will be involved and provide them with adequate financial and staff support," Mancusi recommends. "Let the lending staff know that the program has the support of senior bank officers and the board of directors. Set up policies and procedures. The policy needs standards to identify the levels of risk. They need not parallel regulatory definitions, although that might be the most productive approach in the long run. It's important to know the risk associated with a particular loan, as well as to have information about collectibility, economic conditions, sources of your bank's loan demand, and the historical rate of collection on loans."

Components of an internal loan review program

"The loan officer's role is to alert the loan review officer of any and all developing credit problems," says Mancusi. "He or she should identify the nature of the problem, recommend a risk rating, and outline a plan of action in a problem loan report. The originating loan officer generally has the responsibility for collecting the loan." Mancusi even suggests that the ability of loan officers to identify and refer problem credits in a timely manner be used as one basis for evaluating job performance.

"The loan review officer reviews problem credits referred by loan officers and decides whether to agree with the recommended risk rating. He has the authority to change the rating but should first discuss the decision with the loan officer. The loan review officer is also responsible for conducting an ongoing review of the loan portfolio. The focus of the review should be to determine compliance with the bank's own policies and procedures (including documentation requirements), to determine compliance with applicable laws, regulations, and rulings, and to assess the quality of the loan portfolio.

"The loan review officer will determine the scope and scheduling of the internal loan review program, but it should include a quarterly review of all loans identified as problem

283

loans by examiners and internal reviewers. The loan review officer should also provide monthly reports to senior management and the board of directors.

"While there must be initial identification of problems by the loan officers, they also must have an ongoing responsibility to update the loan review officer of any changes in the status of problem loans. There should be a schedule for performing loan reviews, such as a quarterly review of certain types of loans. The goal is to review a certain percentage of all nonproblem loans annually, including consumer and non-commercial real estate loans.

"These action plans must be prepared and monitored," Mancusi notes. "Keep management up to date on what's being done to address problems. Develop information systems to keep bank management and the board informed—a brief summary is fine. The examiners' conclusions about your loans should basically parallel those of your loan review staff. There will be differences, but be sure it's worth arguing about. Know when you should hold out for your interpretation."

Setting Up a Loan Review Program: One Bank's Experience

A bank can count a good loan review program among its most useful assets. While all loan review programs share certain common elements, each program should be tailored to an individual bank's needs. J. Barry Cary, director of the loan review program for Northern of Tennessee Corporation's four subsidiary banks, identified the following issues that arise in the course of establishing a loan review program.

Establishing goals

"Our loan review program was introduced in early 1987 for all four of our subsidiary banks, including our lead bank, North-

284

ern Bank of Tennessee," says Cary. We wanted to minimize our loan losses and provide an accurate assessment of the loans in our reporting. You can turn an average-performing bank into a high-performing bank if you can control your loan losses. One of our primary goals was to identify problem loans prior to their being identified by external parties, such as bank examiners. We developed a comprehensive written loan review policy which was adopted by all of our banks. We set up the program to rate and judge all our credits using the same criteria. The only area of reference is the cutoff point for reviewing credits, which is $100,000 at our lead bank and $25,000 at the smaller subsidiary banks."

"With this program in place, we're reviewing our problem loans more often," Cary continues. "We're also strengthening our documentation levels. In the past eight months, we've corrected many technical exceptions. In general, we feel that the program is working. The main thing is to minimize loan losses and to have no surprises regarding our large lines of credit. We want to know where we stand—if we can see where the risks are, we can spot potential problems."

The holding company's lead bank, Northern Bank of Tennessee in Clarksville, has $192 million in assets. "The customer base is small- and mid-sized businesses that need up to $1 million in credit," Cary explains. "We provide consumer credit, and a nearby military installation also brings in new money each month. The other banks under the holding company umbrella are community banks; two are located near the Nashville metropolitan area."

Overcoming obstacles

The idea of a loan review program had been discussed for several years, according to Cary. "After we made the decision to establish a loan review program, it took 30 to 60 days to get the policies written and approved by the board and then put

285

into place," he says. "At first, some lending officers viewed the loan review program as a potential threat. So there was a good deal of selling the program, both at the board of directors level and at the loan officer level. The program has the strong support of the holding company president, however, as well as that of the board of directors. The loan officers came to realize that the progam is there to help them manage the risks.

"With any new program you face the problem of allocating sufficient resources," says Cary. "We're a small organization, so our staff expansion for the program was limited to a program director at the holding company level and two others at the lead bank. We don't yet have sufficient on-site staff at our other, smaller banks to keep the program operating at the level we'd like. Our goal is to eventually have one loan review person at each bank—someone with the technical and documentation expertise, such as a former bank examiner. At this point, it's easier for us to hire that expertise than to train it. The person in charge of loan review must be able to point out errors without turning people off, because the bank president won't be looking over people's shoulders forever to be sure they're supporting the program."

Reaping the benefits

"The program is still in its early stages, and we're adjusting things as we go along; but we've received positive reactions from our subsidiary banks," Cary notes. "We're involved in participation activity with them and we use the loan grading system we've developed to assign the element of risk. This gives the other participating banks a certain degree of comfort. As a by-product of the loan review program, we see the opportunity in two or three years to provide a portfolio analysis service to other banks in our market area.

"We've studied other banks' loan review programs, and we

286

find that ours provides a more detailed analysis," says Cary. "We have a very conservative board of directors who like to see the facts behind the grading. When we review the loans every month, we try to provide the documentation for them in layman's terms, because the board members aren't bankers. Loans are graded either 'A,' 'B,' 'C,' or 'D.' The 'A'-quality loans are reviewed once a year, as are 'B' loans. We provide the board with a list of 'C' and 'D' (classified) loans once a quarter when they're reviewed. On the 'D'-grade loans, we make specific allocations for expected losses and earmark them in our reserves."

"We've found that the loan review program has been a benefit to the bank examiners. It helps them to see which loans we consider problems, so they can concentrate on finding anything we might have missed. With the loan review program in place, we have developed information for them that lets them know what our problem credits are. Too many banking companies don't know which of their credits are bad. I would encourage anyone setting up a loan review program to use a conservative approach in assigning degrees of risk to credits—that way it's harder for people to argue with your assessments."

Loan Review Programs: The Benefits and How to Set One Up

The three main factors driving the banking industry are competition, deregulation, and the economy—and all three have direct impact on a bank's loan portfolio. "The importance of loan portfolio quality cannot be overemphasized," says George Freibert, president of Professional Bank Services. "A quality loan portfolio preserves the bank's capital account, protects the depositors' funds, protects and enhances the value of shareholder investment, and assists the bank in fulfilling its responsibility to the community. It also provides what I call 'regulatory tranquility' with the bank examiners. Most problems with regulators involve the loan portfolio," says Freibert, speaking from his years of experience as a bank examiner for the Federal Deposit Insurance Corporation. This article will explain why banks should think of a loan review program as a form of quality control. It provides tips on designing a loan review program, and also covers the documentation and reporting aspects of a loan review operation.

A loan review program can also reduce the amount of time that senior management devotes to the examination process. "If the examination process is a total disruption to the operation of your bank—not just an inconvenience—you may have problems with loan documentation, as well as the operational end of the bank. The smoother and better organized the bank, the less the examination process will disrupt the normal operation of your bank.

"Bankers must take exams more seriously than they did several years ago. Today, because of overwhelming negative statistics, the momentum is in the regulators' court. They can inundate you with statistics about how many banks have failed, how many banks are on the problem bank list, civil money penalties that have been levied, etc. It's hard to argue with all the numbers. It certainly behooves you to keep things squared away and avoid such drastic regulatory remedies. Additionally, the regulatory forces are a lot like the industry—they're strapped for people. There are more problem banks, but field forces are smaller and less experienced. Younger examiners with less experience tend to go more by the book. Therefore, loans that are arguably good but lack complete documentation may be classified. Banks are subject to tougher regulatory scrutiny, and a solid, objective loan review program will go a long way in reducing criticisms in the loan area."

288

Designing a loan review program

After you've considered the benefits of a loan review program, how do you design one? Freibert suggests seven important considerations: Policy drafting and approval; the size and condition of the bank and its loan portfolio; staffing and support for the program, the timing of the program; scope of the reviews; grading or classifying of the assets; and reporting of findings.

"Like any bank policy, the loan review policy should be in writing," says Freibert. "It should be subject to considerable advanced discussion at the senior management level. It should be drafted to fit the actual needs of the bank. It also should be reviewed and approved in advance by the bank's board of directors."

"The size of the institution and its loan portfolio will generally dictate whether full-time personnel are devoted to the program or whether it's set up as part of the audit department or the loan function. You must also decide how much of the portfolio is to be reviewed on a recurring basis. The size of the institution should not be used as an excuse for failure to establish an effective loan review program." Freibert suggests periodic use of outside firms as a solution for community and small regional banks.

"Getting a program started is probably one of the most difficult phases. The quality of the bank's portfolio and the organization of the loan department will directly affect the initial startup time and cost. If you have poor documentation, disorganized files, weak loan policies, poor quality credits, or inadequate loan supervision, it will take longer to get the loan review program well organized and functioning."

Why you need it

"An internal loan review program is distinguished from the regulator's review in several ways. Bank examiners come in

289

infrequently and take a snapshot of your loans. An internal program, however, is more of a movie that provides an ongoing review of the portfolio for reasons other than just classifying loans. The loan review program has several purposes, the most important being the maintenance of credit quality. Second, it ensures compliance with laws and regulations. The focus now is on safety and soundness, rather than on compliance. Regulators assure me that compliance will be back, but right now it's not as important as credit quality." Freibert suggests that banks should nail down compliance problems in order to preclude lawsuits from disgruntled consumers looking for a reason not to repay their loans.

"Another function of the loan review program is to ensure that your credit department is adhering to bank policy and that documentation is adequate. A program also assists in assuring the accuracy of a bank's financial statements. Loan review will help you assure that call reports are accurate; it's very important that loan loss reserves be adequate and that other statistics be accurate so that reports do not have to be refiled. A progam also provides an objective measure of the ability and performance of the people in the loan department. If your loan review consistently turns up a list of problem credits all made by the same loan officer, it should tell you something about that officer's ability. Finally, a program can assist in strategic planning through analysis of loan portfolio trends, loan profitability, earnings forecasting, capital planning, and liquidity planning.

"Loan review programs are recommended by regulators, who encourage banks to have a program that identifies problem credits. It facilitates the examination process, for a number of reasons. First, it saves time: The examiners can go directly to your loan review files and, while they're not going to agree or disagree exactly with them, it gives them a point of departure. If the examiner believes he can rely on the bank's loan review program, he will probably reduce the scope of his examination of loans. A loan review program also adds to a professional relationship with the examiner." According to Freibert, the loan review program will also reduce examination time. "It may, in effect, reduce the number of examinations that you have. If the regulators have a high degree of comfort with your ability to run your bank, identify your problems, and straighten them out, you'll probably see often a lot less of them than if they have to come in and dig everything out from under every rock on their own and cross-examine your people to figure out what is going on.

"The most important part of the process is the people assigned to it—like a bank, a program will only be as good as its people. It starts with the board and with senior management: They must be dedicated to it and must support it. Staffing and supporting the loan review function are two of the most important considerations of the entire program. Management must make it clear that it supports the program, and experienced, credible personnel should conduct the reviews. The people assigned to the program shouldn't be overly zealous about criticizing others, but they should not be too shy about pointing out deficiencies that need correction.

"The frequency and scope of the loan review will be determined by the size of the bank, the number of people assigned to the program, and the resources allocated to it. Some banks have tailored their loan review programs around periodic reporting—such as annual reports to shareholders, or quarterly call reports. Loans may be reviewed before or after the disbursal of the funds. Most reviews are conducted after the loan is made.

"Few institutions can afford the time and resources necessary to review the entire portfolio on a regular basis, so the process must focus on areas of greatest risk," Freibert says. "Larger lines of credit would be one of the priority areas. The program should examine all aggregated indebtedness of a single borrower above a certain dollar amount or percentage of the bank's capital." Freibert also recommends examining the loans of related borrowers—perhaps those depending on the same livelihood or the same company or collateral.

Also review loans with a history of exhibiting weaknesses—classified, loans on non-accrual, past due, or loans in litigation, for example. Other special situations should receive attention: concentrations of credit, OREO (other real estate owned), industrial development bonds, and insider loans. "Insider transactions attract a great deal of scrutiny from regulators. Insider loans should be the best loans in the bank—in terms of credit quality and adherence to policies and regulations."

To effectively summarize results for management, the review officer will have to summarize the quality of the credit through a classification or grading system. Freibert does not recommend using regulatory terms. "It's better that the bank establish its own system of grading standards. Some bankers use narratives or number/letter combinations, but substance should take priority over form in this area. Identifying and reporting areas of weakness in the portfolio and in loan administration is the purpose of the review."

Documentation and Reporting: The Paper Trail

George Freibert also stresses the importance of the "paper trail" in the loan review program.

Workpapers

Accurate and complete workpapers are critical to the loan review process. Workpapers should follow each loan under review from review date to review date. The loan review staff should note any changes that have occurred in the credit between review dates. These changes would include increases or decreases in loan balances, changes or substitution of

292

collateral, the addition or deletion of co-makers, and expiration of financing statements. Workpapers should also reflect any specific action that has been taken to shore up the loan. Workpapers should be kept on file in an orderly manner so the loan review officer can utilize them from review date to review date without "reinventing the wheel" each time. Accordingly, workpapers should be completed according to standards set in the loan review policy. This precludes each loan review person from inventing his or her own method of designing or completing workpapers. Standardized, pre-printed workpapers are strongly recommended.

Workpapers should be completed in such a manner as to adequately document the decision of the loan reviewer as it relates to that particular loan or line of credit. For example, objective data should be thorough and accurate so anyone looking at the workpaper could make an objective overview of the loan. This would include such data as the original dates, original amounts, current balances, dates of filing of security instruments, co-makers, appraised value, insurance, and other data which can be picked up from the note or bank documents themselves. Any subjective analysis, such as the reviewer's narrative comments or decisions drawn from the objective data or loan discussions with lending officers, should also be documented on the workpapers via written narratives or notes.

Management reporting

Periodically, according to the bank's loan review policy, the workpapers should be distilled into a "big picture report" to the board of directors or a designated committee. The report generated by the review process should be concise, clearly written and should focus on major findings of the review. The report should address such items as the volume and type of loans reviewed, general trends in the portfolio, patterns of weakness in specific areas (such as a high past due ratio in one particular type of loan), improvements since the previous review, the volume of criticized loans versus the total of loans reviewed, and overall past due ratios.

The report should be written so the reader can understand it. Bear in mind that directors and, in some instances, the chief executive officer, may not be loan technicians. These reports should also make recommendations for changes in policy and procedure, training, or, as necessary, observations concerning the effects of previous changes.

It is important that reports concerning loan review be submitted to the board or its designated committee on a recurring periodic basis, so the board or committee will expect the report in its normal course of business. Traditionally, these reports are submitted monthly, quarterly, or semiannually, depending on the frequency of the review. Should the board or committee have any specific questions about the loan review process, they should have the ability to direct these questions to the loan review officer in the same manner in which they would communicate with the bank's internal or external auditor.

Independence of the loan review function

The loan review staff must be independent of those whose work it reviews, and it must have at least the ability to report directly to the board. This does not necessarily mean that loan reviewers report exclusively to the board, but there should be a channel free of intimidation so loan review staff are able to communicate directly with the board should they feel the need to do so. If the loan review function is part of the internal audit department, independence should not be a problem.

However, if loan review is part of loan administration, the situation may be different in that loan review personnel may feel intimidated by their peers. Some banks have adopted a

294

policy of rotating people in the loan review function, wherein a loan officer one month may be the loan reviewer the next month. This procedure is not recommended as it seriously lessens independence and probably will not be an acceptable procedure to the bank's regulator. If the loan review area is attached to loan administration, it should be attached only organizationally and administratively, not for the purpose of supervision and direction. Regardless of whether loan review is in the audit department, the loan area, or another area of the bank, the critical elements are independence and ability to communicate directly with the board or its designated committee.

Simplicity

A significant element of most successful loan review programs is simplicity of execution and communication. If a loan review report does not hold the attention of the reader because it dwells on insignificant details, it is unlikely that the board, its committee, or senior management will react in a meaningful manner to that report. People have to understand communications before they can act effectively upon the communicated information. Accordingly, the loan review report must focus on the big picture: the scope of the review, the findings of the review, and recommendations to effect improvements in the quality of the portfolio or changes in policy.

9
Lender Liability

The proliferation of lender liability suits throughout the banking industry causes every banker to feel some degree of concern. Suits involving multimillion-dollar judgments against banks, with the amount awarded the plaintiff far in excess of the amount of the loan involved, have struck fear into the hearts of banks. If the bank loses such a case, the result will be a multimillion-dollar judgment against the bank. Even if the bank prevails in court, it will still be a loser, since it will have substantial legal fees often amounting to hundreds of thousands of dollars. In addition, bank's senior management will have spent an inordinate amount of time dealing with this litigation, and generally, the bank will have been subjected to considerable adverse publicity.

As a result of lender liability concerns, most banks' relationships with their borrowers will have undergone a fundamental change, with the bank much less inclined to counsel the borrower regarding the operation of his business. Also, the bank will be more hesitant to make a marginal loan or to attempt to rehabilitate a troubled borrower. When a loan problem develops, the bank will make greater efforts to give the borrower adequate notice, strive to be more reasonable in its approach, and work to ensure that its actions exhibit good faith and fairness.

It does appear that the lender liability pendulum is swinging in favor of lenders. A number of substantial damage awards made by juries have been reversed upon appeal. In addition, a number of states have enacted legislation that makes verbal loan commitments unenforceable, and a number of other states are considering such legislation. This is significant because most lender liability suits involve allegations that the lender made a verbal commitment to loan additional funds to the borrower that it failed to honor.

This section contains three articles addressing lender liability issues. The first covers general topics, such as good faith and fair dealing, interference and undue control, and misrepresentation and fraud. The Uniform Commercial Code requires every party to a commercial transaction to act honestly and fairly. Most lender liability cases involve allegations that the lender has failed to deal fairly with the borrower, that the bank has changed its position without notice to the borrower, or that it has failed to honor verbal commitments. Allegations of interference and undue control involve the issue of whether the bank became too involved in the management of the debtor's business, or through its actions had so restricted the operations of the business that it could not operate successfully. Allegations of misrepresentation and fraud involve the issue of whether the bank, either deliberately or through its negligence, misled the borrower or a third-party obligor, such as a guarantor, by untruthful statements.

The second article contains seventeen criteria that a lender may use to identify a potential lender liability claimant, who is usually a longstanding customer of the bank. Potentially troublesome borrowers may display several specific characteristics, which may alert the observant banker to a potential lender liability problem. This article also discusses several common misconceptions about director's and officer's insurance and explains why many bankers have little confidence that their D & O policy will protect them if a lender liability suit is filed against them or the bank. Finally, the article makes suggestions for dealing with a troubled borrower that will assist the bank in avoiding lender liability exposure.

The final article in this section discusses the so-called Penthouse case, which resulted in a $129,000,000 judgment against Dominion Federal Savings and Loan Association and its law firm. To the relief of lenders all over the country, this case was overturned on appeal. This article also discusses a number of concerns that a bank should have in dealing with its customers and makes specific recommendations for minimizing the risk of lender liability claims.

A New Debtor Defense—Suing the Lender

Every banker is aware of a new phenomenon in the banking industry: the proliferation of lender liability suits. These usually involve a debtor in financial trouble who defends his liability on the debt by alleging that his problem has been caused by some misconduct on the lender's part. In most cases the debtor will also file a counterclaim against the bank for actual and punitive damages for the irreparable injury done to his business by the bank's actions.

The widely publicized filing of a $3.6 billion lawsuit by the Hunt brothers of Texas against 23 of the nation's largest banks has resulted in a flood of media coverage of the lender liability problem. While most bankers are aware of the problem, many do not recognize its seriousness or that recent court cases are causing a significant change in traditional relationships between the commercial borrower and lender. Banking practices that were acceptable just a few years ago are now resulting in multimillion-dollar verdicts against banks. Although many middle-market bankers seem to feel that this is a problem for the "big banks," there are currently numerous lawsuits against small banks.

For example, a debtor who lost his land through foreclosure filed an $82 million suit against a small Illinois bank, its president, its legal counsel, and a director who had been involved in a real estate transaction with the debtor. The case is fairly typical—the complaint alleges that the defendants engaged in fraud, conspiracy, negligent misrepresentation, legal malpractice, and the intentional infliction of emotional

299

distress on the debtor. Although these are traditional theories of liability in tort and contract litigation, they are relatively new to lender liability and are proving to be increasingly effective for debtors.

It is important that every banker understand the basic issues involved in most lender liability cases. This article will discuss some of these basics and will also make recommendations that may help the bank analyze its current practices.

Good faith and fair dealing

The Uniform Commercial Code (1-203) requires every party to a commercial transaction to act honestly and fairly. Since these are subjective standards, a judge or jury will usually define what constitutes good faith and fair dealing—or lack thereof—in a particular situation. Recent court decisions indicate that lenders will be held to relatively high standards in this regard. However, lenders have even been held liable for conduct which was specifically authorized by their underlying loan documents. In other words, the lender must be constantly aware that the manner in which it exercises its rights and remedies may ultimately be scrutinized by a jury whose perception of good faith and fair dealing will be decisive.

Many cases involving the bank's alleged failure to act in good faith involve a "course of dealing" established or tolerated by the bank. If the bank has, over a period of time, acquiesced in certain actions by the borrower without objection, it may have established a course of dealing which it is obligated to continue unless it gives the debtor adequate advance notice of an intended change.

A case in point is that of *KMC Co., Inc. v. Irvine Trust Company* (757 F.2d 752 [1985] CA6 Tenn.). In 1979, KMC, a Tennessee wholesale and retail grocery business, arranged for a $3 million line of credit with Irving Trust. The indebtedness was evidenced by a demand note and secured by KMC's accounts receivable. In 1980 this line of credit was increased to $3.5 million. In March 1982, KMC requested a loan disbursement of $800,000, which Irving Trust refused to advance, even though it would have left KMC's total borrowings below the $3.5 million limit. Shortly thereafter, KMC failed and subsequently filed suit against the bank. KMC contended that the bank should have given notice it was about to cut off the line of credit, and that failure to do so was a breach of good faith by Irving Trust. KMC also alleged that the bank's misconduct was the specific and direct cause of its failure. Irving Trust maintained that KMC was already on the verge of financial collapse and that its conduct was not only reasonable, but specifically permitted under the provisions of the loan documents involved. The trial jury agreed with KMC and awarded damages of $7.5 million, a verdict later affirmed on appeal.

The KMC case holds a number of lessons. First, a demand note may not be callable at the whim of the lender; rather, a decision to call the note may have to be justified by evidence that the lender's position would be impaired if the note were not called. Second, it appears that advancing funds under an established line of credit is no longer in the sole discretion of the bank. Instead, the bank may be under a legal obligation to provide funds to the borrower unless it can justify the decision not to do so. A lender unable to provide a satisfactory factual basis for its decisions may become liable for substantial damages, with the bank's liability being measured by the fiscal impact on the borrower, not by the amount of the loan involved.

In addition, the default provisions in most loan documents will generally include an insecurity clause, which gives the lender the right to deem itself insecure, accelerate maturity, and demand full payment. Recent court decisions indicate that these provisions must also be applied fairly and in good faith. In determining what is fair, the court will again consider the lender's "course of dealing" with the borrower. If the lender has consistently tolerated certain actions by the debtor, then the lender may not be allowed to alter its position and deem itself insecure unless it gives adequate advance notice that such actions of the debtor will no longer be tolerated. The same is true for specific events of default that have been tolerated by the lender.

In addition, the bank will be required to act fairly and reasonably when engaged in workout negotiations. The lender should avoid threatening to call a loan or to begin collection proceedings to induce the debtor to comply with the bank's demands, when, in fact, that decision has not been made. Always exercise caution in handling a workout and consult legal counsel prior to making any demands on the debtor as part of the negotiation process.

Interference, coercion, and undue control

When the quality of the loan begins to deteriorate, the lender has a natural instinct to get more directly involved in the management of the borrower's business in an attempt to solve its problems. However, the debtor may view this conduct as unreasonable and an attempt by the lender to take control of the business. In a suit against the lender, the debtor may allege that the lender's interference with management was in fact the cause of the ultimate failure of the business. The debtor may suggest that the lender used economic duress in the form of threats to call the loan, to repossess collateral, or to close the business in order to compel the debtor's execution of agreements that were unduly advantageous to the lender and detrimental to the debtor. Such an agreement might require the pledging of additional collateral, execution of individual guaranties, or major changes in the operation of the business. The prudent bank will also refrain from trying to influence the stockholders' choice of management, will not countermand decisions made by management, and will avoid becoming involved in the day-to-day operations of the business.

A case in point is *State National Bank of El Paso v. Farah Manufacturing Company,* one of the early lender liability cases (679 S.W.2d 661 [Tex. App. 1984]). Farah sued the bank claiming fraud and duress arising from the bank's demand that the company dismiss a number of its present directors, including its founder, and replace them with directors more acceptable to the bank. As a result of this alleged misconduct, Farah was awarded $19 million in damages, an award later sustained on appeal. Interestingly, Farah was not in default at the time the bank made its demands. However, the bank informed company management that it had decided to call the loan if its demands were not met—even though the bank's records indicated that such a decision had not actually been made.

In many cases involving allegations of duress or undue interference, it appears that a personality conflict existed between company management and the loan officer handling the loan. As a rule, the debtor will attempt to capitalize on this situation by contending that the bank's actions were really based on the loan officer's dislike for the borrower, rather than on any real belief that the bank was in jeopardy.

In most instances, the debtor's attorney will also use the bank's own credit files to his advantage. For example, even if a bank asserts in court that the credit was rapidly deteriorating, its own credit files may lack any information regarding deterioration, the bank's concern, or attempts to communicate with the borrower. In such cases the judge or jury may be inclined to believe that the bank's position is not corroborated by the information reflected in its credit files. In many banks, inadequate consideration is given to comments that are placed—or not placed—in the credit files. Every lender should be aware that file contents are subject to the discovery process in litigation and will be ultimately made available to the debtor's attorney.

Misrepresentation and fraud

If a banker fails to deal honestly with a borrower or with third parties concerning the borrower, liability may arise for misrepresentation and/or fraud. Problems arise because bankers are much too casual in their verbal assertions to both borrowers and third parties making inquiries about the debtor. A number of legal precedents indicate that oral statements made by a lender to a borrower may constitute a binding contract, even though it varies the terms of the written agreement. Therefore, vague assurances and representations made by a loan officer during casual conversation with a debtor are dangerous. Because of concern about lender liability suits involving debtor allegations that a lender violated a oral commitment, a number of states have recently enacted legislation that makes oral loan commitments unenforceable.

The bank is also required to be truthful in its dealings with third parties—such as guarantors and other lenders or creditors—who inquire about the debtor's financial status. A lender must fully disclose all the pertinent facts in response to specific questions from a potential guarantor. Failure to do so may provide the guarantor with a defense to payment and also create a serious liability exposure for the bank. A bank has no obligation to provide information to third parties who request credit information concerning a borrower. However, if the bank discloses information, a third party may be legally entitled to rely upon it. Therefore, a bank must be cautious when it responds to credit inquiries, since incomplete or misleading information may result in liability to third parties who acted in reliance upon the information furnished.

Banker malpractice?

Several recent court decisions suggest that bankers, like doctors and attorneys, have an obligation to their customers to the level of professional knowledge they purport to have, or which the customer might normally expect. If the lender proves to be negligent or incompetent, liability for damages may arise. Such is the case in a Florida decision in which a debtor won a $12 million judgment against a bank where the bank represented itself as having considerable expertise in the field of asset-based lending. According to the evidence, the bank had only recently entered that field, and had only one experienced asset-based lender with suspect credentials. When the debtor developed problems, it sued the lender, alleging that the bank's lack of expertise had contributed to the failure of the company.

Cases of this type are causing considerable concern in the banking industry, especially since bankers, unlike attorneys and physicians, generally cannot purchase personal malpractice insurance. The bank officer, therefore, must rely on the fact that his bank carries directors' and officers' liability insurance, and that the bank is ultimately willing to indemnify him in the event there is a damage award against the individual officer.

In summary, bankers need to be much more sensitive to the many situations that could needlessly expose them to lender liability. Similarly, bankers need to make a concerted effort to review existing policies and procedures and make changes that minimize the risk to the bank.

How to Recognize a Potential Lender Liability Claimant

In the past, when a banker referred to a "problem loan" or "troublesome customer," this was an expression of concern about a nonperforming loan and a possible charge-off. Now when a banker uses these same terms, he is probably just as apprehensive about becoming a defendant in a lender liability suit as he is about incurring a charge-off. With a tidal wave of lender liability suits sweeping the country, every banker is aware of the possibility that both he and the bank may become the target of such a suit.

Filing a lender liability suit is generally a troubled debtor's defensive move in response to the bank's efforts to collect a loan. The debtor usually alleges that his financial problems were caused by the bank's actions—not by his own mismanagement. The debtor typically claims that the bank failed to act in good faith, interfered with the operation of his business, exercised duress, failed to keep commitments to loan additional funds, and engaged in misrepresentation and fraud. The bank, the loan officer who handled the loan, the bank's CEO, other bank officers, board members, and even the bank's attorney will often be named as defendants. Because many of these suits have resulted not only in the award of compensatory damages but also in multimillion-dollar awards of punitive damages, the prospect of being involved in a lender liability suit strikes fear into the heart of most bankers.

Banks used to take comfort from the fact that they were covered by director's and officer's insurance. However, D&O premiums have skyrocketed in the past few years, making it difficult for many banks to purchase adequate D&O coverage, if they are able to obtain it at all. Because a number of former D&O insurers have pulled out of that field, there is little competition for this type of business. Current D&O policies are also characterized by high deductibles and a proliferation of new exclusions, which minimize the bank's coverage. In most current D&O policies, for example, claims by regulatory bodies such as the FDIC or the Comptroller of the Currency are not covered. An "insured vs. insured" exclusion eliminates coverage in the case of a suit by officers and directors against other officers and directors, or in a case where the bank sues its former officers and directors. If the bank has had substantial loan problems, the insurance company may also include a past due/classified assets exclusion, which excludes coverage of claims involving past due loans or loans classified by examiners. These, of course, are the very loans which have the greatest potential for a lender liability suit. As a result of these changes, most bankers have little confidence that their policy will give them adequate protection if a lender liability suit is filed against them or the bank.   Banks prevail in the majority of lender liability suits. From the bank's standpoint, however, involvement in a lender liability suit is always a no-win situation. According to insurance industry statistics for 1984, the average defense cost of suits litigated that year was $385,000. These legal costs may be only partially covered by D&O insurance. In addition, the bank will have spent a tremendous amount of officer time preparing for the suit, will have suffered damage to its public image, and will have seen customer confidence in the bank shaken. In view of these facts, the best defense is to avoid becoming involved in this kind of litigation in the first place. The bank must develop the ability to identify at an early stage the customers who may become potential liability claimants.

Dealing with troubled borrowers

Troubled borrowers are the customers who represent the greatest exposure to the bank. As a borrower's performance deteriorates, the bank is usually inclined to become involved in the management of the borrower's business. This may lead to accusations that the bank has exercised undue control over the borrower's affairs or interfered with the operation of the business. The bank, especially in a case where it has had a long-standing relationship with the borrower, may have established a "course of dealing," and be required to give adequate notice prior to changing its relationship. If the bank has been too casual in its discussions with the borrower, it may be accused of lack of good faith if it fails to honor verbal assertions which the borrower has construed to be binding commitments. To avoid such problems, the bank must ensure that it has an arm's-length relationship with a troubled borrower. It should also review the manner in which the loan has been handled to identify its potential lender liability exposure.

In many cases, a bank that formerly might have been inclined to try to rehabilitate a troubled loan may decline to make the attempt rather than incur the liability involved in such actions. The bank's concern about lender liability will result in the bank instituting collection action on loans that it might otherwise have attempted to rehabilitate. The bank should very carefully examine its relationship with each troubled borrower. Since many potential lender liability claimants have common identifiable characteristics, banks should become adept at identifying them and proceed with caution when it appears the borrower fits the profile of a typical lender liability claimant. Workout negotiations are especially fraught with peril from a lender liability standpoint, so the bank should always handle such negotiations very carefully.

Profile of a typical claimant

Since many lender liability claimants have common characteristics—including certain attitudes, personality traits, and a certain "style" in handling their transactions—it is possible to develop a profile of the typical claimant. If your borrower exhibits the following characteristics, you may be at risk for a lender liability claim:

1. Has difficulty accepting advice about anything, including his business and finances.
2. Has a tendency to overreact to minor problems, turning them into major difficulties.
3. Has a confrontational approach to everyone he deals with—including his friends.

4. Tends to blame everyone else for his problems and assumes no fault on his part.

5. Has complained to top management about the "actions" of various loan officers and often accuses the bank of making "errors" in handling his loans and accounts.

6. Constantly complains that the bank doesn't understand his business—which is quite unique in his view.

7. Is critical of various provisions in the bank's loan documentation and accuses the bank of not trusting him.

8. Has ongoing problems with his family and personal life.

9. Fails to follow through when the bank recommends he hire a consultant, financial advisor, or lawyer.

10. Uses his attorney as a "stalking horse" in an attempt to intimidate the bank and its officers.

11. Seems to change lawyers and accountants with increasing frequency.

12. Fails to keep appointments and return telephone calls, claiming he never received the bank's letter or message.

13. Is extremely critical of the other banks and lenders he dealt with before he became your customer.

14. Usually is slow or unable to provide the bank with required current financial information, and objects to being asked for it.

15. Has an unrealistic perception of the worth of his business, consistently overvaluing assets and underestimating or overlooking liabilities.

16. Is irate when the bank questions his projections of future performance, even though past projections have never been met.

17. Feels that the bank is absolutely obligated to continue

doing business with him, because of family history, social connections, or long relationship with the bank.

If troublesome potential lender liability situations can be identified early enough, your bank and your legal counsel may be able to take significant steps to improve the bank's position and to repair damage done by the bank's past handling of the loan.

Guidelines for workout negotiation

1. Get your attorney involved at an early stage.

2. Have *two* bank officers sit in on all discussions with the borrower to corroborate what is said.

3. Don't threaten the borrower! Be reasonable and businesslike in your approach.

4. State the bank's position clearly. Explain fully what you are asking the borrower to do.

5. Don't make unrealistic demands or set unreasonable deadlines.

6. Do not discourage the borrower from bringing his attorney and/or accountant to any negotiations. In many cases, the bank should actively encourage this step.

7. Don't lose your composure! A confrontation with the borrower will be detrimental to the bank's position.

8. If you are deadlocked, adjourn for a day or two and try again.

9. If an agreement is reached, immediately confirm it in writing to all parties involved.

10. Be sure that one bank officer acts as "mission control" to ensure the bank is consistent in its statements and actions.

Liability: Lenders Win One

To the relief of lenders all over the country, the Court of Appeals for the Second Circuit in New York has overturned a record $129 million judgment against Dominion Federal Savings & Loan Association and its law firm, Melrod, Redman & Gartlan. The original judgment, in favor of *Penthouse* publisher Robert Guccione, had threatened the solvency of both Dominion and the law firm. According to a *Wall Street Journal* report, in this case, as in many others, the judge and jury apparently disregarded the loan agreements written to protect the bank and focused on apparent bad-faith dealing by the lender.

The appeals court, however, gave weight to the written terms of the loan agreements, disparaged the so-called lost profits theory used to calculate damages, and agreed with federal banking regulators that lender liability suits are a potential threat to the safety and soundness of the banking system. Because Second Circuit rulings are influential in business matters, this ruling is expected to have a broad impact on future lender liability cases and is being viewed by many banking lawyers as a favorable development for lenders.

Dominion originally agreed to loan $35 million to Guccione to build an Atlantic City casino. When the bank had trouble finding other lenders to participate in its commitment, it allegedly schemed to delay the loan closing to get out of the commitment, thus acting in bad faith. Dominion denied these charges, arguing that it was simply taking precautions to protect itself from loss. The Second Circuit ruled that much of Dominion's behavior that the trial court found "shoddy" occurred after the expiration of the commitment, and was not relevant to the case.

Issues in lender liability

Richard G. Smolev, partner with the Chicago law firm of Sachnoff, Weaver & Rubenstein, Ltd., offered some lender liability pointers in a panel discussion at American Bankers Association Small Business Banking Conference. "First of all, assume that anything you write down will be read to a jury three, four, or five years from now. Be careful about what you put in the loan files. The question about giving a borrower advice is tough. How far do you go? Are you a lender, or have you begun to exercise control over the business? Attending the borrower's board meetings leaves the bank open to charges that the borrower was acting under the bank's control, and other parties dealing with the borrower can use this argument in their own lawsuits.

"As for a bank taking equity positions in a company, if you take a pledge of stock, the question is will you exercise voting rights? Take the stock, but consult your legal counsel," Smolev recommends. "Another issue is whether demand instruments are really payable upon demand. Make sure the documents fit the deal. Don't put in provisions you don't plan to enforce. Look at your own forms and boilerplate and go over them with counsel. Don't act inconsistently with your loan agreements and documents. When a bank client tells you he wants to declare bankruptcy, you can avoid potential liability by imposing conditions and getting them approved by the court. Oral commitments that were never reduced to writing have been the basis for lawsuits. When there's a change in loan officers, document the fact that there has been no deviation from the loan agreements on file at the bank.

"Environmental liability is another important issue," Smolev notes. "One of the problems is that cleanup costs have no relation to the size of the loan. Before you finance a real estate venture or a project with environmental implications, look at the laws of the state, and the risks of having that property on your hands."

Minimizing the risk of liability claims

When initially making the loan commitment, Smolev recommends that lenders take the following steps:

- Avoid oral promises or comments that could obligate the bank, particularly those a prospective borrower might act in reliance upon.

- Assure that proposal letters remain letters of intent and are not construed to be binding commitments to lend.

- Advise the potential borrower at the proposal stage, of information or loan provisions you will be requiring that could be costly or time-consuming, such as environmental audits, certified audits, or prepayment penalties.

- Once a commitment is in place, avoid unilateral changes to that commitment. Keep in mind that a negotiated change must be supported by consideration and often requires a concession to the borrower.

- Where a committed loan fails to close, unless it is clearly the fault of the prospective borrower, consider obtaining a release of claims, even if it means returning all or a portion of an otherwise nonrefundable commitment fee.

To avoid problems in administering the loan that could expose the bank to lender liability suits, Smolev offers these guidelines:

- Assure that the loan agreement accurately reflects the loan terms.

- Avoid oral modifications of the loan.

- When changing loan officers, create a paper trail establishing that there have been no modifications of the credit terms.

313

- Avoid establishing a course of conduct (over–advances, acceptance of late payments, etc.) that could be implied to constitute modifications of the loan covenants.

- Avoid threats regarding enforcement of loan covenants.

- If loan terms are to be modified, consider obtaining releases or other concessions from the borrower in consideration of the changes.

- When terminating the credit, provide ample advance notice, if possible, to afford the borrower an opportunity to obtain other financing.

- Assure that payroll taxes are current. Never fund net payrolls only, particularly into a payroll account.

- To avoid liability as an information supplier, respond to credit inquiries truthfully and accurately. Avoid inducing others to act in reliance upon alleged misstatements.

- Where dealing with participants, provide all credit information on the credit to the proposed participant, and allow the participant to make an independent credit evaluation.

- Assume anything you reduce to writing and place in a file will be read to a jury.

If the bank is in the position of collecting a problem loan, there are steps it can take to avoid lender liability problems, according to Smolev:

- Avoid taking excessive control of a borrower's operations.

- Recommend, but do not mandate, retention of consultants. Give the borrower several potential consultants to choose from.

- Remain a lender and not a borrower. Stay off the board of directors and avoid day-to-day management decisions.

- Obtain possession of and liquidate all collateral in a commercially reasonable manner. Assure that default is declared and that collateral is preserved and maintained. Make sure that collateral is prepared for and offered for sale in a sufficiently broad market. Give notice in writing to all necessary parties, including the borrower, guarantors, and junior lienholders who have given notice.

Bankers (and their counsel) who are interested in the issue of lender liability may find a book from Practicing Law Institute (PLI) quite helpful. *Lender Liability Litigation: Recent Developments* was prepared for a PLI seminar and includes discussions of lender liability theory as it relates to bankruptcies and leveraged buyout financing, and avoiding lender liability. The book is available from PLI, 810 Seventh Avenue, New York, NY 10019, 212-765-5700.

315